Practical QlikView

MARK O'DONOVAN

Copyright © 2012 Mark O'Donovan
All rights reserved.
ISBN-10: 1478158603
ISBN-13: 978-1478158608

DEDICATION

I dedicate this book to my parents, Ita and Larry.

For listening to me talk about writing this book and for all their help.

20th March 2012

CONTENTS

Copyright Page 9
Disclaimer 9

How to use this book 10
An overview of this book 10

Section 1: Teach me QlikView 14

1. Tell me something about QlikView. 15
What is this book about? 15
What does QlikView actually do? 15
Who might find this book useful? 16
Who produces QlikView? 16

2. Getting Started 17
Installation overview 17
    What version of QlikView is used in this book? 17
    What are the system requirements for QlikView? 17
    Where can I get the software and how much does it cost? 18
Installing QlikView 19
Summary 24

3. My First QlikView Document 25
Create some sample data 25
Import your sales data into QlikView and start using QlikView 26
    Step 1 26
    Step 2 27
    Step 3 27
    Step 4 27
    Step 5 28
    Step 6 28
Summary 36

4. Creating QlikView Documents 37
Data Sources for QlikView 37
    Table Files 37
OLE DB and ODBC 44
    Which should I use OLEDB or ODBC ? 44
How to setup ODBC connection 44
    Create an ODBC Connection in QlikView 49
    Create an OLE DB connection 51
    Read data using OLE DB\ODBC connections 54
ODBC Connection to an Access database 55
    Select Tables from your Access database 58

5. Manage data loaded into QlikView 61
Link Tables 63

Read less data..65
    Filter the data: WHERE...65
    Grouping data: GROUP BY..65
  Add some expressions..66
    Where can I use expressions?...66
    Expressions in the Load Script...67
    Useful Script Functions...69
  QlikView Help...72
  Useful menu options...72

6. Charts and Tables 73
  What types of Charts can I create?...73
  Pivot Table...74
  Compare QlikView with Excel..77
  Straight Table...78
  Other Chart Types 83
    Bar Chart...83
    Line Chart..84
    Pie Chart..84
  Chart Expressions...85
    Synthetic Dimension Functions..86
  Chart Groups..88
    Cyclic Group...88
    Drill-down Group..90
  Chart Style...92
  Animate...94
  Trellis...95
  Fast Type Change..97

7. QlikView Development Tips..99
  Wizards..99
  User Preferences..99
  Themes..100
  Sharing your QlikView Document...104
  Reports..105
  Other Useful Options..107
    Detach\Attach..107
    Clone...107
    Menu options...107
    Section Summary..107

Section 2: Practical Examples...108

Section 2: Overview 108

1. Everyone...108
  Track your spending...108
  Football Scores...118
    Calculation condition..121

2. Personal Computer 122
What is happening on your computer: Events 122
How well is my computer running: Computer Performance 125
    Group Chart Expressions 132

3. Database 134
Sql Server Reporting Services (SSRS) 134
SQL SERVER – database versions 138
    Database compatibility level 140
    Mapping – ApplyMap function 140
    Load Data from SQL Stored Procedures 142

4. Websites 143
Google Analytics – website data 143
    Multiple Axes 145

Section 3: Advanced Topics *146*

1. Partial Reload - for large amounts of data 146

2. Set analysis 149

3. Dual Function 152

4. Calendar Tables 153

5. Powershell and QlikView 154
QlikView command line 154
    Reloading a QlikView document 154
    Automate Tasks in QlikView 154

Section 4: Going Further with QlikView *156*

1. Business Intelligence (BI) - What is it? 156
2. Microsoft Business Intelligence 156
3. Employment and QlikView 157
4. Is QlikView just for IT\geeky people? 157
5. Link QlikView and Microsoft Office documents 158
6. What else has QlikTech to offer? 159
    QlikView Desktop 159
    QlikView Server 159
    QlikView Publisher 159
    Collaboration 159

Appendix *160*

Appendix A: Terms Used 160
QlikView Document 160
Data Source 160
Qlikview file (.qvw) 160
QVD file 160

Appendix B: Other QlikView Sheet Objects 161

Input Box 161
    Input Box - DESCRIPTION 161
    Input Box - REASON TO USE 161
    Input Box - EXAMPLE 161
Statistics Box 164
    Statistics Box - DESCRIPTION 164
    Statistics Box - REASON TO USE 164
    Statistics Box - EXAMPLE 164
Bookmark Object 166
    Bookmark Object – DESCRIPTION 166
    Bookmark Object – REASON TO USE 166
    Bookmark Object – EXAMPLE 166
Button 169
    Button – DESCRIPTION 169
    Button – REASON TO USE 169
    Button – EXAMPLE 169
Current Selections Box 170
    Current Selections Box – DESCRIPTION 170
    Current Selections Box - REASON TO USE 170
    Current Selections Box – EXAMPLE 170
Search Object 171
    Search Object - DESCRIPTION 171
    Search Object - REASON TO USE 171
    Search Object - EXAMPLE 171
Slider calendar object 173
    Slider/Calendar object - DESCRIPTION 173
    Slider/Calendar object - REASON TO USE 173
    Slider/Calendar object – EXAMPLE 173
Line arrow object 175
    Line arrow object – DESCRIPTION 175
    Line arrow object - REASON TO USE 175
    Line arrow object - EXAMPLE 175
Container 176
    Container - DESCRIPTION 176
    Container - REASON TO USE 176
    Container - EXAMPLE 176

Appendix C: Useful Websites 178
QlikView sites 178
Sql Server sites 178
Learning Sql 178
Index 179

Copyright Page

All rights reserved.
No part of this publication may be reproduced or transmitted in any form or by any means without written permission from the author.

Disclaimer

Although the author and publisher have made every effort to ensure that the information in this book was correct at press time, the author and publisher do not assume and hereby disclaim any liability to any party for any loss, damage, or disruption caused by errors or omissions, whether such errors or omissions result from negligence, accident, or any other cause.

Information sold in this book is sold without warranty, either expressed or implied.

Title: Practical QlikView
Version: 1.1

How to use this book

I think the best way to use this book is to work your way through the chapters of Section 1, then you can start creating your own QlikView documents with more confidence.

You can start by looking at the chapters in Section 2 that you are most interested in, there is no need to cover the chapters of Section 2 in order.

Next I will give a brief overview of the different sections contained within this book.

An overview of this book

Section 1:

First we will teach you how to create your own sample data in Excel and create your first QlikView document.

Then once you have created your first example we will give you examples of connections to various different sources of data such as text files and databases.

Next we will look at how you can manage the data once you have loaded data from the data source. For example how you can filter\group records and add your own expressions.

Tables are all well and good but what most people want to see are charts displaying the data so we will cover Charts in QlikView in more detail as well as Pivot tables.

In the final chapter of this section we will cover tips to help with the development of your QlikView documents such as using Themes to provide a consistent look and feel to your QlikView documents and some useful User Preferences options.

Section 2:

In this section we will cover practical examples of how you might use QlikView.

Everyday

We will start with everyday examples by showing how you can use QlikView to track your own spending. We hold no responsibility for what this reveals if you are following the examples with your own spending data.

The 'Track your Spending' example is useful because it shows you how to read multiple Excel Worksheets into your QlikView document.

Next we will look at analyzing Premier Football League results. In this example we highlight how to display data in a table only when certain criteria have been reached using a 'Calculation Condition'.

The 'Football Scores' example also demonstrates how to create a row number for each record read into your QlikView document.

Personal Computer

We now move from Everyday examples to examples based on your computer performance and events that are happening on your computer. These examples are useful to discover if there are any problems on your computer that you should be aware of related to performance or applications causing errors.

The first 'Personal Computer' example analyses the EventLog. This log is on the Windows operating systems but most people rarely look at it. You can export the data and analyze it to discover if there are any errors that are occurring on your computer that need investigating.

People often remark that their computer is running slow. But there are many reasons why this could be the case. The next example called 'Computer Performance' in which we gather data about how the computer processor and memory is performing and analyze this data in QlikView.

The 'Computer Performance' example also shows how you can group chart expressions so you can easily switch between charts displaying different expressions over the same dimension.

Later in the 'Google Analytics' example we will demonstrate how you can plot 2 different y-axes on the same chart.

Database

At first this might seem an example just for Sql Server users but it covers how you can map data to another value using a lookup table within QlikView. This technique is useful for all users to learn.

The first example demonstrates how you can use QlikView to monitor what the compatibility version of the databases on your server. For example some databases may be compatible with Sql Server 2005 commands whereas others might be compatible with Sql Server 2008\2008 R2 commands.

To finish the 'SQL SERVER' example we show you how to call stored procedures from QlikView to load your QlikView document with data.

Websites

The final example in this section covers analyzing websites using data gathered from Google Analytics.

The 'Google Analytics' example also shows you how you can plot multiple y-axes on a chart. This is important if you are plotting 2 expressions that have values that vary greatly for example: one is in the 10000's and another expression never going above 10.

Examples in this book

Below are the websites where sample data was used in the examples within this book.
For more information on QlikView , this book and sample data please go to the website
http://practical-qlikview.com.

Sample data used for examples

We show you how to generate sample data for the initial examples yourself.
This is very good for demonstration and learning purposes.

Access database
AdventureWorks.zip file from http://adventureworksaccess.codeplex.com.

Sql Server databases

If you do not already have access to a sql server database or reporting services database and would like to learn some more I would suggest you get Sql Server Express(a free download from Microsoft) with Advanced Services which will allow you to create reports using SSRS.

http://www.microsoft.com/download/en/details.aspx?id=25174

Excel Sample Sales data

Download the Sample Data: Excel 2002 Sample: PivotTable Reports
The reason for using this data is that the Pivot Tables and Chart are in the Excel documents so you can compare them against what you have done in QlikView.
Go to http://www.microsoft.com/download/en/details.aspx?id=14738

Practical Examples

Track your spending

We will show you how to create your own excel spreadsheet. It is your decision whether to make up data (as I have done in the example) or use data from your own spending habits. I guess it depends on who you will show the finished QlikView document.

Football Scores

You can download the Premier Football league scores for Seasons 1996/1997 to 2010/2011.
You can download the spreadsheet used in this example from:

http://www.clearlyandsimply.com/clearly_and_simply/2010/05/combine-tables-and-charts-on-excel-dashboards.html

Computer Performance

The data from these examples comes from your own computer. The reason for this is that we want to make the examples as useful as possible and it is no use seeing how slowly my computer is running.
The screenshots are from Windows XP with notes on getting the same data from Vista.

Next are a couple of links on how to get to the Event Log\Performance Monitor in Windows 7:

Windows 7 Event Log:
http://windows.microsoft.com/en-US/windows-vista/Open-Event-Viewer

Windows 7 Performance Monitor:
http://blogs.msdn.com/b/securitytools/archive/2009/11/04/how-to-use-perfmon-in-windows-7.aspx

Databases

These 2 examples require access to a Sql server with reporting services for one of the examples.

Even if you do not have a sql server this example does cover a useful example of mapping functions as described in the section overview.

Google Analytics

This example uses data from Google Analytics website but it is easy to replicate the data as shown in the example.

Section 3:

In this section we cover some of the more advanced topics in QlikView for example: partial reloads of data to improve performance, set analysis, dual functions, calendar tables and using Powershell and QlikView.

Section 4:

In section 3 we cover what Business Intellgience (BI) is and compare QlikView with Microsoft BI. We also cover what other products QlikView has to offer.

Section 1: Teach me QlikView
Overview

Chapter 1

In this chapter you will be introduced to QlikView and we will describe ways in which you can use QlikView.

Chapter 2

Then we will describe how to download and install QlikView.

Chapter 3

You will create your first QlikView document. This will include generating some sample data in Excel, Import the data into QlikView and display the data in a bar chart and table.

Chapter 4

In this section we will demonstrate how you can connect to and get your data from different sources such as databases and text files.

Chapter 5

Once you have your data loaded into a QlikView document this chapter will show you how to manage that data from filtering the data to creating expressions and more.

Chapter 6

People love charts. Mostly everyone would prefer to look at a chart to understand what is happening to data rather than look at a table of data. So this chapter will examine how to create charts as well as tables of data such as pivot tables.

Chapter 7

The final chapter of this section delves into tips that will make your life even easier when creating QlikView documents (and hopefully more fun). We will show you how to create themes to create a consistent 'look and feel' to your documents. Themes are an important aspect to understand especially if your intention is to eventually use QlikView in your working life.

We will also examine options that are open to you to share what your reports look like even using the QlikView Personal Edition (QVPE).

1. Tell me something about QlikView.

What is this book about?

This book is a practical introduction to QlikView.

First we will look at the basic concepts used in QlikView so you can start using the software quickly and then we will explore different examples where QlikView might be used. Finally we will discuss how you can take this new knowledge further.

What does QlikView actually do?

Although QlikView is becoming more and more popular and even being requested in job advertisements many people might wonder what QlikView actually does.

With QlikView you can analyze data in sources such as Excel Spreadsheets, Databases, or text files. You can create charts from your data, you can search through your data very quickly, you can explore your data easily which can help you make decisions or many just confirm what you thought.

QlikView is part of a category of software called 'Business Intelligence'.

This is not to say that it cannot be used by people in their everyday lives. But instead that it is normally used for analyzing business data so that more informed decisions can be made.

For example: If you are using data about the orders customers have placed you might want to answer the question 'Which of my customers placed the largest total order in the last 6 months?'

QlikView makes it easier to answer such questions.

Or in everyday life you might ask 'Where did I spend most of my money in the last 6 months?' QlikView makes it easier to answer such questions.(if you have data about where you are spending your money.)

Who might find this book useful?

Anyone who currently uses a spreadsheet, text file or database to save information and thinks it might be useful to analyze this information.

This could be the everyday person who wants to track their personal finances or how they are progressing in their exercise\weight loss program.

This could be the IT user who wants to explore sql backup data, web server logs or sql server reporting services (SSRS) logs.

This could be the finance person who wants to use QlikView to explore Revenue Information or Invoice Details.

Some reasons to use QlikView after you have learnt the basics from this book and tried some examples:

- It makes it easier to explore data and make decisions.
- It is helping you with your goals in life such as budgeting.

- You are using it to monitor your computer performance.
- You are using it at work whether in IT, Finance or another department.

- You might find that it helps you save you money.
- You see it more and more in job advertisements and feel it is something you should learn.

The main reason to use QlikView is that you think it is a useful tool.

Who produces QlikView?

Below are a few details about QlikTech

- QlikView was developed by a Swedish company called QlikTech.
- QlikTech was founded in 1993.
- QlikTech has over 24,000 customers.
- QlikTech has over 1000 Employees.

If you have never heard of QlikView or QlikTech before then hopefully the points above should satisfy you that QlikTech is by no means a small company.

Next we will look at getting the software and installing it on your computer.

2. Getting Started

At last you are coming to installing the software. The reading about how great QlikView is and how it might change your life forever is done (for now at least).

Installation overview

What version of QlikView is used in this book?
The examples produced in this book were created using QlikView Personal Edition Version 11(QVPE).This is not a time limited product.

QlikView Personal Edition can only open QlikView documents created with that copy of QlikView Personal Edition (QVPE). **If you try to open QlikView documents created by another user you will get the following warning. If you recover this file you will no longer be able to open documents you created.**

> This QlikView document was created by another QlikView Personal Edition user. Since you are using a QlikView Personal Edition, you may only open files that you created yourself. You may recover the file if you created it on a different computer, but doing so will use one of your 4 remaining recovery attempts.
>
> However, if you recover the file, you will no longer be able to open files created with your current user key.
>
> Do you want to continue and recover the file?
>
> ☐ Yes, I want to continue (not recommended)

What are the system requirements for QlikView?

Below is a table of system requirements for QlikView installation:

	32 Bit	64Bit
Operating System	Windows XP SP3	Windows XP Professional x64 SP2
	Windows Vista	Windows Vista x64
	Windows 7	Windows 7 x64
	Windows Server 2003	Windows Server 2003 x64
	Windows Server 2008	Windows Server 2008 x64
		Windows Server 2008 R2
Memory	1GB Minimum	2 GB Minimum
Disk Space	250 MB total required to install	300MB Total required to install

NOTE: These are the minimum system requirements and more memory and diskspace would be required depending on the amount of data you are analysing.

Where can I get the software and how much does it cost?

It's Free!
Well for the 'Personal Edition' anyway.

This is always the best price when you want to learn how to use some software.

http://www.QlikView.com/us/explore/experience/free-download/

1. Fill in the form and click on the 'Download Now' button you will be presented with a confirmation screen as shown:

Thank You for Registering

Thank you for your interest. Download QlikView Personal Edition now.

And after you have installed QlikView, be sure to check out the New to QlikView section on QlikCommunity – Our large online community for QlikView developers and business professionals to interact, learn and share their experiences.

2. Click on the 'Download QlikView Personal Edition now.' Message.
3. Select the Language and Version of Windows you require.
4. Tick the box to accept the user license.
5. Then click on the 'Download QlikView Now' button.

Download QlikView

QlikTech invites you to download a full version of QlikView, including a Personal Edition License that enables you to create unlimited QlikView documents for your own personal use.

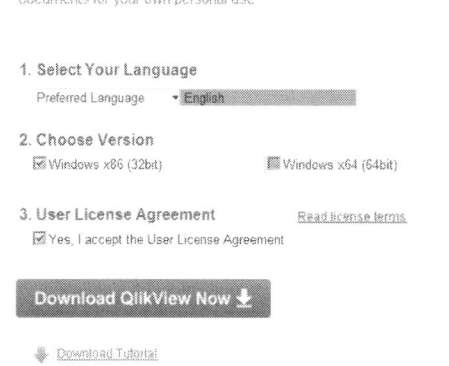

1. Select Your Language
   Preferred Language: English

2. Choose Version
   ☑ Windows x86 (32bit)   ☐ Windows x64 (64bit)

3. User License Agreement   Read license terms
   ☑ Yes, I accept the User License Agreement

   [Download QlikView Now]

   Download Tutorial

Installing QlikView

Once you have downloaded the version of QlikView for your required language \ computer double click on the file to run the installation program.

1. If you get a 'Security warning' click on the Run button.

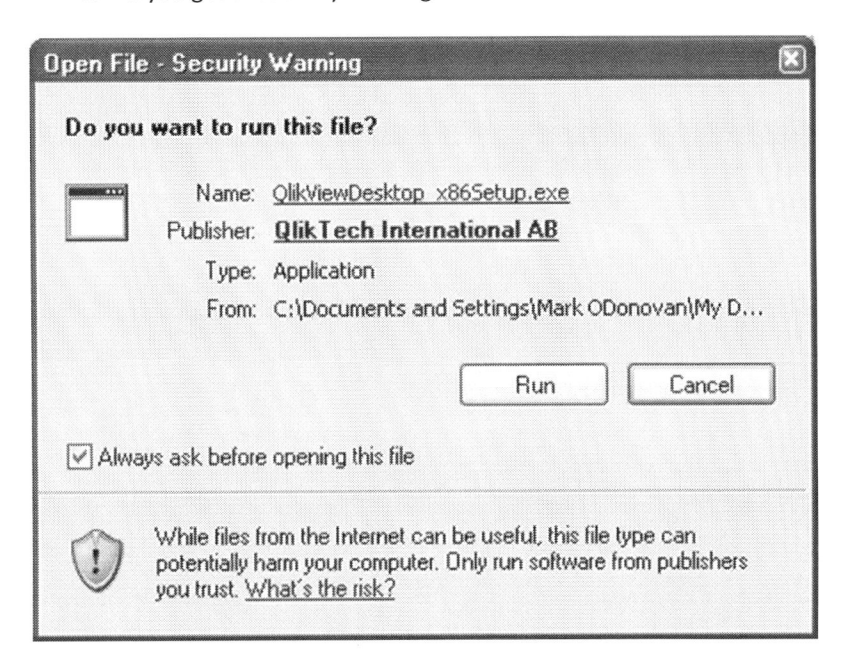

2. Select the language and click OK.

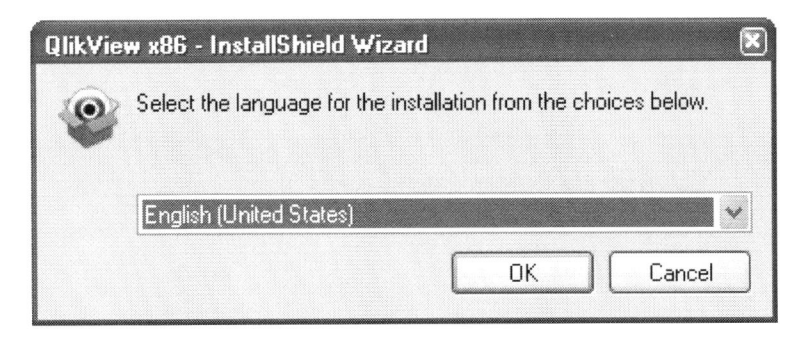

3. The QlikView installation wizard will then be displayed.
4. Click the Next button.

Getting Started - CHAPTER 2   19

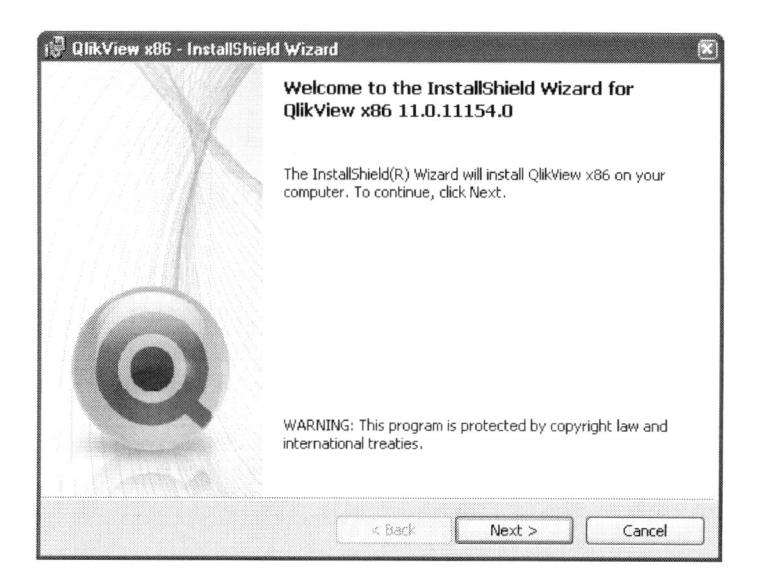

5. Accept the license agreement.
6. Click the Next button.

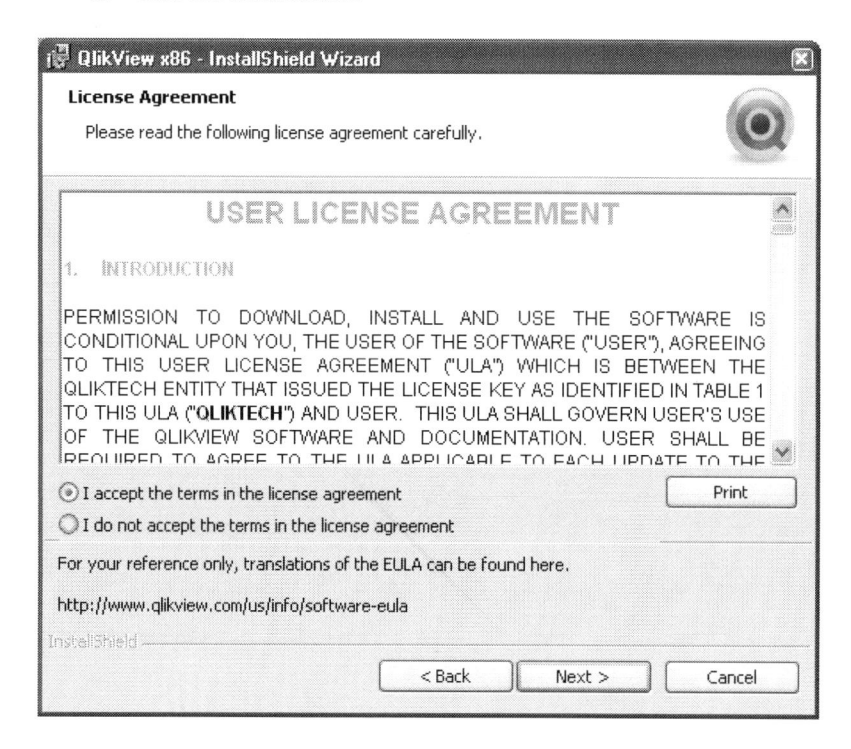

7. Enter your Name and Organization details

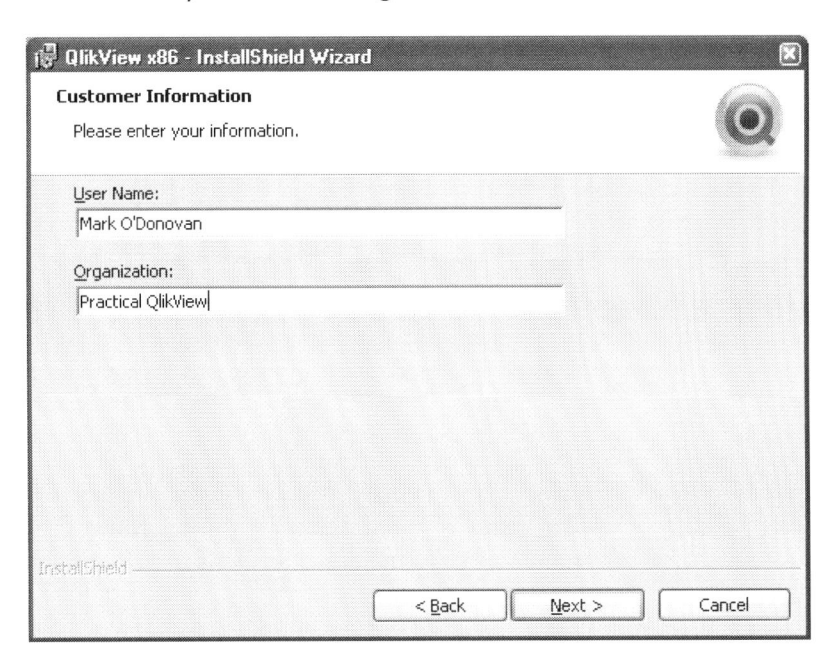

8. Check that QlikView is going to be installed on the correct drive.
9. You should check you have enough disk space on this drive.
10. Change the location where QlikView will be installed by clicking on the **Change** button and selecting another folder.

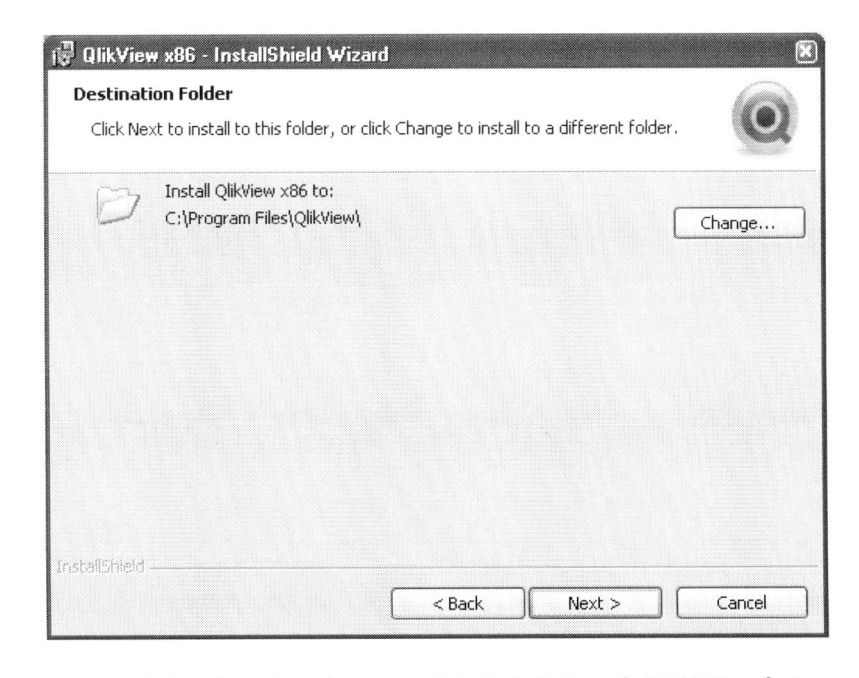

11. Select **Complete** for a complete installation of all QlikView features.

Getting Started - CHAPTER 2   **21**

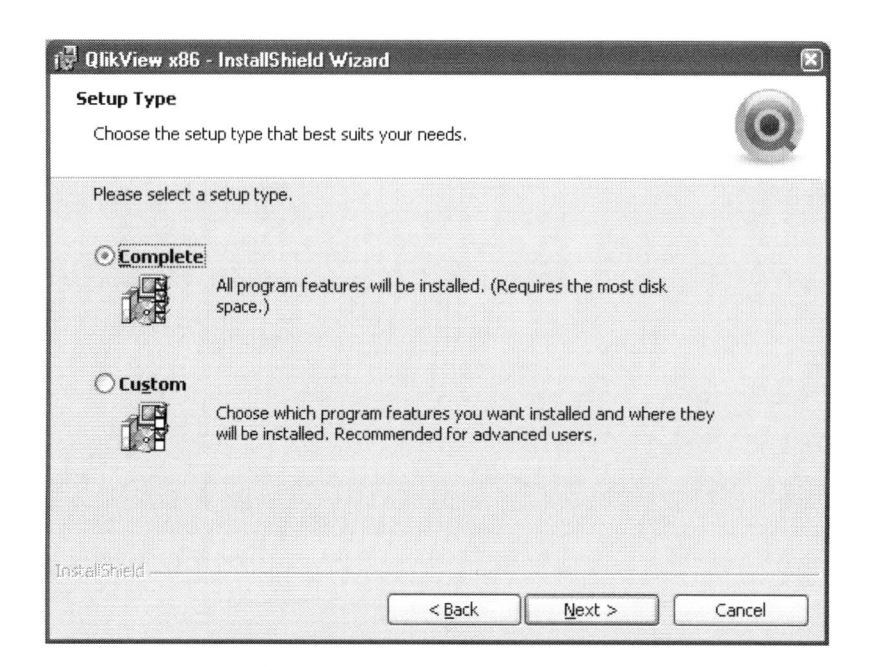

12. If you selected the **Custom** install you could choose not to install Examples, Plugins, Themes and Documentation in order to reduce the amount of space required for the installation.

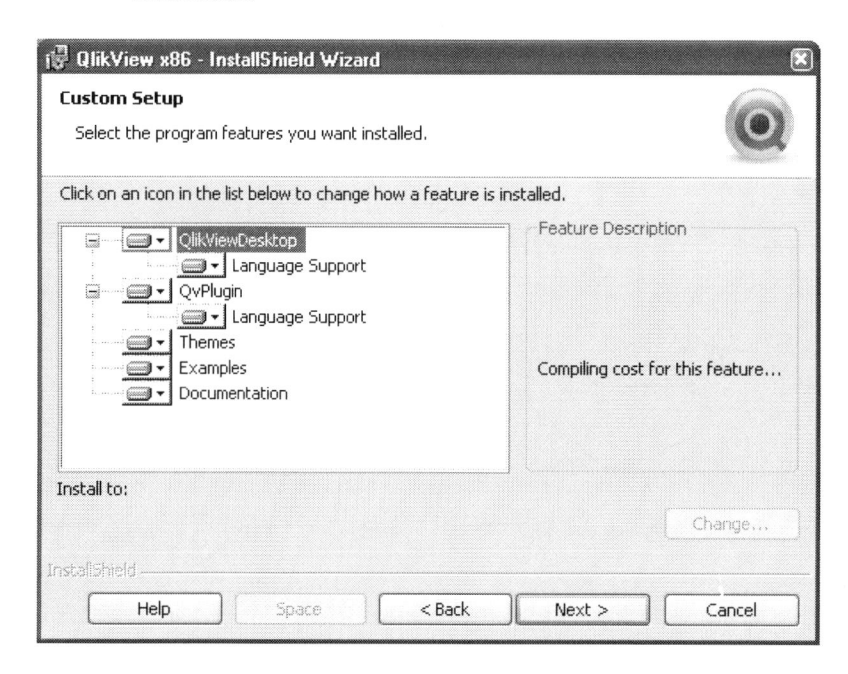

13. On 64bit Operating Systems you will have the extra option of the 64bit version of the QlikView plugin as you can see from the next screenshot.

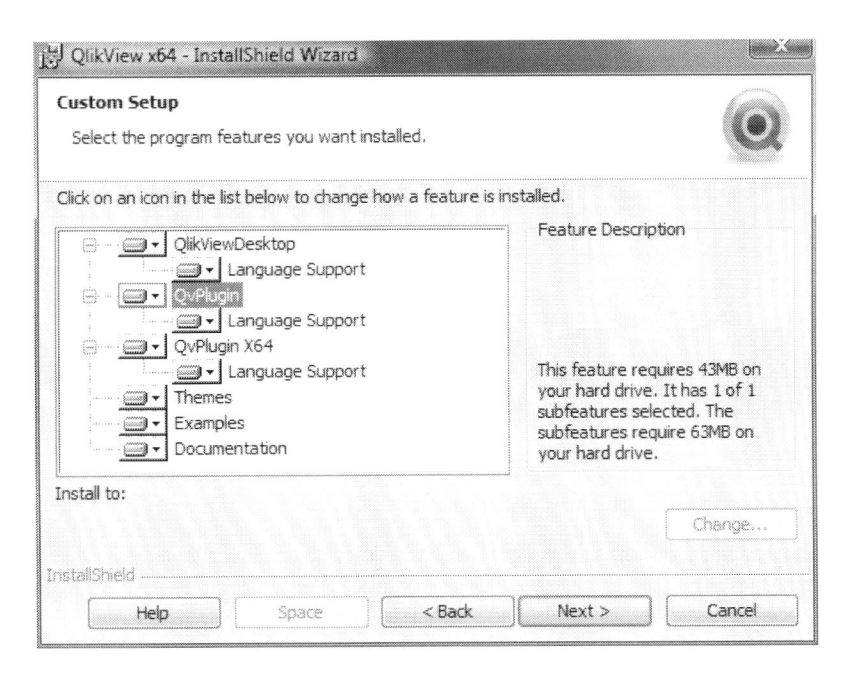

14. In this example we will continue with the full installation.
15. Click on the **Next** button.

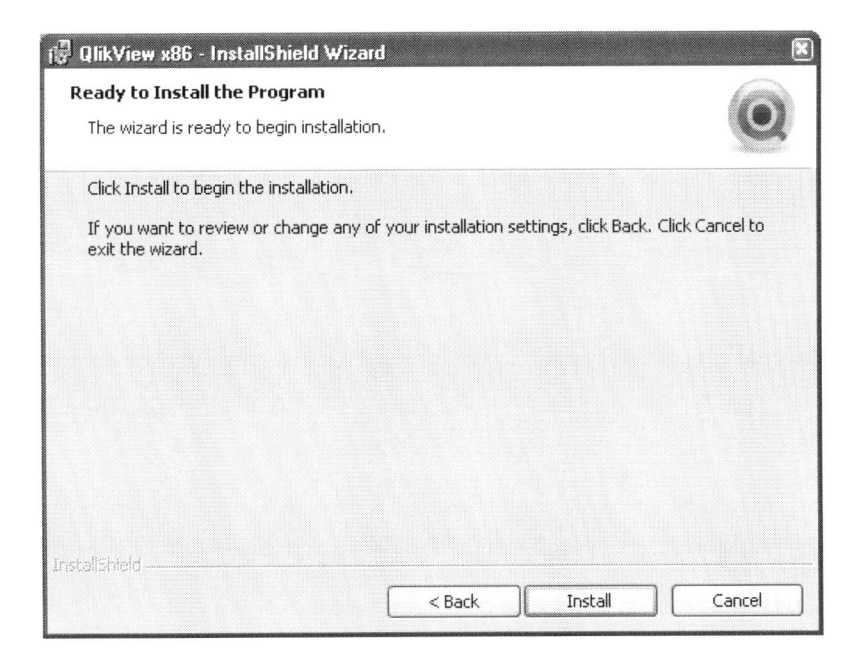

16. Click on the **Install** button.
17. Once the installation has completed the following screen will be displayed:

Getting Started - CHAPTER 2   23

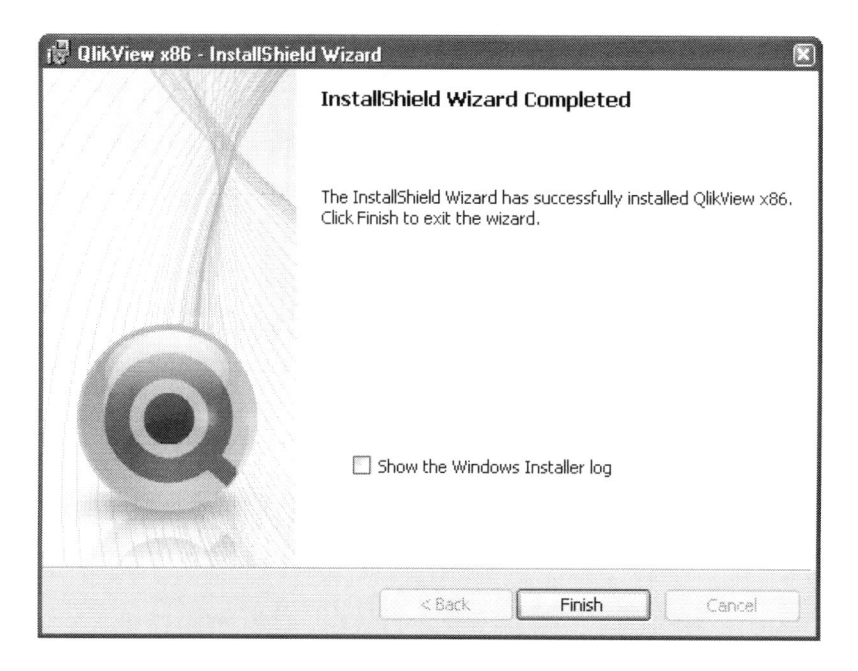

18. Click the **Finish** button.
19. Now you can click on the Start button, go to 'All Programs, find the QlikView folder and click on the 'QlikView 11' application.

Summary

In this chapter we covered the system requirements for QlikView as well as the limitations of the QlikView Personal Edition.

You have downloaded QlikView and installed the application.

In the next chapter you will start using QlikView and create your first application which will include creating some simple sample data, importing the data into QlikView and creating a chart from the data.

3. My First QlikView Document

In this chapter we are going to perform the following tasks:

- Setup some data in an Excel spreadsheet using a couple of simple formulas.
- Import the data into a QlikView document.
- Display the data in a table
- Create a chart from the imported data.
- Create a table of calendar month names within the QlikView document so that there is a link between the imported data and this new table created within QlikView.
- Update the Chart and Table to display the month names.

Create some sample data

In this example we are going to create some sample sales data in Excel.
In the other examples within this book data will be downloaded from the internet.

1. Open the version of Excel that you are using.
2. Create 4 column headers of ID,TOTAL,MONTH and YEAR:

    - **ID** - Type 1 in the row below the ID header.
    - **TOTAL** - Enter the following: =RAND()*(100-10)+10
    - **MONTH** - Enter the following: =(CEILING(RAND()*12,1))
    - **YEAR** - Enter the following: =(CEILING(RAND()*10,1))+2000

    For the first row below each of the header fields perform the following 3 points to create the sales data :
3. Move the mouse to the bottom right corner of the cell (the cursor will change into a + sign).
4. Press the control key and drag the cursor down.
5. Create above 50 rows of data.

NOTE: Your data will be different as the numbers are random.

	A	B	C	D
1	ID	TOTAL	MONTH	YEAR
2	1	22.34414	5	2005
3	2	25.85694	5	2007
4	3	20.77137	9	2006
5	4	42.20922	7	2003
6	5	70.39827	7	2010
7	6	10.62519	4	2008
8	7	72.04885	9	2005
9	8	57.29614	12	2005
10	9	46.62975	10	2008
11	10	57.9066	10	2008
12	11	30.30061	10	2003
13	12	81.23921	5	2001

a into QlikView and start using QlikView

ady open click on the Start button, go to 'All Programs', find the
click on the 'QlikView 11' application.
, select 'New'.

el File where you created your sample sales data and select the file.
ton.

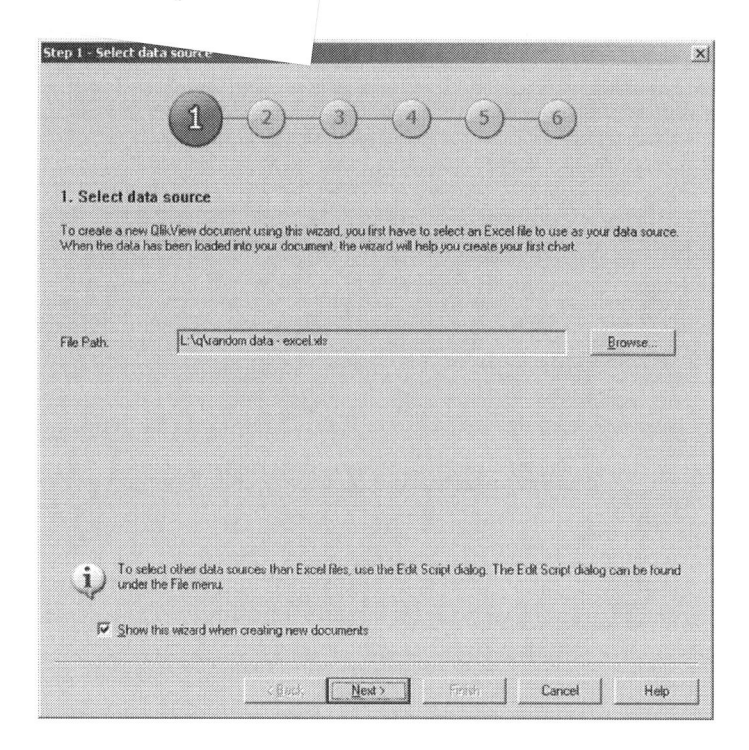

26   CHAPTER 3 - My First QlikView Document

Step 2
5. Select the option 'Use column header from data file'.
6. This option will use the headers that you have already in your excel spreadsheet.
7. Click the Next button to continue.

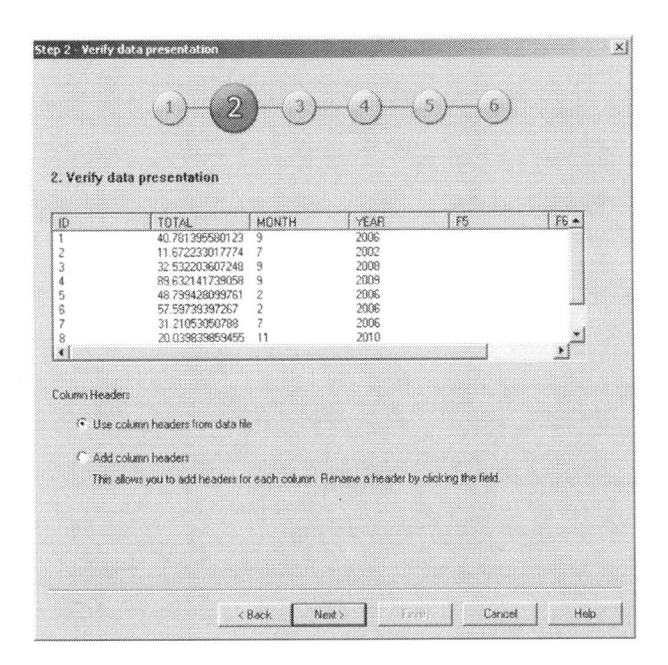

Step 3
8. Save your QlikView document and click Next. The file will end in .qvw.

Step 4
9. Select the 'Straight table' chart. This type of chart will display the data in the Excel spreadsheet that you created.

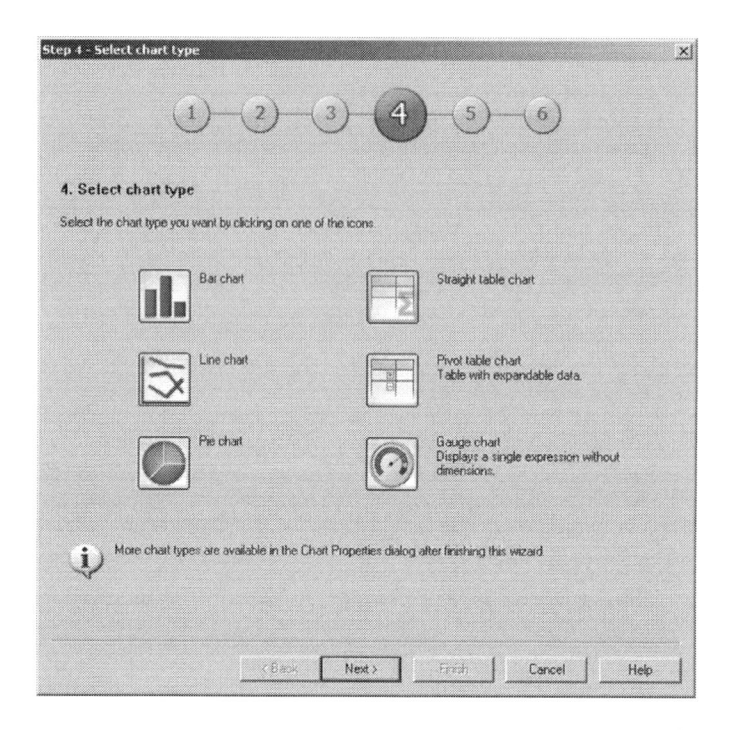

Step 5
10. Select the dimension you wish to use to group the data.
11. Set the 'First Dimension' to **MONTH**.

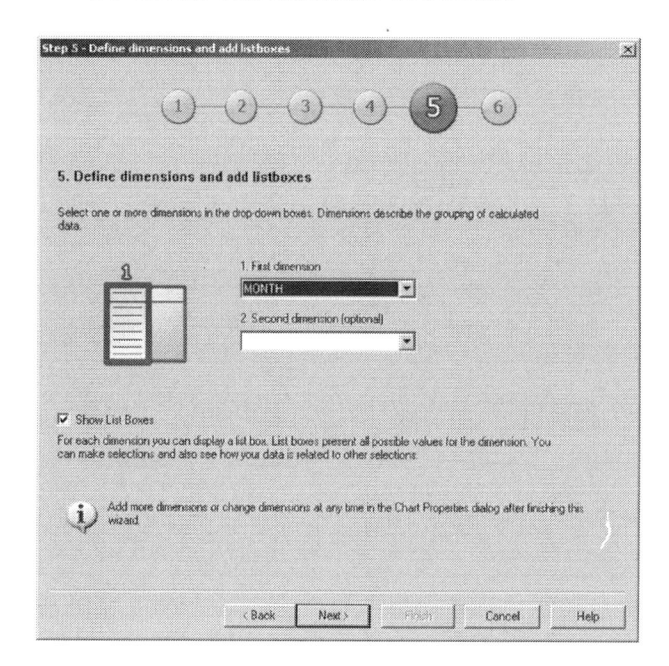

Step 6

12. Set the 'Calculate the sum of' option to **TOTAL**.
13. This will display the sum of the TOTAL field.

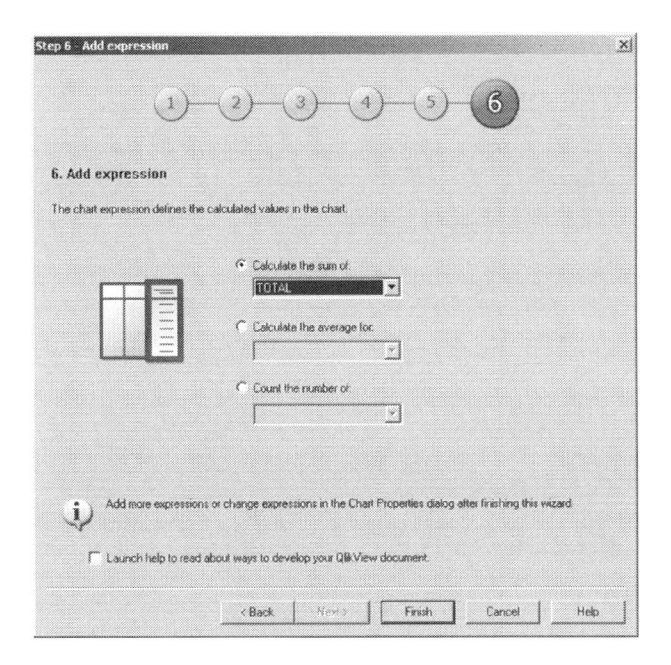

14. Click on the **Finish** button.
15. Below is a screenshot of what your first QlikView document should look like.
16. You will see the Month list and the 'Straight Chart table' contains the Sum of TOTAL values grouped by the Month Dimension.

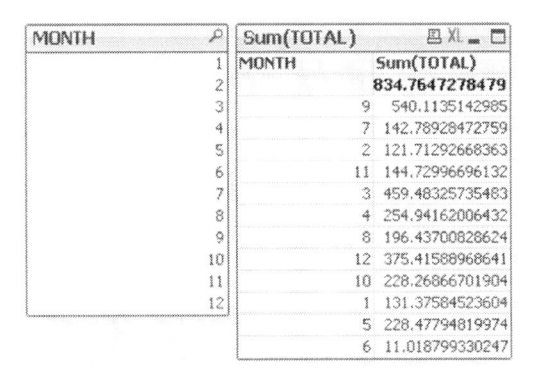

MONTH	Sum(TOTAL)
	834.7647278479
9	540.1135142985
7	142.78928472759
2	121.71292668363
11	144.72996696132
3	459.48325735483
4	254.94162006432
8	196.43700828624
12	375.41588968641
10	228.26866701904
1	131.37584523604
5	228.47794819974
6	11.018799330247

17. You can filter the values by selecting a MONTH value.
18. To remove the filter, click the 'CLEAR' button in the toolbar.

My First QlikView Document - CHAPTER 3

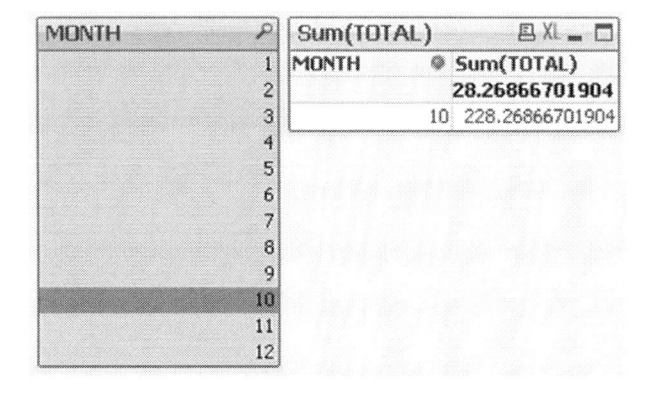

Next we will create a **Bar Chart**.

1. Right click on a blank area of the sheet.
2. Select 'New Sheet Object', then Chart.

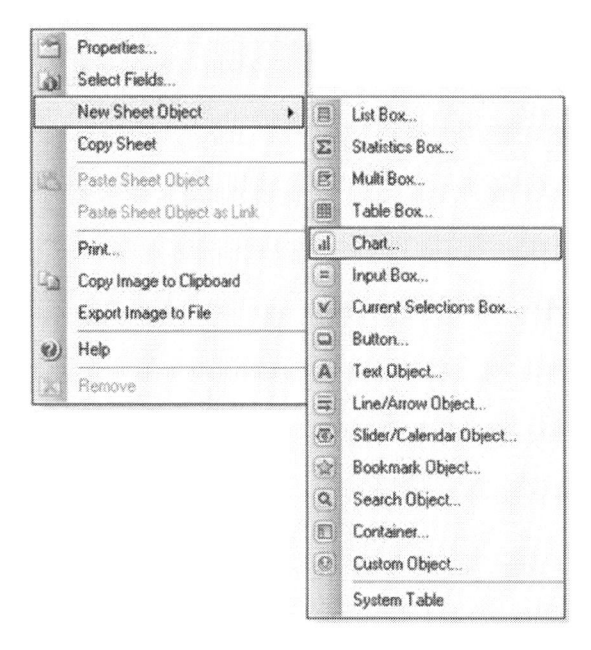

The chart wizard will start.

3. Enter a name in the Window Title textbox: My First Chart.
4. Select the icon for the Bar Chart in the 'Chart Type' area.
5. Click **Next**.

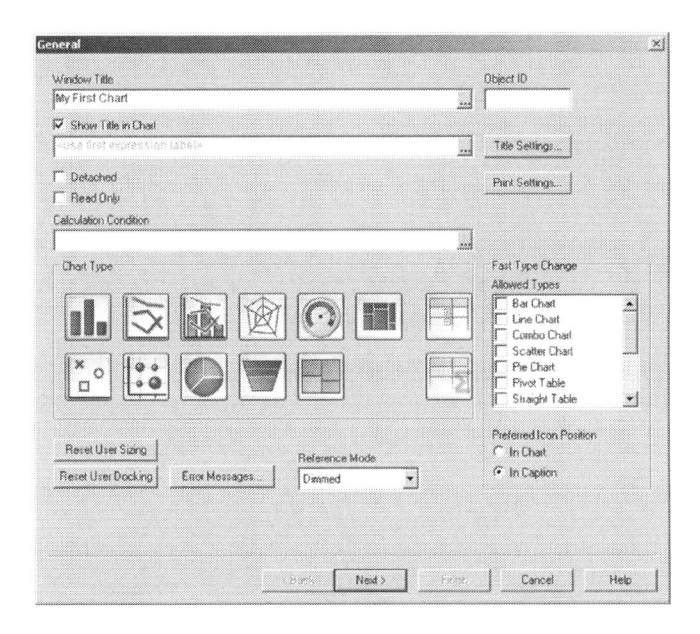

Dimensions

6. Dimensions determine how the data will be grouped in the chart (the X axis).
7. Select MONTH from the 'Available Fields/Groups' list and click the Add button so that the option is moved to the 'Used Dimensions' list.
8. Click **Next**.

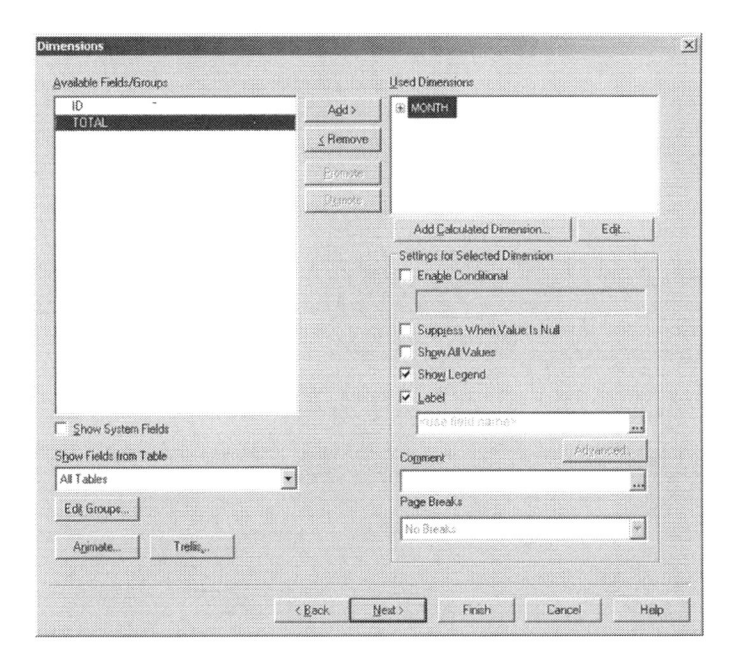

Expressions

9. The expression will determine what value is plotted on the y-axis of the chart.

My First QlikView Document - CHAPTER 3   31

10. In this example we will use the sum of all the total values for each month.
11. In the 'Edit Expression' dialog enter the text:

    SUM(TOTAL)

    Where TOTAL is the name of the field in your table that contains the sales totals.

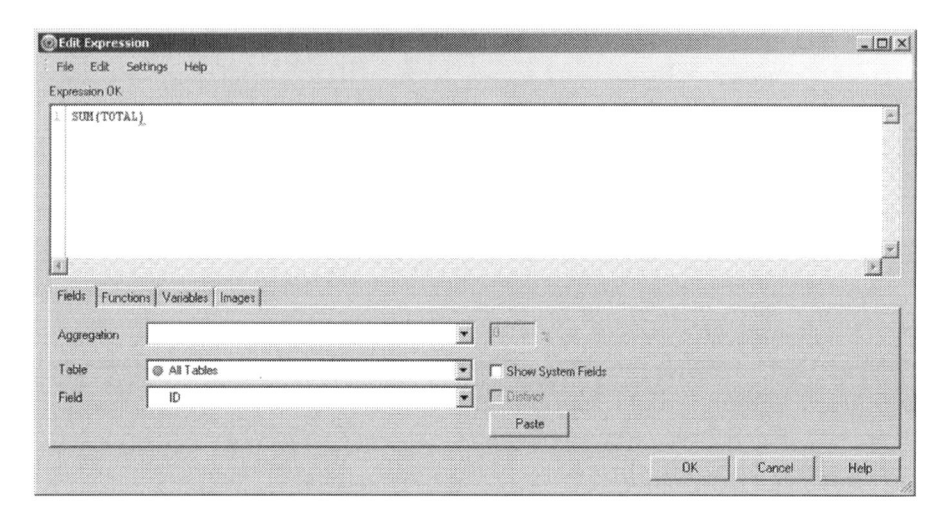

12. Click OK, then click on the Finish button and your chart will be displayed and should look similar to the screenshot below.

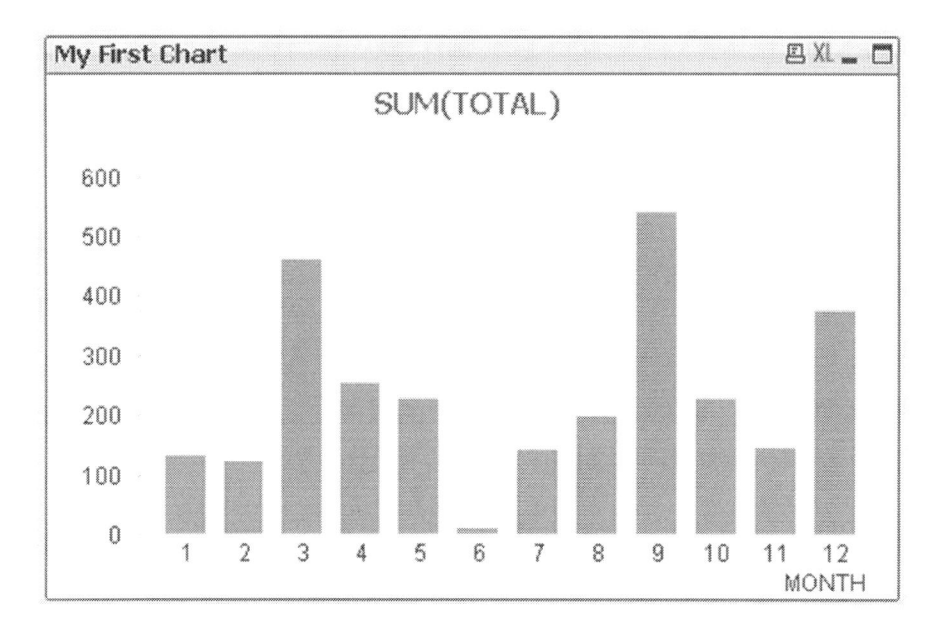

13. Now if you select a MONTH value from the MONTH list the 'Straight table' and the Chart will be updated to only display the selected months.

You can select multiple months from the MONTH list by holding down the CTRL key when you select each record.

14. A table that is defined and stored in QlikView is called an **Inline table**.
15. Next we are going to add an **Inline table** so that we can convert the Month numbers into abbreviated month names such as Jan, Feb, Mar etc...
16. Press Ctrl + E to open the load script.
17. Go to the **Insert** menu.
18. Select the **Load Statement** option.
19. Select Load Inline.

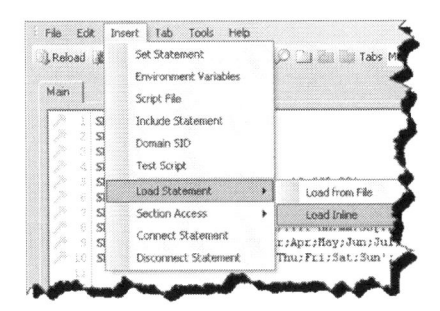

20. A grid will be displayed.
21. Change the F1 and F2 field names to Num and Name as in the next screenshot.
22. In the Num column enter the numbers from 1-12.
23. In the Name column enter the abbreviated month name such as Jan for January.
24. Click **OK** and view the code added to the Load script.

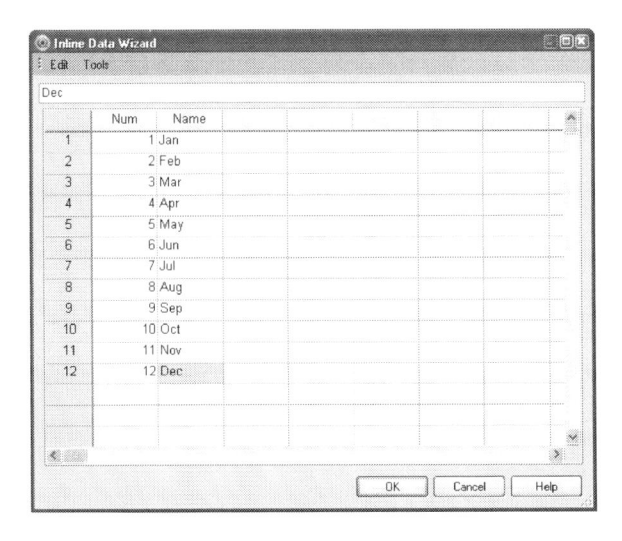

25. Below is the code that was added for our **Inline table**.
26. You can see the headers and the values that you added.
27. **LOAD** * INLINE [
    Num, Name

My First QlikView Document - CHAPTER 3   33

          1, Jan
          2, Feb
          3, Mar
          4, Apr
          5, May
          6, Jun
          7, Jul
          8, Aug
          9, Sep
          10, Oct
          11, Nov
          12, Dec
       ];

28. You can add a name to this table by entering the table name followed by a colon in the line before the load statement.
29. In this example we have called the table 'Calendar'.

IMPORTANT: Links between tables are created when field names are the same in both tables.

30. The fields in the first table were:

    ID
    TOTAL
    MONTH

31. The inline table has the fields:

    Num
    Name

32. QlikView would create no link between these tables, we can easily change the fieldnames on the inline table by just renaming the header names as in the example :

Calendar:
LOAD * INLINE [
   MONTH, MONTHNAME
   1, Jan
   2, Feb
   3, Mar
   4, Apr
   5, May
   6, Jun
   7, Jul
   8, Aug
   9, Sep
   10, Oct
   11, Nov

   12, Dec
];

LOAD ID,
   TOTAL,
   MONTH
FROM
[C:\random data - excel.xls]
(biff, embedded labels);

33. We have changed the fields in this table from Num and Name to MONTH and MONTHNAME.
34. Reload the data.
35. If we now go to the table viewer (File->Table Viewer) we can see that QlikView as created a link between the 2 tables using the MONTH field.

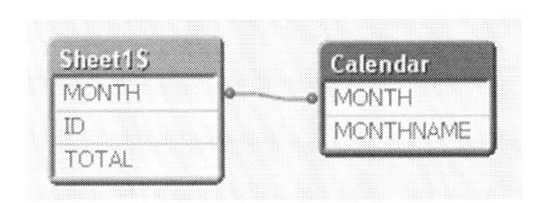

Next we are going to update the Chart we created to use the MONTHNAME field

36. Right click on the Chart and select **Properties**.
37. Select the **Dimensions** tab.
38. Remove the MONTH dimension from the Used Dimensions list.
39. Then add MONTHNAME to the Used Dimensions list.

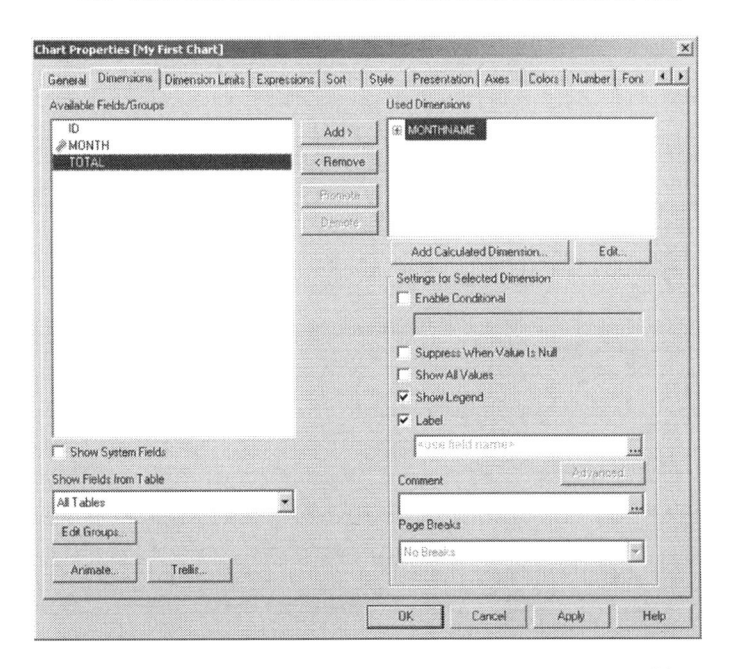

My First QlikView Document - CHAPTER 3   35

40. Click the **OK** button to apply the changes.

41. Now instead of the numeric value of the month in the chart the MONTHNAME showing the abbreviated month will be displayed.

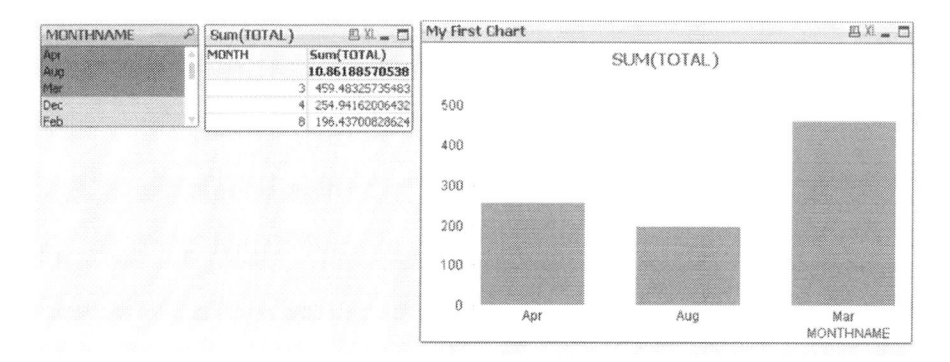

Summary

Using this simple example we have covered:

- How to create sample data when you want to learn a new function of QlikView.
- How to import data from an Excel spreadsheet.

- How to display data in tables and a simple bar chart.
- How to create tables of data within your QlikView document.

- How tables are linked together in QlikView.

In the next chapter we are going to look at the QlikView document in more detail.

We will look at some of the following areas:

- Different data sources that you can use.
- How you can change the imported data using expressions.
- Different types of Charts that you can display.
- Creating reports from your QlikView document and saving it.

4. Creating QlikView Documents

Data Sources for QlikView

A data source is where you are get the data you wish to analyze.

Different types of data sources need to be setup in different ways.

I will describe each of the main data sources for QlikView.

The first data source you will have already encountered if you are following the examples is the Excel file. Excel files are one of a group of files you can import into QlikView called 'Table Files'.

Table Files

You can import various types of text files into QlikView using the 'Table Files' button from the Load Script.

Here is a list of the files that can be imported.

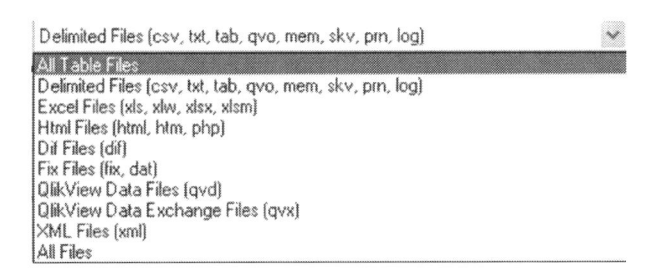

```
Delimited Files (csv, txt, tab, qvo, mem, skv, prn, log)
All Table Files
Delimited Files (csv, txt, tab, qvo, mem, skv, prn, log)
Excel Files (xls, xlw, xlsx, xlsm)
Html Files (html, htm, php)
Dif Files (dif)
Fix Files (fix, dat)
QlikView Data Files (qvd)
QlikView Data Exchange Files (qvx)
XML Files (xml)
All Files
```

When starting to use QlikView you will mostly use this option to import Excel or Delimited files such as csv (comma separated files) or plain text files such as a log.

Excel

This is the data source that everyone uses first when learning QlikView.

When you select the File->New menu option and the wizard to create new documents starts, the first step is to select an Excel data source.

Please refer to the 'My First QlikView Document' chapter for an example of using this wizard.

Once you gain more confidence in creating QlikView documents you may wish to turn off this wizard.

This can be done by selecting the Settings Menu, then the 'User Preferences' option.

In the top-right part of the screen under the 'General' Tab you will see the following option:

☑ Show "Getting Started Wizard" when creating new document

If you remove the tick from this box and click the OK button you will not longer get the wizard the guides you through setting up your new QlikView document when you select the File->New menu option.

At any other time you can import Excel files using the 'Table Files' option from the Load script.

Excel Example

In this example we are going to:

- Download some sample data
- Import the data into QlikView

Download the Sample Data: Excel 2002 Sample: PivotTable Reports

The reason for using this data is that the Pivot Tables and Chart are in the Excel documents so you can compare them against what you have done in QlikView.

Go to http://www.microsoft.com/download/en/details.aspx?id=14738

1. Download the Reports.exe file
2. Double Click the Reports.exe file
   Enter the folder where you wish extract the files to, for example: C:\sample_pivot_tables.
3. Click the Yes button to create the folder if it doesn't already exist.
4. Once the extraction has completed Click the OK button.
5. Go to the folder where you extracted the Excel files to : C:\sample_pivot_tables
6. Open each of the spreadsheets to have a quick look at the contents.
7. You will see a Worksheet in each one called 'Source Data'.
8. This is the data that you will be loading into your QlikView document.

9. You will also see pivot tables\charts that use this 'Source Data'.
10. Next you will see how you are able to create the pivot tables\chart in QlikView and explore the data easier and even export the results to Excel.

Read Source Data into QlikView

11. From the Load Script click the 'Table Files...' button.
12. Navigate to the folder where to saved the Excel files (C:\sample_pivot_tables).
13. Select the file: SampleCustomerReports.xls, then click the Open button.

    Check the following:
14. The 'File Type' is set to Excel(xls).
15. The Tables field is set to **Source Data$**
16. The Labels field is set to Embedded Labels (this will use the first row of the worksheet as the labels for each column).
17. Click on the Next button.

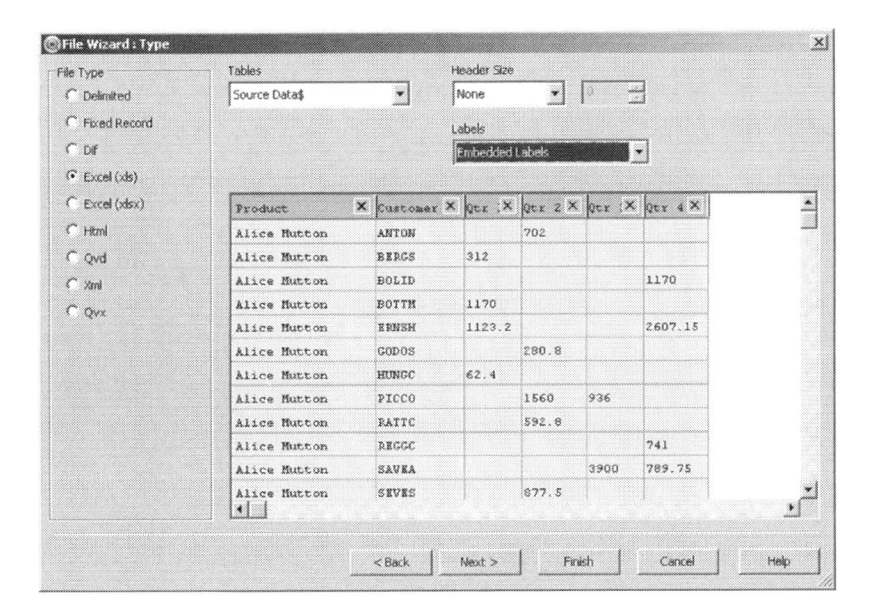

18. Click the Next button.
19. Click the Next button again.
20. From this Options screen you can set the WHERE clause.
    The WHERE clause is used to restrict the number of rows that are returned from the Excel spreadsheet and is useful if you are dealing with large amounts of data and only require rows that meet certain criteria.

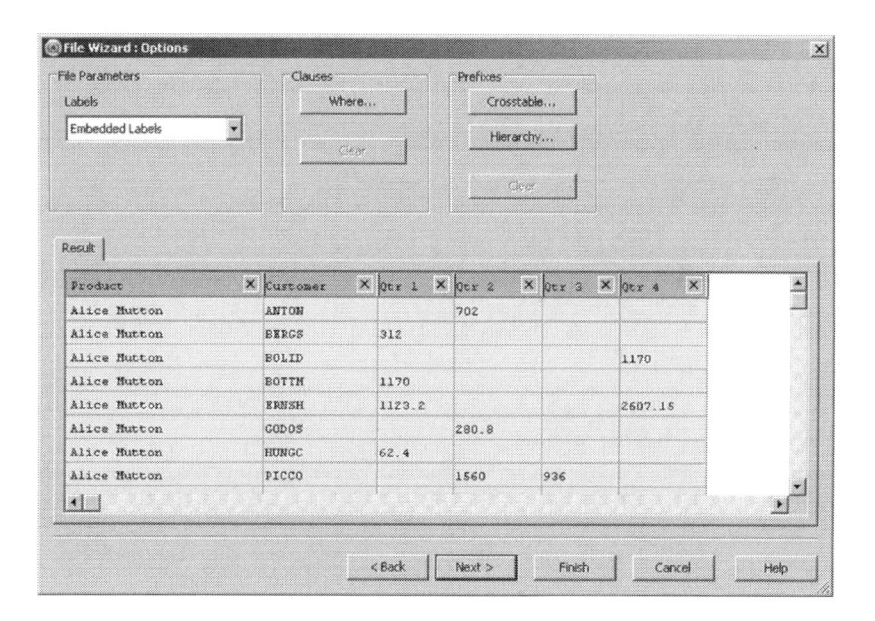

21. You can also change the table headers within this screen by clicking on the header, change the name and then click on one of the rows of data below the header to change the header.

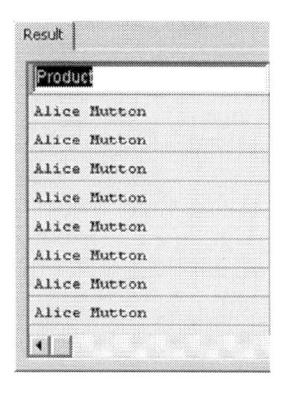

CrossTable

1. The crosstable option is used to combine data several columns.
2. Examples of using the crosstable will be covered later in this book. In particular in the example 'Tracking your spending' in section 2.
3. Click the Next button once more. Click Finish.
4. The following script that will be added to your Load script.

   LOAD Product,
      Customer,
      [Qtr 1],
      [Qtr 2],
      [Qtr 3],
      [Qtr 4]
   FROM
   C:\sample_pivot_tables\SampleCustomerReports.xls
   (biff, embedded labels, table is [Source Data$]);

5. Click the Reload button.
6. Save the QlikView document if required.
7. The 'Sheet Properties' screen will be displayed.
8. In the Fields tab, a list of fields read from the Excel file will be displayed.
9. If you move any of these fields into the 'Fields Displayed in Listboxes' a listbox will be added to your QlikView document for each field.
10. Click the OK button.

Text files

There are several reasons to import text files into QlikView. For example all your data might be in a csv (comma separated value) file or you do not own Microsoft Office.

In this example we are going to import a list of years.

1. Open the load script by selecting File->Edit Script.
2. Click the 'Table files...' button.
3. Select the text file you created with the years on each line and click the 'Open' button.
4. A similar screenshot to the next one will be displayed.
5. Click the header of the data and change @1 to YEAR.

YEAR X
2003
2006

6. Click the Finish button.

   The following LOAD statement is added to the load script.

Creating QlikView Documents - CHAPTER 4   41

```
Directory;
LOAD @1 as YEAR
FROM
d:\years_to_display.txt
(txt, codepage is 1252, no labels, delimiter is '\t', msq);
```

7. The Directory statement specifies which folder to look for the file in such as :
   Directory c:\mytestdata\;
8. Click the RELOAD button. If there were no errors the 'Sheet properties' screen will be displayed.
9. Select File->Table Viewer.

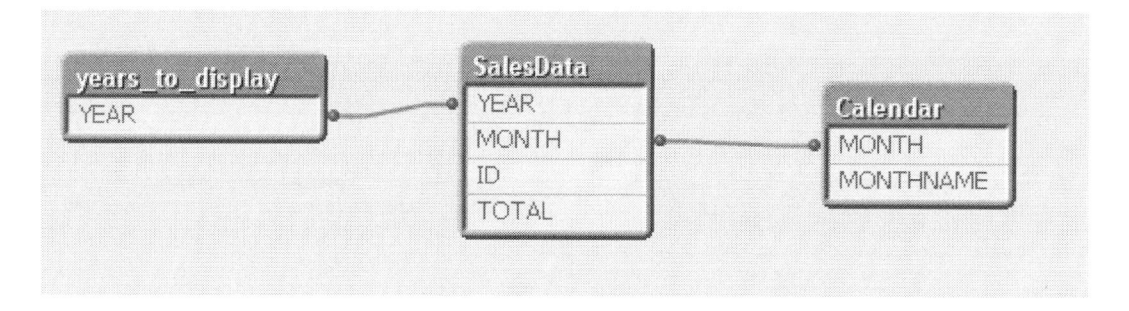

10. You will see there is a link between the SalesData table and the text file we imported. This is because we changed the field when importing the text file data to match the YEAR field in the SalesData table.

INNER JOIN

1. If you wanted to display only the years listed in your text file you could create a join between the tables as in the following example:
2. I added a name to the text file we imported just below the 'Directory;' command.
3. To only display the years listed in the text file I added the following 'INNER JOIN' command before the SalesData table is read.

   INNER JOIN (years_to_display)

4. This command means that data will only be read from the SalesData table where there is a matching record in the years_to_display table.
   In this case the years_to_display and SalesData tables are linked using the YEAR field so only years listed in the years_to_display will be displayed.

Sum(TOTAL)			
MONTHNAME	YEAR		Sum(TOTAL)
			534.04434891376
Apr		2003	16.069285304157
Mar		2003	93.742318500653
Oct		2003	97.583177013191
Jul		2006	31.21053050788
Aug		2006	72.61322387103
Feb		2006	106.39682207243
Sep		2006	116.42899164442

years to display
2003
2006

5. The 'years to display' list box lists the records in the YEAR field.
6. Example code:

```
Directory;
years_to_display:
LOAD @1 as YEAR
FROM
d:\years_to_display.txt
(txt, codepage is 1252, no labels, delimiter is '\t', msq);

INNER JOIN (years_to_display)
SalesData:
LOAD ID,
    TOTAL,
    MONTH,
    YEAR
FROM
[C:\random data - excel.xls]
(biff, embedded labels);
```

OLE DB and ODBC

Which should I use OLEDB or ODBC ?

It is generally agreed that ODBC is the old way to connect to databases.

- OLEDB - can improve data access performance.
- OLEDB - is easier to setup than ODBC.
- OLE DB - has evolved from ODBC.
- OLE DB - accesses all types of information.

- ODBC - requires setup of the DSN (Data Source Name).

Make sure you use the correct drivers for the version of the program you are using.

64bit - can use 32\64bit version of drivers.
32bit - can only use 32bit version of drivers.

How to setup ODBC connection

1. Open the ODBC Data Source Administrator.
   (These might differ on other versions of Windows)
2. Open the ODBC Administrator. You will find this option in the Control Panel.

For Vista Users: Click the Start button and select the 'Control Panel', then select 'System and Maintenance', then 'Administrative Tools', then Data Sources (ODBC).

For XP Users: Click Start. Click Control Panel. Double-click Administrative Tools. Double-click Data Sources (ODBC).

3. Click on the Drivers tab and confirm the correct driver is installed so that you can connect to your data source.
4. There are different types of DSN that you can setup:

System DSN - anyone on the machine can access this DSN.
User DSN - single user can access this DSN.
File DSN - in text file .DSN. Files don't need to be on the local computer.

5. The default location for the file DSN is:
   C:\Program Files\Common Files\ODBC\data sources
6. If the driver is not installed this will need to be done before you try to create your DSN.
7. The drivers can normally be found on the installation software or support section of the website for the software you are try to connect to.
8. Once you have confirmed the correct drivers are installed perform the following tasks to create a new System DSN:

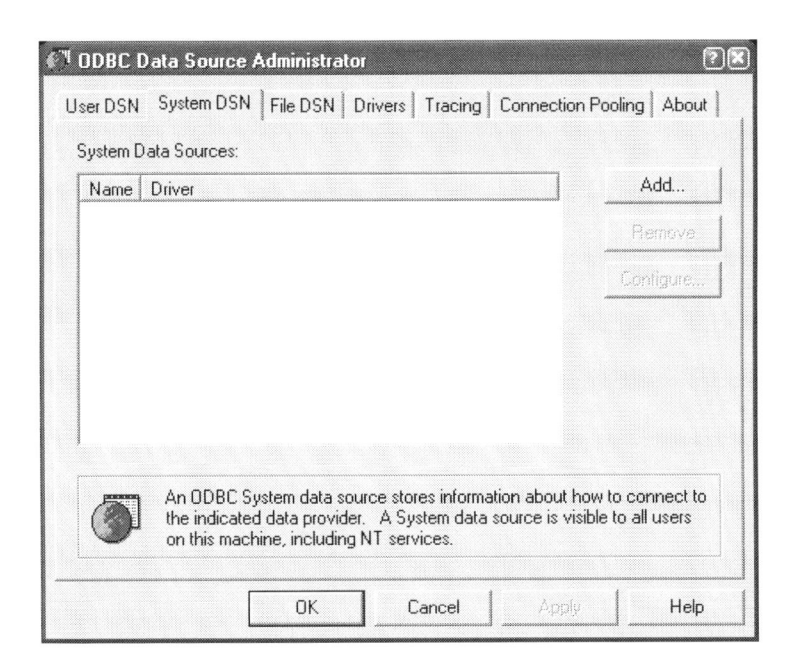

9. From the ODBC Data Source Administrator carry out the following tasks:
10. Click System DSN tab and click Add button

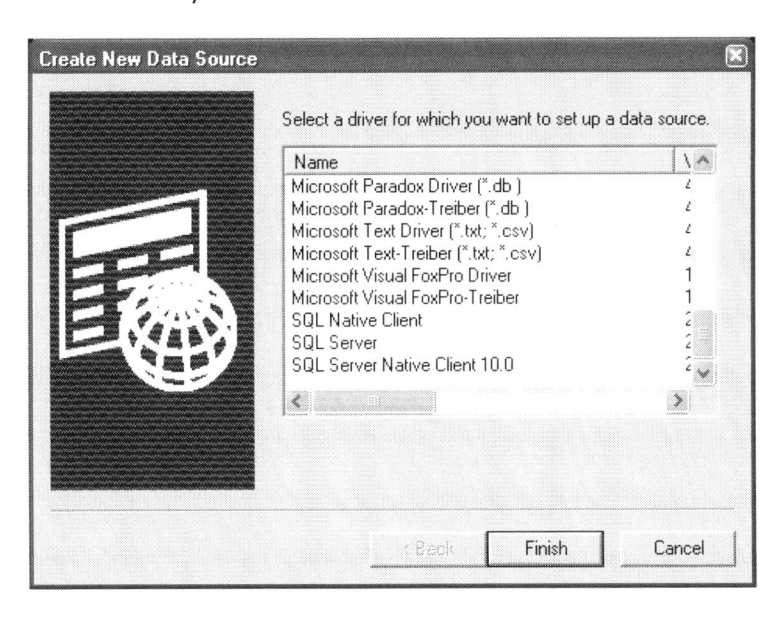

11. To create a new DSN for an Microsoft SQL Server, select the 'SQL Server' driver and click Finish.

Creating QlikView Documents - CHAPTER 4   45

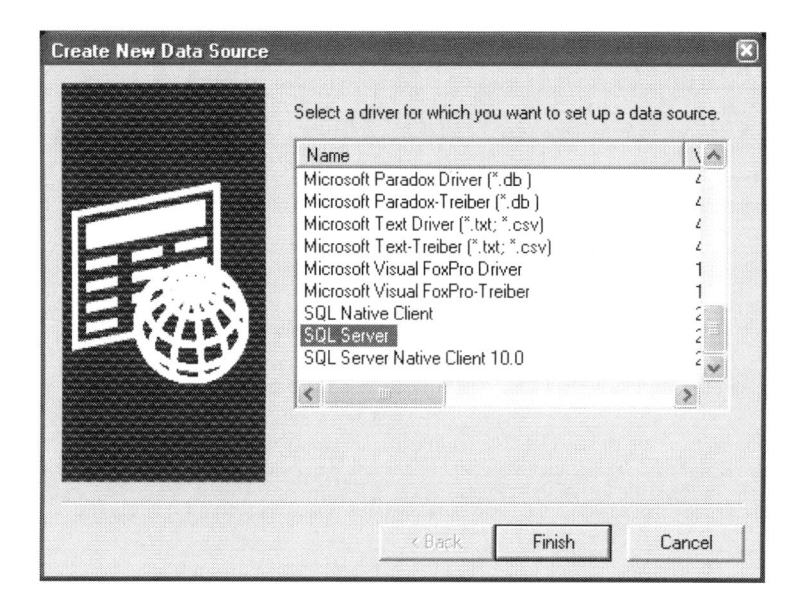

12. In this example I am using DSN name as MyTestDSN.

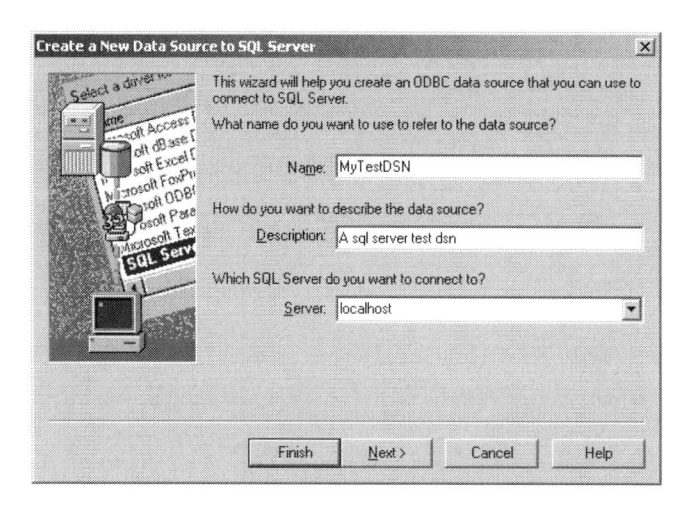

13. Enter the host name or IP Address of the machine your server is installed on and click Next.
14. Choose your authentication method.
15. (In this example we are using "SQL Server authentication")
16. Enter your Login ID and Password to connect to SQL Server and Click the Next button.

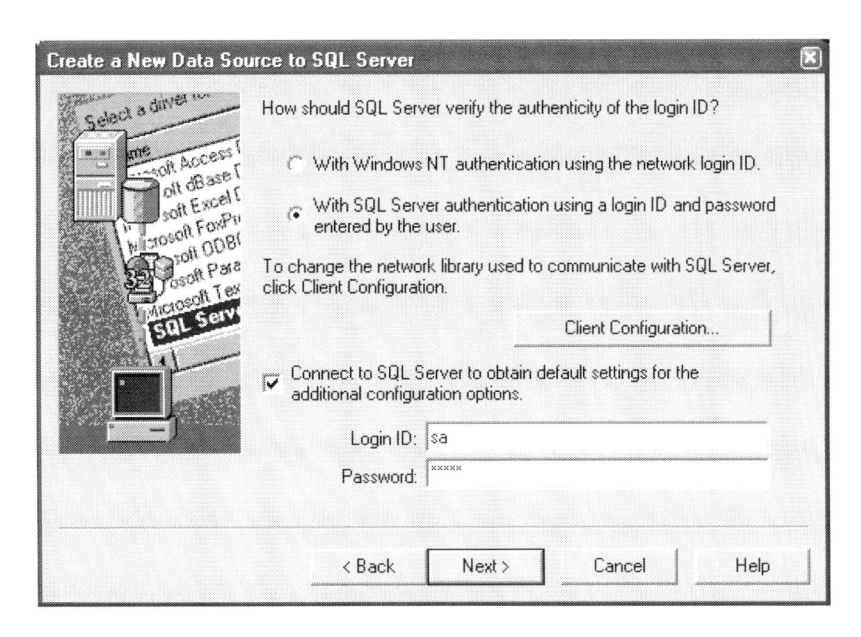

17. Click 'Next' two times to skip next Screen, then Click Finish.

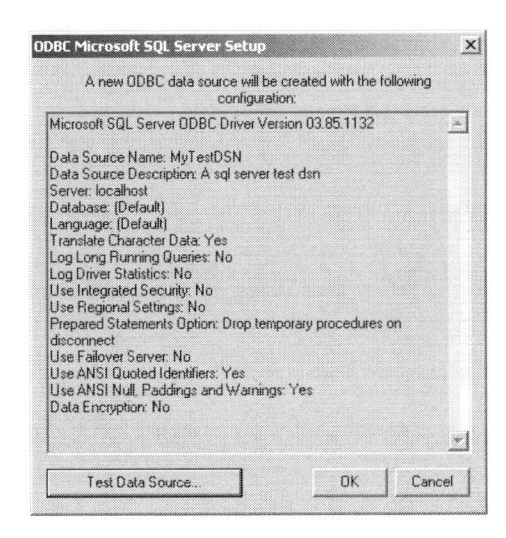

18. If you click the 'Test Data Source...' button the following screen should be displayed to confirm that you have setup your DSN correctly.

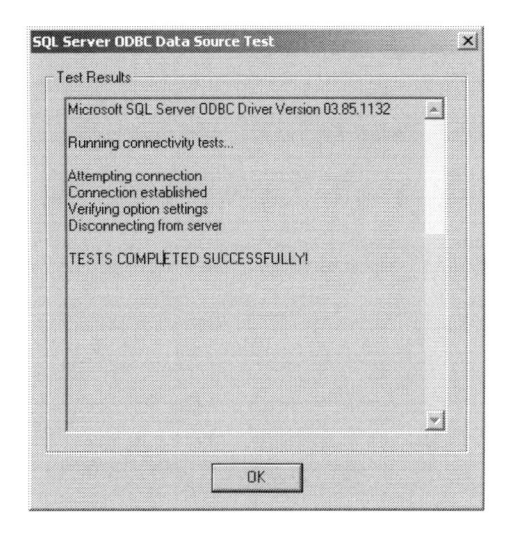

19. Click the OK button.

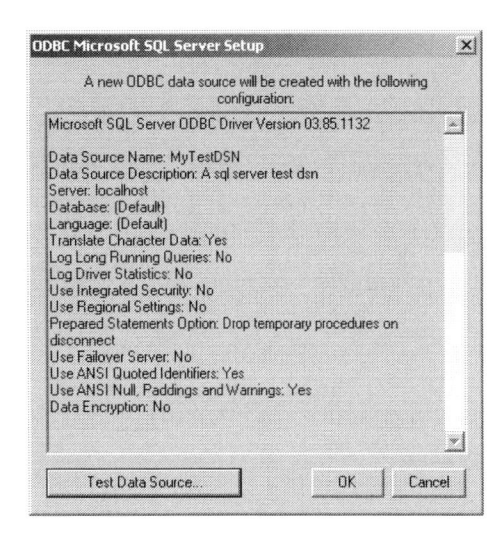

20. Click the OK button.
21. The 'System DSN' should now include the DSN you have just created:

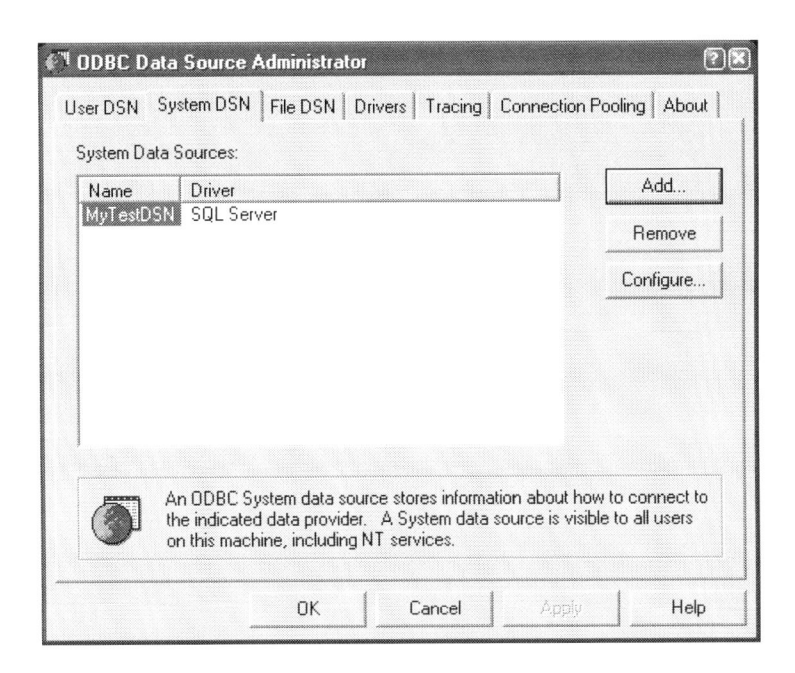

22. You can connect to various data sources using the Microsoft OLE DB providers for ODBC Drivers.

Create an ODBC Connection in QlikView
1. Open your QlikView application.
2. Select the File Menu, then select Edit Script.
3. Select 'ODBC' from Database dropdown list and then click the 'Connect...' button.
The 'Connect to Data Source' screen will be displayed.
4. All System DSN's will be displayed, if you need to see any User DSN's you need to select the 'Show User DSN's checkbox at the bottom of the screen.

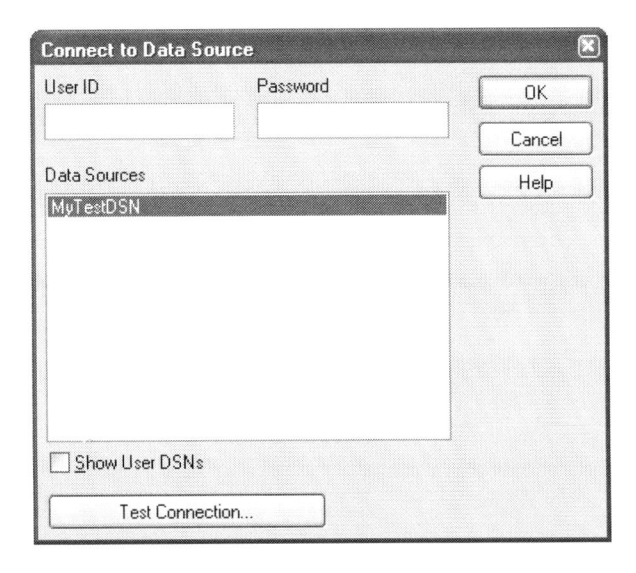

Creating QlikView Documents - CHAPTER 4   49

5. Enter the username and password for the DSN you have selected.

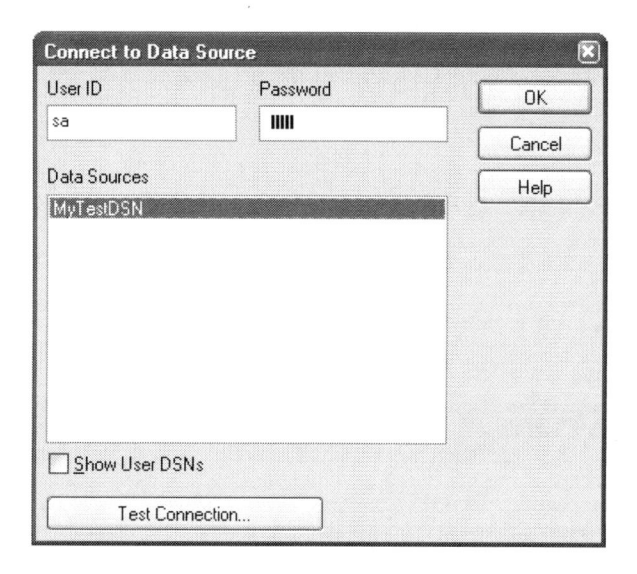

[Connect to Data Source dialog showing User ID "sa", Password field, Data Sources list with "MyTestDSN" selected, Show User DSNs checkbox, and Test Connection button]

6. Click on the 'Test Connection...' button to verify that the ODBC connection is setup correctly and that you are using the correct username and password.

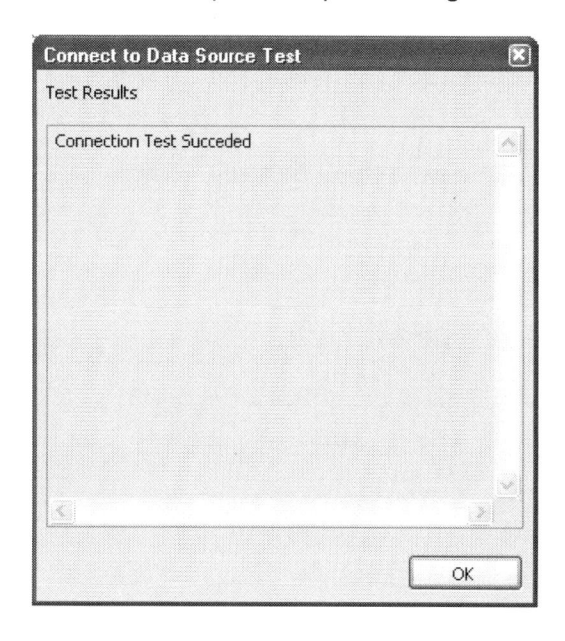

[Connect to Data Source Test dialog showing Test Results: "Connection Test Succeded"]

7. Click OK on both screens then the 'ODBC CONNECT' command will be added to your load script. You can see from the example below that the username\password have been encrypted.

ODBC **CONNECT** TO MyTestDSN (XUserId is fWSDQZFMeD, XPassword is LcTfCRFMLLZEHHC);

8. To test these connections click on the 'Debug' button in the toolbar.

50 CHAPTER 4 - Creating QlikView Documents

9. If you have not already saved your QlikView app you will get a message asking you to save your document before continuing.
10. Click on the OK button and save the document.
11. Then the Debug screen will be displayed.
12. To run the full Load Script just click on the 'Run' button'.
13. You will see a 'Connected' message at the bottom of the screen.
14. This confirms that the script has connected to the database using your ODBC connection.
15. If you are reading the data from your load script you can use the 'Limited Load' feature to only read a set number of rows of data.
In the example only 10 rows of data would be read when the 'Run' button was clicked.
This is very useful when you are using data sources with a large amount of data.

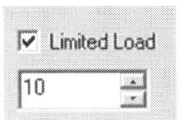

16. Click on the Close button and the following screen will be displayed.
17. There is nothing in the 'Available Fields' list because there is no select command in your load script to read your data.
18. Click on the 'OK' button.
19. Select the File->Edit script menu option to return to the load script.
20. The CONNECT command will now be added to your load script.
21. Next we will look at creating OLE DB connections and then how you can read data using ODBC \ OLEDB connections.

Create an OLE DB connection

22. Select the File Menu, then select 'Edit Script',
23. Select 'OLE DB' from Database dropdown list and then click the 'Connect...' button.

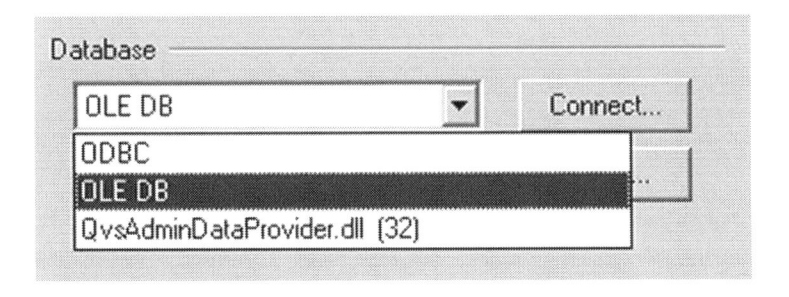

24. The Data Link Properties page will be displayed.

Creating QlikView Documents - CHAPTER 4 51

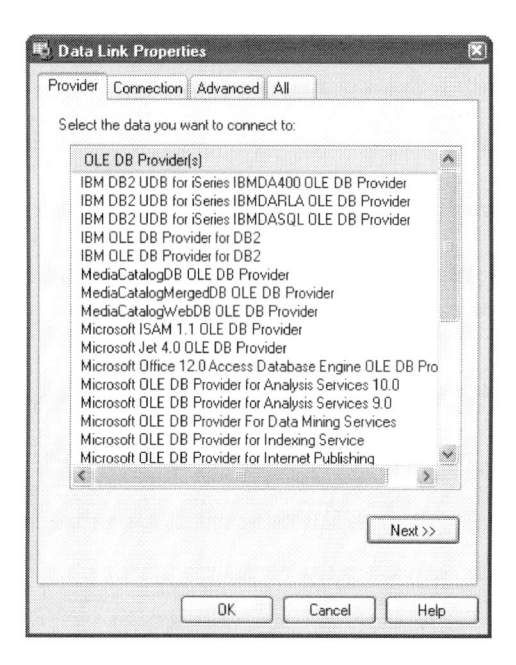

Provider tab:
25. A list of OLE DB providers will be displayed.
26. Select the provider you wish to use.
27. In this example we are going to connect to a SQL Server so select 'SQL Native Client'.
28. Click the **Next** button.

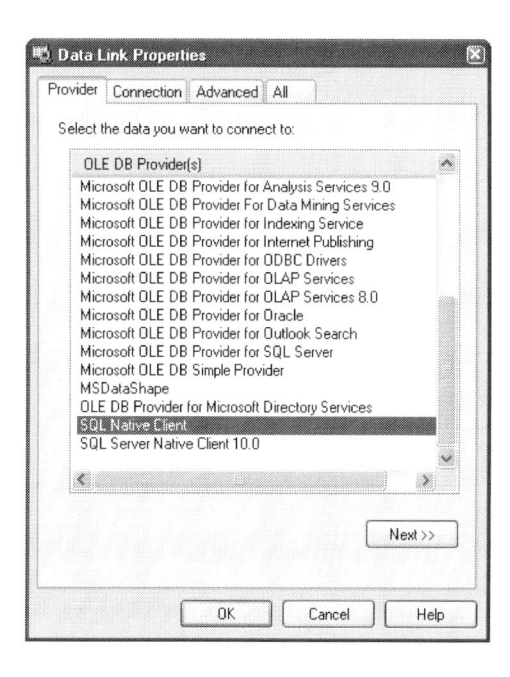

Connection tab:
29. **Data Source**: This is the name of the server where the SQL Server is installed. Localhost is for the local machine ie: the machine you are using.

30. **Initial catalog**: This is the database that you will connect to, in this example the database is called 'mytestdatabase'.

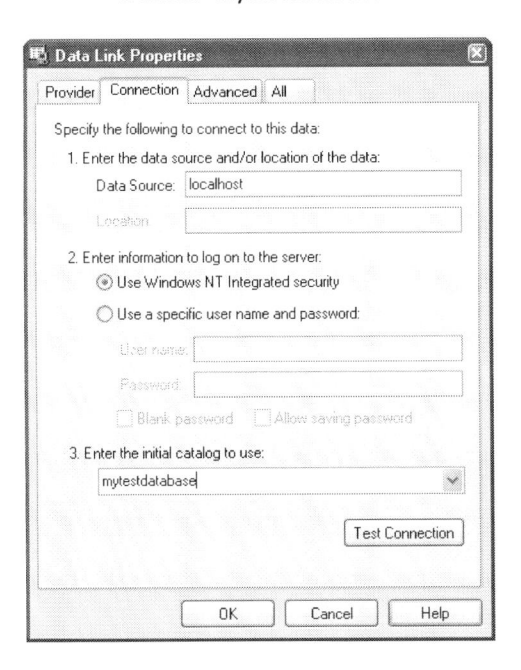

(To use sql authentication select 'Use a specific user name and password')

31. In the example below the username is set to 'sa'.

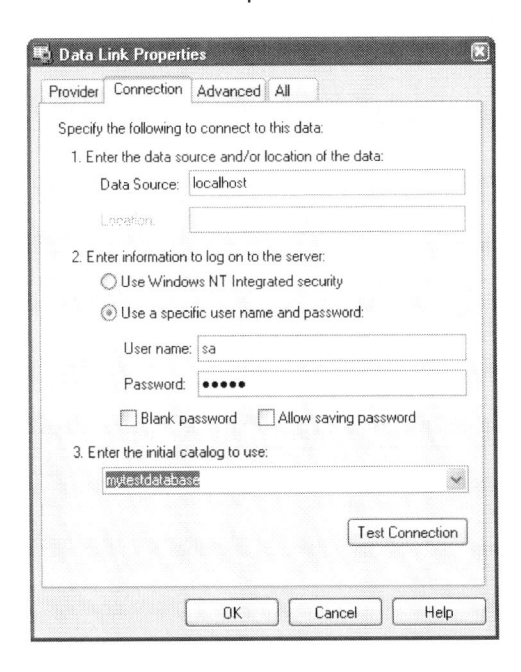

32. Click the 'Allow saving password'. Make sure the 'Blank password' option is **not** selected.

33. Click on the 'Test Connection' button. This will check that the username and password are correct and have access to the database specified in the initial catalog.

34. Click OK, then an 'OLEDB **CONNECT** TO' command is added to the load script.
35. The format is:

    'OLEDB **CONNECT** TO' [<the connection string>]

Read data using OLE DB\ODBC connections

A CONNECT command on its own in your load script is not very useful.
You need to use a SELECT statement to read some data into your QlikView application.

1. Open your Load script (Ctrl + E for the shortcut).
2. Click the SELECT button.
3. The 'Create Select Statement' screen will be displayed.
4. For each table you want to read data into your QlikView application:
5. Select the table from the 'Database Tables' list.
6. Select the Fields you wish to add from the Fields list. If you select all fields as '*' then click on the 'Preceding Load' option so that all fields are displayed in the script.
7. Click the Add button.
8. Once you have finished adding tables click the OK button.

ODBC Connection to an Access database

In many respects this example is similar to the ODBC connection to the sql server database. But not everyone uses sql server.

1. First download the AdventureWorks.zip file from:
   http://adventureworksaccess.codeplex.com.

2. Unzip the database which is an accdb file.
3. The Access database will be saved into the folder c:\qv_access_db.
4. Open the ODBC Administrator. You will find this option in the Control Panel.

   For Vista Users : Click the Start button and select the 'Control Panel', then select 'System and Maintenance', then 'Administrative Tools', then Data Sources (ODBC).
   For XP Users: Click Start. Click Control Panel. Double-click Administrative Tools. Double-click Data Sources (ODBC).

   ### Add a DSN for Microsoft Access
5. Click on the 'System DSN' tab.
6. Click the Add button.

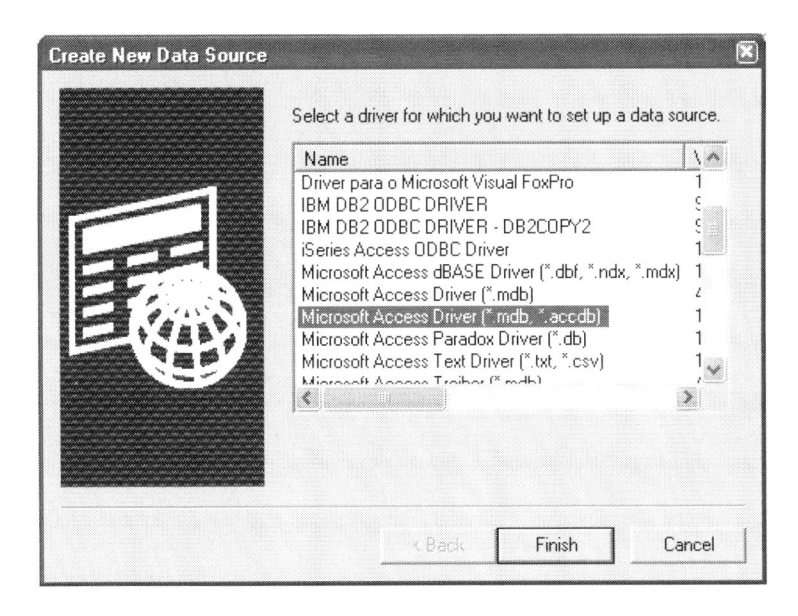

7. Highlight the 'Microsoft Access Driver (*.mdb, *.accdb)' option, then click 'Finish'.
8. The '**ODBC** Microsoft Access Setup' screen will be displayed.

Creating QlikView Documents - CHAPTER 4   55

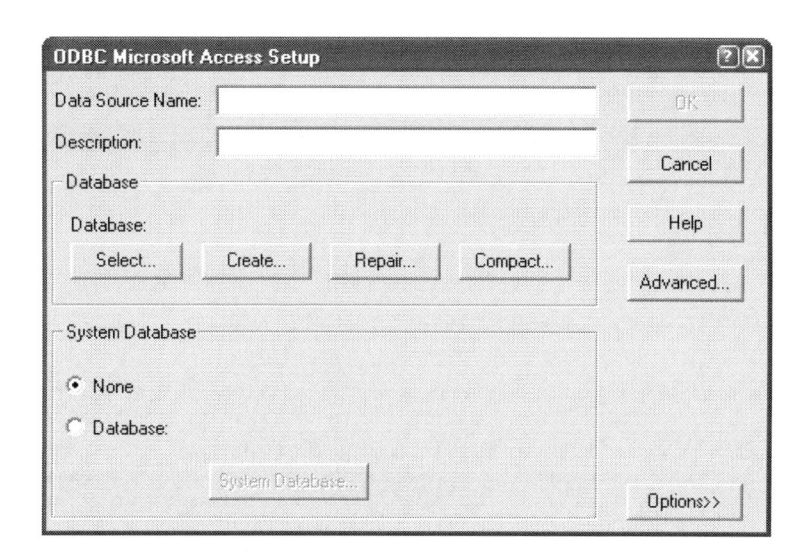

9. Click the 'Select' button and browse to your Access database.
10. Click the OK button.

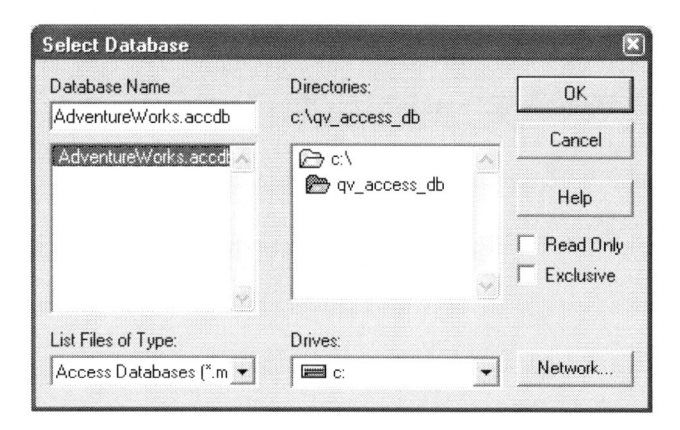

11. Give your DSN a name such as : my_test_access_db.
12. Click the OK button.

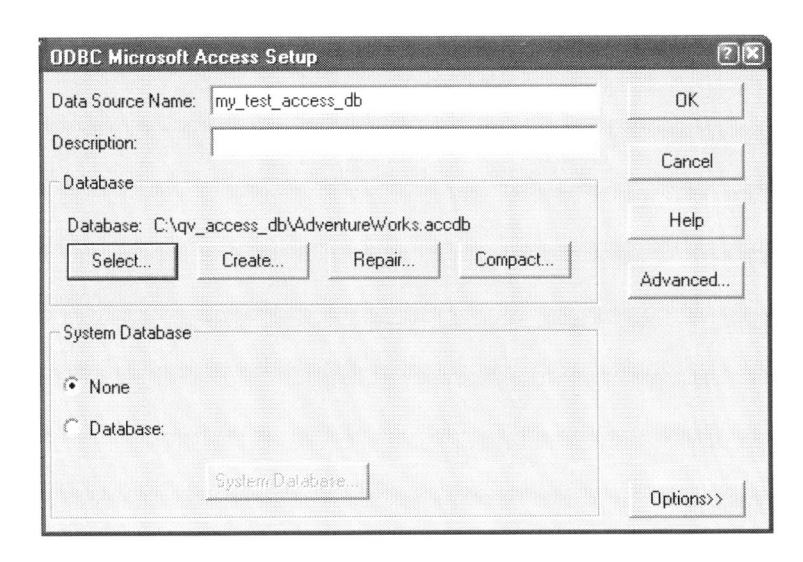

13. You now can see your new DSN for Microsoft Access in the list of System DSNs. If you do not have a driver for accdb files you download it from :

    http://www.microsoft.com/en-us/download/details.aspx?id=13255

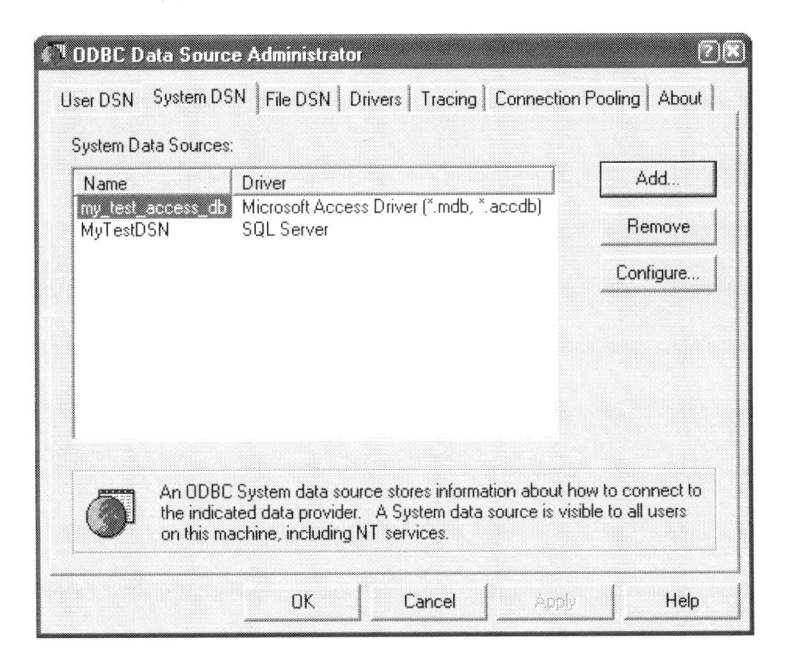

14. Now open QlikView and select the File->New option.
15. If the wizard starts press the cancel button.
16. Select the File->Edit Script option. This will display your load script.
17. Select 'ODBC' from Database dropdown list and then click the 'Connect...' button.
18. The 'Connect to Data Source' screen will be displayed.
19. All System DSN's will be displayed, if you need to see any User DSN's you need to select the 'Show User DSN's checkbox at the bottom of the screen.

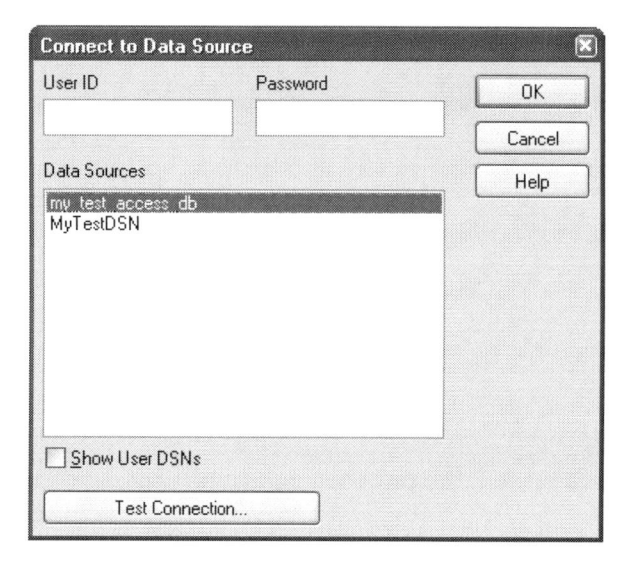

20. You do not require a username \ password for this Access database so you can click the 'Test Connection...' button to check your DSN is setup correctly.
21. You should see the screenshot below if there are not problems with your DSN.

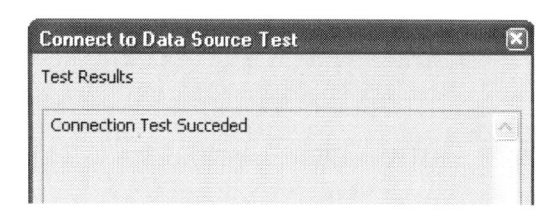

22. Click the OK button in both the 'Connect to Data Source Test' screen and 'Connect to Data Source' screen.
23. The ODBC CONNECT statement should be added your load script like the one shown next:

    ODBC **CONNECT** TO [my_test_access_db;DBQ=C:\qv_access_db\AdventureWorks.accdb];

Select Tables from your Access database

24. Open your Load script (Ctrl + E for the shortcut).
25. Click the SELECT button.
26. The 'Create Select Statement' screen will be displayed.

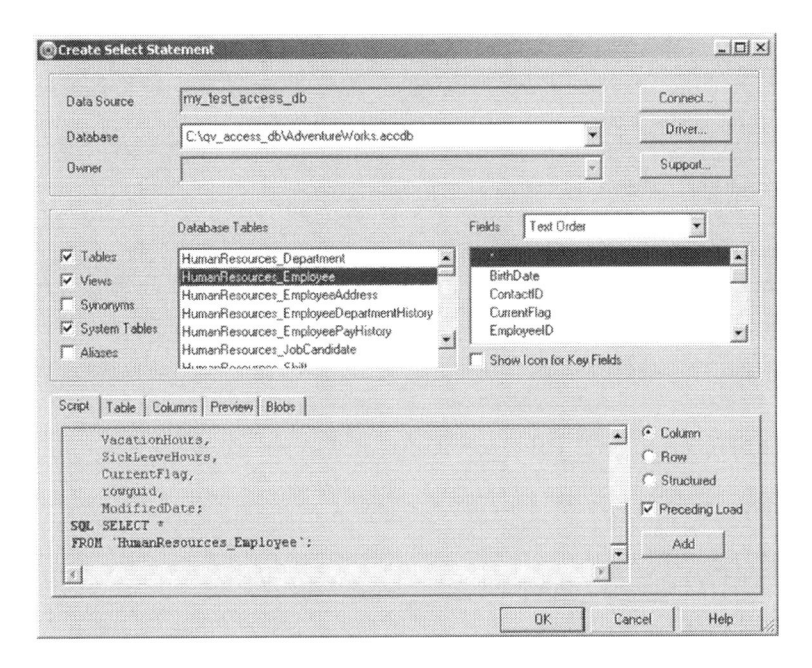

For each table you want to reload data into your QlikView application:
27. Select the table from the 'Database Tables' list.
28. Select the Fields you wish to add from the Fields list.
29. If you select all fields as '*' then click on the '**Preceding Load**' option so that all fields are displayed in the script.
30. Click the Add button.
31. Once you have finished adding tables click the OK button.
32. Below is an example of the CONNECT and LOAD statement used to add the HumanResources_Employee table from the database to your QlikView document.

CONNECT TO [my_test_access_db;DBQ=C:\qv_access_db\AdventureWorks.accdb];
 LOAD EmployeeID,
  NationalIDNumber,
  ContactID,
  LoginID,
  ManagerID,
  Title,
  BirthDate,
  MaritalStatus,
  Gender,
  HireDate,
  SalariedFlag,
  VacationHours,
  SickLeaveHours,
  CurrentFlag,
  rowguid,
  ModifiedDate;
SQL SELECT * FROM `HumanResources_Employee`;

33. Click on the RELOAD button to read the data into your QlikView document.
34. Hold down the CTRL key and select some fields , then click the add button to move the fields into the 'Fields displayed in listboxes'. See the next screenshot.

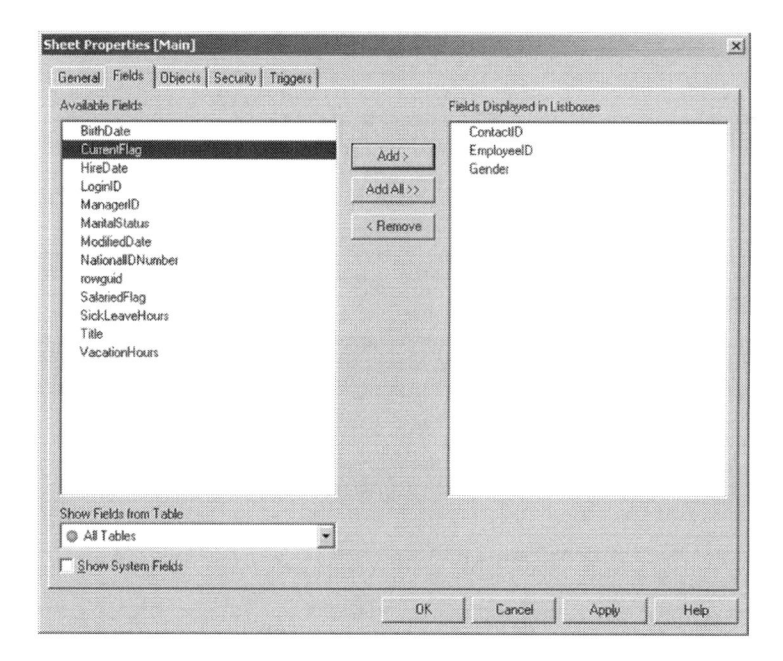

35. Click the OK button to see the data of the fields you selected.
36. Select and drag the list boxes into a better order (see next screenshot).

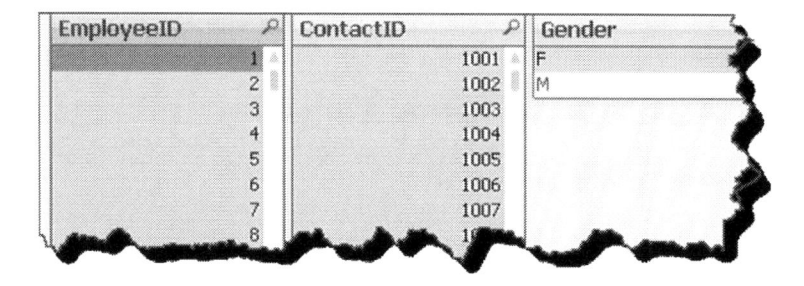

37. In this example I selected 'Employee Id' 1.
38. The fields that are not greyed out in the other list boxes tell me that this Employee has a Contract ID of 1209 and Gender is Male ('M').
    Next we will look at how to manage the data you have loaded into your document.

5. Manage data loaded into QlikView

Once you have created the right links between your tables creating the charts\tables from that data is relatively easy.

In this chapter we will examine how QlikView creates links between tables and how we can prevent QlikView from creating unwanted links between tables.

We will also cover the use of expressions in QlikView to manage your data.

Next we will look at how you can preview the data you have loaded into your QlikView document using your load script.

You can explore the data you have loaded by going to the File Menu then selecting the 'Table Viewer' option (CTRL+T).

This is the table that we used in the previous example of an ODBC connection to an Access database.

If you right click on a table you will have the option to Preview the data that is loaded into your QlikView document.

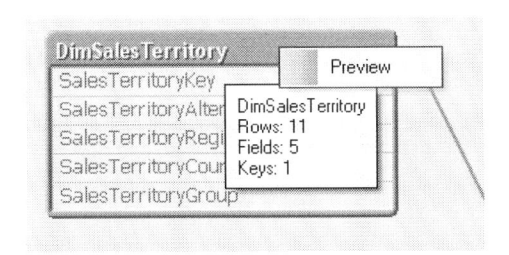

For a more complex view of several tables linked together see the next screenshot.

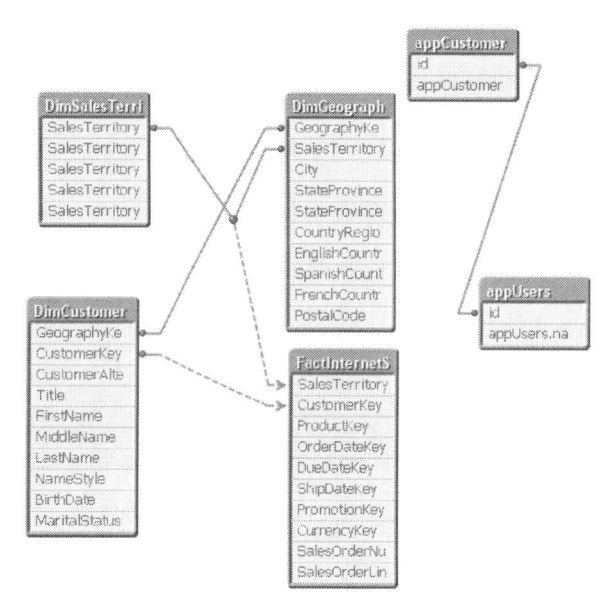

NOTE: The tables with links between the fields have the same field name.
Dashed lines in the Table viewer means that there is a Circular reference between tables.

The problem with circular references is that they can lead to unpredictable results.

The example below shows the links between tables that cause a circular reference :
DimCustomer(GeographyKey) -> **DimGeography**(GeographyKey)

DimGeography(SalesTerritory) **FactInternetSales**(SalesTerritory)

Back to:
FactInternetSales(CustomerKey) -> **DimCustomer**(CustomerKey)

To avoid Circular references firstly you need to decide if we need all the fields in each table.

If you can remove fields from the load script that are not required this might break the circular reference.

If all fields are required we can make changes to the way tables are linked together using the QUALIFY statement which we will cover next.

Link Tables

QlikView creates links between tables of data where there are identical field names in both tables. It is that simple.

But with that simplicity there can sometimes be problems that need to be resolved. Such as when QlikView creates a link between 2 tables that you do not want.

Luckily there are a couple of ways that we can fix these problems:

1. Using the AS clause to rename field names.
   The format of the AS clause is:

   <original fieldname> AS <new fieldname>

   For example: If you had the 2 tables below in your load script.

   appUsers:
   LOAD id,
      name;
   SQL SELECT *
   FROM testdb.dbo.users;

   appCustomers:
   LOAD id,
      name;
   SQL SELECT *
   FROM testdb.dbo.customers;

   The 2 tables would be linked together because of the identical field names.
   Therefore you can simply change name of the fields that are causing the link in one table as we have done in the appUsers table.

   appUsers:
   LOAD id as userid,
      name as username;
   SQL SELECT *
   FROM testdb.dbo.users;
   appCustomers:
   LOAD id,
      name;
   SQL SELECT *
   FROM testdb.dbo.customers;

2. Use the QUALIFY statement

This works by prefixing the table name to each field:

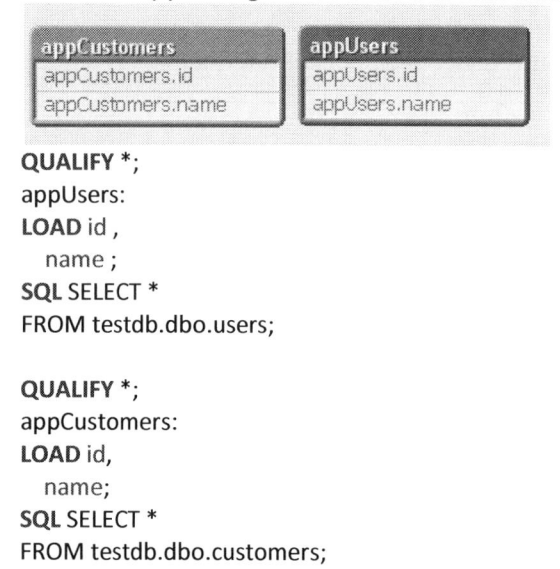

appCustomers	appUsers
appCustomers.id	appUsers.id
appCustomers.name	appUsers.name

QUALIFY *;
appUsers:
LOAD id ,
   name ;
SQL SELECT *
FROM testdb.dbo.users;

QUALIFY *;
appCustomers:
LOAD id,
   name;
SQL SELECT *
FROM testdb.dbo.customers;

If you need to link the tables you can use the UNQUALIFY statement to prevent the table name from being prefixed to the field listed in the UNQUALIFY statement.
As in the next example where the id field is linked by using the UNQUALIFY statement.

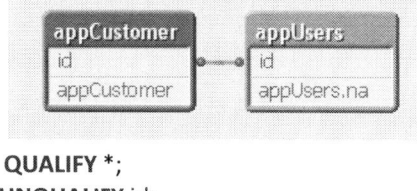

appCustomer	appUsers
id	id
appCustomer	appUsers.na

 QUALIFY *;
UNQUALIFY id;
appUsers:
LOAD id ,
   name ;
SQL SELECT *
FROM testdb.dbo.users;

QUALIFY *;
UNQUALIFY id;
appCustomers:
LOAD id,
   name;
SQL SELECT *
FROM testdb.dbo.customers;

Read less data

You might not require all the data in the spreadsheet\text file\database that you are loading into your QlikView document.

Next we will cover ways in which you can filter and group your data.
If you have used sql commands before these concepts will be familiar to you.

Filter the data: WHERE

The WHERE clause can be used with SQL SELECT statements.

In this example we are only reading the EmployeeIDs that are less than 10.

ODBC **CONNECT** TO [my_test_access_db;DBQ=C:\qv_access_db\AdventureWorks.accdb];

```
Employees:
LOAD EmployeeID,
    NationalIDNumber,
    Gender,
    rowguid,
    ModifiedDate;
SQL SELECT *
FROM `HumanResources_Employee`
WHERE EmployeeID<10;
```

NOTE: When adding a WHERE clause to your SQL SELECT statement remember to move the ';' to the end of the WHERE clause.

Grouping data: GROUP BY

In this example we will show how you can group data for example we can group the number of Employees by Gender using the code below.

Place this code below the script for the Employee table.
The RESIDENT command specifies that you are using a table that has already been loaded.

```
Employees:
LOAD EmployeeID,
    NationalIDNumber,
    Gender,
    rowguid,
    ModifiedDate;
SQL SELECT *
FROM `HumanResources_Employee`
WHERE EmployeeID<10;
```

GenderCount:
LOAD
Gender,
COUNT(Gender) as GenderCount
Resident Employees
GROUP BY Gender;

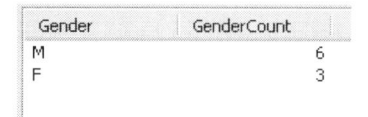

Gender	GenderCount
M	6
F	3

Add some expressions

Why add expressions to your documents?

You have already used simple expressions such as SUM(TOTAL) to calculate the total of some field. The more complex your documents become the more you will find yourself asking questions that cannot be solved without using expressions.
 We will start by using simple expressions to create calculated fields in the load script.
For example if you wanted to set a field to a different value if it was over some threshold.

Where can I use expressions?

Expressions can be used in various places within your QlikView document.
The examples we are going to cover here are using expressions within:

- The Load Script – You can use expressions to calculate the value of fields.
- Chart Expressions – Each expression is calculated for each dimension.
- Other Objects – Most objects use expressions in some way. For example you can set the Text field in a Text Object using an expression.

1. Right click on the current sheet you are working on. Then select 'New Sheet Object->Text Object'.
2. Click on the '...' button on the right of the Text field.
3. The 'Edit Expression' box will appear.
4. Enter the text:
   =GMT()
5. Click on the OK button.

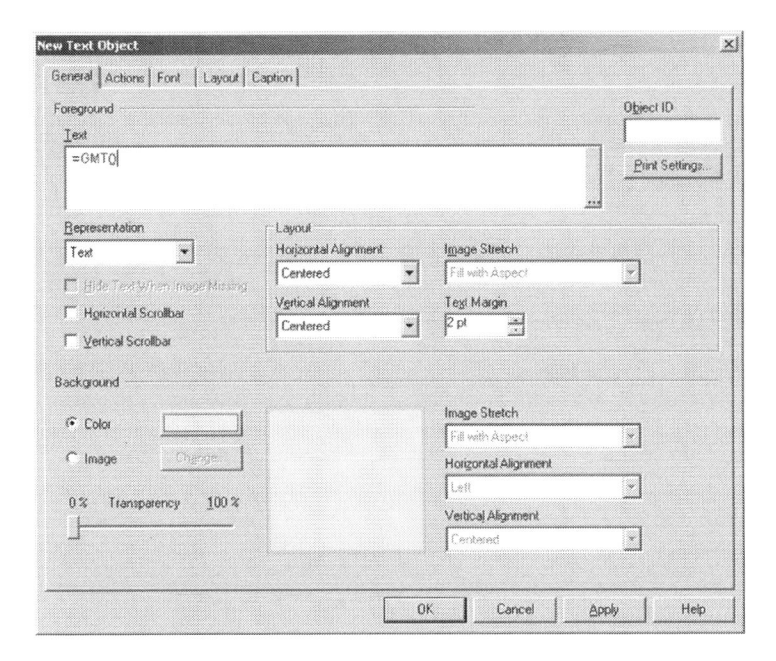

6. You will see the expression in the Text field.
7. Click on the OK button. You will see the current date and time displayed in the text field.

8. When adding expressions the syntax is checked as you type, for example:
9. This is obviously wrong but you also have the message 'Error in expression' informing you that there is an error and the red line under the text as well.

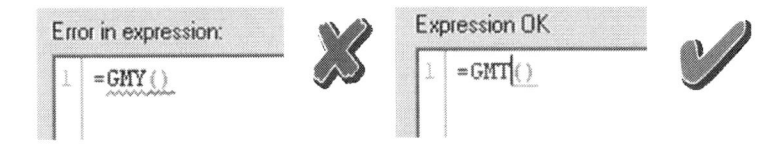

10. Once the syntax is correct the message 'Expression OK' will be displayed.
11. Script expressions are only checked when executed.

Expressions in the Load Script

1. In this example I will show how to create a calculated field in the load script.
2. Select the File->Edit Script option to open the Load Script.

Manage data loaded into QlikView - CHAPTER 5   67

3. In the example below we are using the IF statement to calculate the value of the 'InsideUK' field.
4. The Format of the IF statement is:

   IF(<EXPRESSION>, <TRUE VALUE>,<FALSE VALUE>) as <FIELDNAME>

5. The expression must be either true or false, in this example the expression is:

   CountryRegionCode='GB'

6. The TRUE and FALSE values are strings within single quotes.
   The full IF statement is:

   IF(CountryRegionCode='GB','Inside UK','Outside UK') as InsideUK,

12. Here is an example of the statement from the load script :
    LOAD GeographyKey,
       City,
       StateProvinceCode,
       StateProvinceName,
       CountryRegionCode,
       IF(CountryRegionCode='GB','Inside UK','Outside UK') as InsideUK,
       EnglishCountryRegionName,
       SpanishCountryRegionName,
       FrenchCountryRegionName,
       PostalCode,
       SalesTerritoryKey;
    SQL SELECT *
    FROM AdventureWorksDW.dbo.DimGeography;

13. You can also place calculated fields within the SQL SELECT statement, for example:

    LOAD   ProductKey,
             OrderDateKey,
             UnitPrice,
             OrderQuantity,
              CustomerPONumber;
    SQL SELECT *,
    UnitPrice * OrderQuantity as TotalPrice
    FROM AdventureWorksDW.dbo.FactInternetSales;

Useful Script Functions

Here we will cover some of the more useful scripting functions that are available in QlikView.

Sum
This function calculates the total value.
Ie: Sum(OrderTotal) – might calculate the sum of all orders.

If the expression Sum(OrderTotal) was used in a chart with a Dimension of Customer you would calculate the total amount of orders for each customer.

Min\Max
These functions calculate the smallest and largest values in a set of numbers.
For example to find the min number for SickLeaveHours.

Load Gender, min(SickLeaveHours) as Min_ SickLeaveHours
From MyTable
group by Gender;

FirstValue\ LastValue
These functions calculate the first and last strings in load order.
An example of this function is:

FirstValue(EmployeeID) as first_employee_loaded

CONCAT
This function can concatenate fields together. Must be used with the GROUP BY clause.
This example concatenates the MangerID field separated by a ';'.

CONCAT(ManagerID,';') as ManagerID_list

Below is a full example:

Employees:
LOAD EmployeeID,
   NationalIDNumber,
   ContactID,
   LoginID,
   ManagerID,
   Title,
   BirthDate,
   MaritalStatus,
   Gender,
   HireDate,
   SalariedFlag,
   VacationHours,
   SickLeaveHours,
   CurrentFlag,

        rowguid,
        ModifiedDate;
SQL SELECT *
FROM `HumanResources_Employee`
WHERE EmployeeID<10;

ManagerIDs:
LOAD
Gender,
CONCAT(ManagerID,';') as ManagerID_list
Resident Employees
GROUP BY Gender;

In this example the concat field is grouped by Gender to display a list of managers ids for each Gender.

A preview of the results in the table viewer:

Gender	ManagerID_list
M	109;12;16;263;3;6
F	185;21;3

Count Functions
Count

The COUNT function – calculates the number of records by the GROUP BY clause.

The example shown here counts the number of ManagerID records by Gender:

ManagerIDs_count:
LOAD
Gender,
COUNT(ManagerID) as ManagerID_count
Resident Employees
GROUP BY Gender;

Gender	ManagerID_count
M	6
F	3

If you add the distinct keyword only unique records will be counted.

COUNT(**DISTINCT** EnglishCountryRegionName)

Date Functions
day() - Returns the day when passed a date
month() - Returns the month when passed a date
year() - Returns the year when passed a date.

GMT( ) - returns the current date\time for Greenwich Mean Time.

As you will see in later examples these functions are very useful for grouping data when using aggregation functions as well as exploring data.

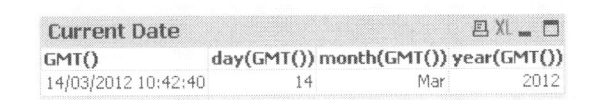

Current Date			
GMT()	day(GMT())	month(GMT())	year(GMT())
14/03/2012 10:42:40	14	Mar	2012

Alt – Provide an alternative

This function provides the first valid number in the list.
If no valid number is found the last parameter is returned.

For example:
Alt ('add','ddd',23,'Error with variables')

This function is especially useful when using variables to check date formats.

Manage data loaded into QlikView - CHAPTER 5

QlikView Help

Here I have described some of the more useful expressions that are used in QlikView app development.

There are many more functions in QlikView than have been mentioned in this book.

Please refer to the QlikView help for an excellent description of the functions and examples.

You can access the **QlikView Help f**rom the Help->Contents menu option.

From within the QlikView help select the following options to find the help on script functions:

Contents tab -> Select the 'Script Management' -> 'Script Syntax' -> 'Script Functions'

There you will find a list of functions arranged by type.

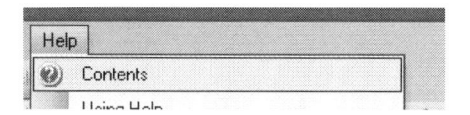

Useful menu options

If you go to View -> Toolbars you can add 2 very useful options to your QlikView screen.

Sheets
This is very useful when you have split your application up into multiple sheets.
This option adds a dropdownlist of the sheet names so you can switch between sheets using the dropdownlist rather than clicking on the tabs.

Bookmarks
This option allows you to add\remove bookmarks from the toolbar.

This chapter has covered the essentials you will need to start managing the data you load into your QlikView document.

It is best to get comfortable with the information presented in these chapters before look at more complex functions and expressions.

In the next chapter we will be covering charts such as line and pie charts and tables such as pivot tables.

6. Charts and Tables

As someone who does not like typing once said "a picture is worth a thousand words" (or it might have been a photo journalist).

So in this section of the book there will be plenty of pictures or as we will be calling them 'Charts'.

In this section I will concentrate of the most popular types of charts that you will be creating in your QlikView application.

What types of Charts can I create?

Most tools for analysing data have a variety of Charts that can be created and QlikView is no exception.

The most popular charts types that we will be focusing on are:

- Bar Chart
- Line Chart
- Pie Chart

These are not charts but are included in the Chart Object:

- Pivot Table
- Straight Table

In the chapter 'My First QlikView Document' we demonstrated how to create a Straight Table and a Bar chart.

Next we will cover other types of charts:
Pivot table (like the Straight table the pivot table is not a chart but setup within the chart object).

Pivot Table

1. Select the File->New option to start the wizard.
2. Select the SampleCustomerReports.xls spreadsheet and click the Open button.
3. Click the Next button. Select option 'Use column headers from data file'.

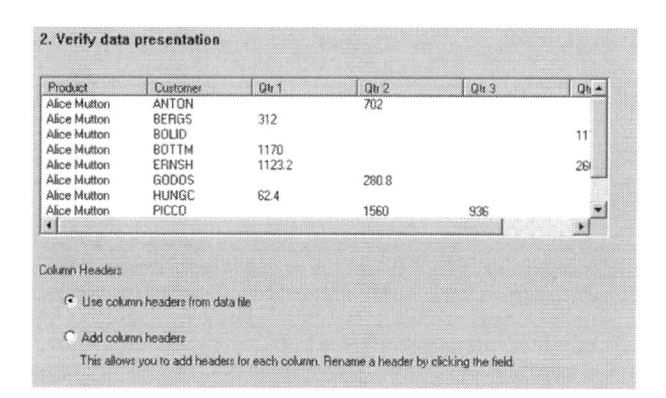

4. Click the Next button. Save your QlikView document
5. Click the Next button. Select the Pivot table chart.

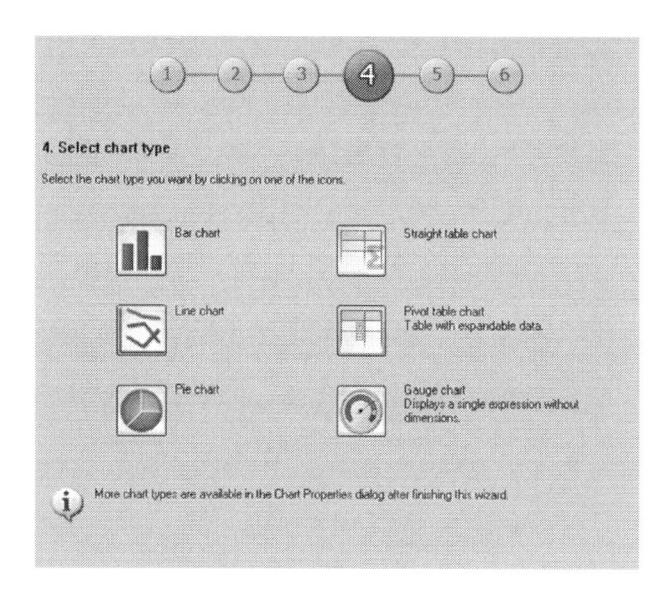

6. Click the Next button. Select the First Dimension as 'Customer'.

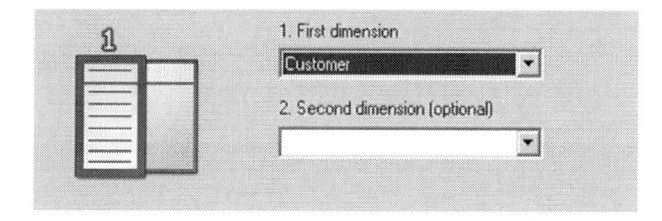

7. Click the Next button. Add the Expression to calculate the sum of field 'Qtr 1'.

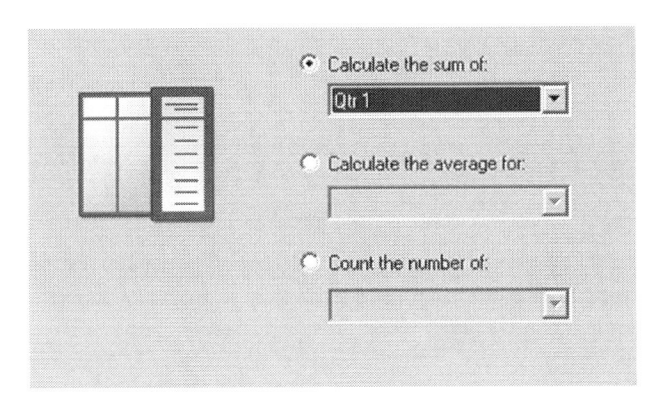

8. Click the Finish button.
9. The QlikView document will have a list box of the Customer dimension and a Pivot table with the totals for 'Qtr 1' by Customer.

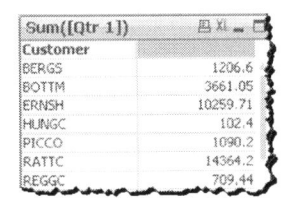

10. Right click on the Pivot table and select the properties option.
11. Select the Expressions tab.
12. Click the Add button
13. Enter the following expression:

    Sum([Qtr 2])

14. Click the OK button.
15. Add the following separate expressions:

    Sum([Qtr 3])
    Sum([Qtr 4])

16. Once you have added all the expressions your screen should look like the next screenshot.

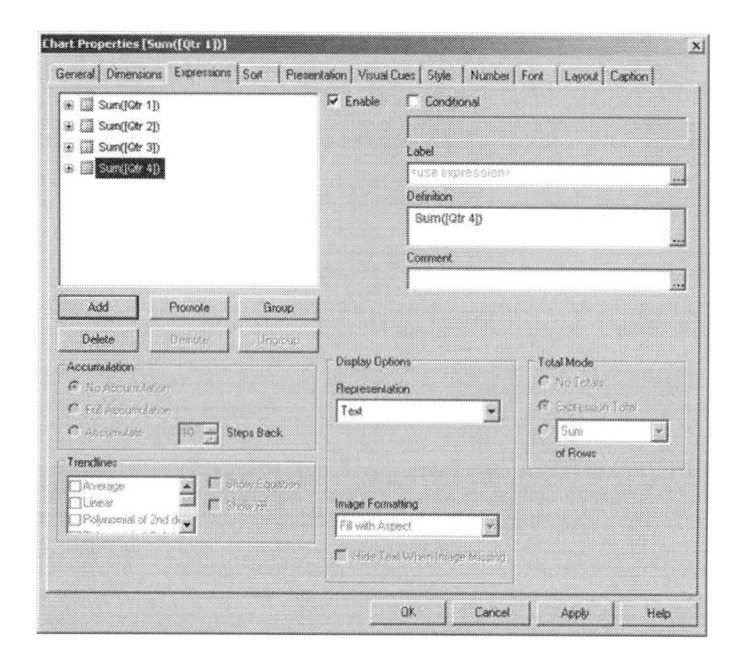

[Screenshot of Chart Properties [Sum([Qtr 1])] dialog, Expressions tab]

17. Change to the Dimension tab and add 'Product' to the 'Used Dimensions'.

[Screenshot of Used Dimensions list showing Customer and Product]

18. Click the OK button.
19. Your Pivot table should now show the Totals for each quarter (Qtr 1, Qtr 2, Qtr 3 and Qtr 4) for each Customer and Product.

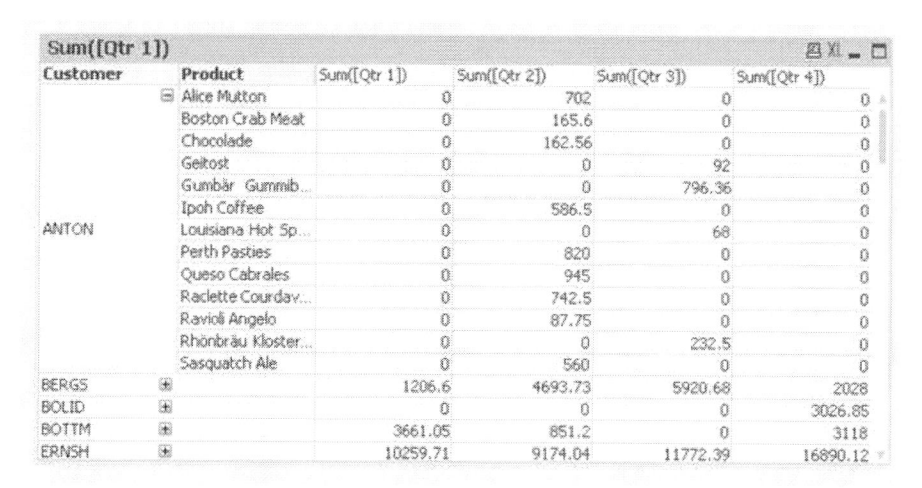

Customer	Product	Sum([Qtr 1])	Sum([Qtr 2])	Sum([Qtr 3])	Sum([Qtr 4])
ANTON	Alice Mutton	0	702	0	0
	Boston Crab Meat	0	165.6	0	0
	Chocolade	0	162.56	0	0
	Geitost	0	0	92	0
	Gumbär Gummib...	0	0	796.36	0
	Ipoh Coffee	0	586.5	0	0
	Louisiana Hot Sp...	0	0	68	0
	Perth Pasties	0	820	0	0
	Queso Cabrales	0	945	0	0
	Raclette Courdav...	0	742.5	0	0
	Ravioli Angelo	0	87.75	0	0
	Rhönbräu Kloster...	0	0	232.5	0
	Sasquatch Ale	0	560	0	0
BERGS		1206.6	4693.73	5920.68	2028
BOLID		0	0	0	3026.85
BOTTM		3661.05	851.2	0	3118
ERNSH		10259.71	9174.04	11772.39	16890.12

20. Right click on the pivot table again and select Properties.
21. Select the 'General Tab'
22. Enter a 'Window Title' such as 'Quarterly Sales Figures'
23. Click on the 'Expressions' tab.
24. Select the first expression in the list of expressions.
25. Click on the Label field and enter a value of 'Q1'.
26. Change the labels for the rest of the expressions so they look like the next screenshot.

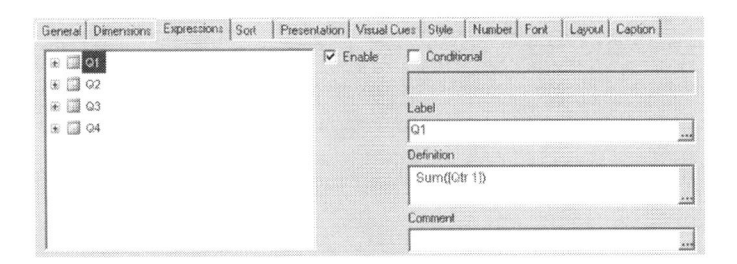

27. Click the OK button to see the improvements you have made to the Pivot table.

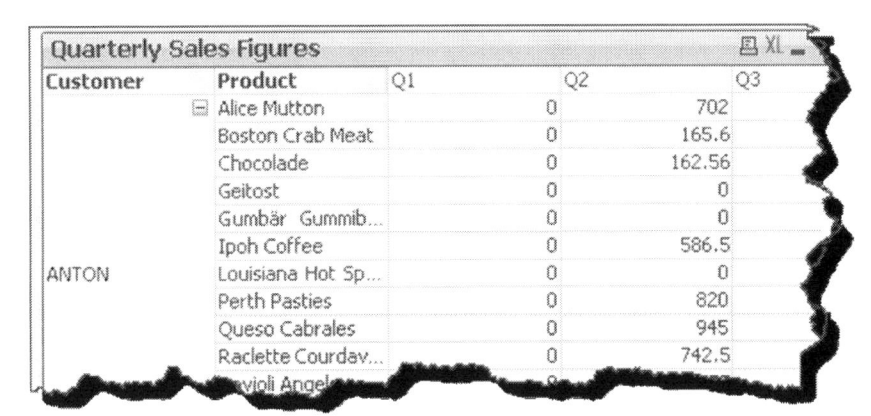

Compare QlikView with Excel

1. Next open the SampleCustomerReports.xls spreadsheet in Excel.
2. Go to the 'Customers' worksheet.
3. This is the same data as displayed in the Pivot table you just created in QlikView.
4. To see the numbers in the same format as the spreadsheet:
    a. Go to the Pivot Table properties.
    b. Select the Number tab.
    c. For each Expression change the 'Number Format Setting' to Money.
    d. See the next screenshot (You can change the currency by replacing the currency symbol in the Format Pattern field.

Quarterly Sales Figures					
Customer	Product	Q1	Q2	Q3	Q4
ALFKI	Aniseed Syrup	£0.00	£0.00	£0.00	£60.00
	Chartreuse verte	£0.00	£0.00	£283.50	£0.00
	Lakkalikööri	£0.00	£0.00	£0.00	£270.00
	Rössle Sauerkraut	£0.00	£0.00	£513.00	£0.00
	Spegesild	£0.00	£0.00	£18.00	£0.00
	Vegie-spread	£0.00	£0.00	£0.00	£878.00
ANATR		£0.00	£0.00	£479.75	£320.00
ANTON		£0.00	£4,771.91	£1,188.86	£0.00
AROUT		£407.70	£2,142.90	£0.00	£3,856.30
BERGS		£1,206.60	£4,693.73	£5,920.68	£2,028.00
BLAUS		£0.00	£615.80	£464.00	£0.00
BLONP		£3,832.72	£2,875.16	£1,110.00	£0.00
BOLID		£0.00	£0.00	£0.00	£3,026.85
BONAP		£1,820.80	£3,368.40	£1,930.40	£4,088.75
BOTTM		£3,661.05	£851.20	£0.00	£3,118.00
BSBEV		£1,714.20	£972.30	£493.00	£0.00
CACTU		£0.00	£225.50	£0.00	£12.50

Straight Table

1. We have covered setting up a straight table in the chapter 'My First QlikView Document'.
2. Here we will cover some of the useful features of the 'Straight Table'.
3. First, create your simple table by right clicking on the sheet, select 'New Sheet Object', then 'Chart'. Enter a name and select the Straight Table Chart type.

4. Click the Next button.
5. Add Dimension of 'Customer' and 'Product' to the 'Used Dimensions' list.

Used Dimensions
- Customer
- Product

6. Click the Next button.
7. Add and expression of:

   Sum([Qtr 1])

8. Click the OK button.
9. From the expressions screen click the add button and add the following expressions:

   Sum([Qtr 2])
   Sum([Qtr 3])

Sum([Qtr 4])

10. For each expression in the 'Total Mode' area on the right side of the screen select the option to 'Sum' the rows as shown:

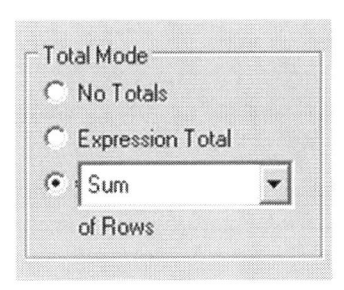

11. Click the Next button.
12. The Sort screen allows you to sort the data in different ways.
13. To sort numeric values simply remove the tick from the Text check box and add one to the Numeric value check box.
14. Load order – This is the order in which the data was read from the data sources.

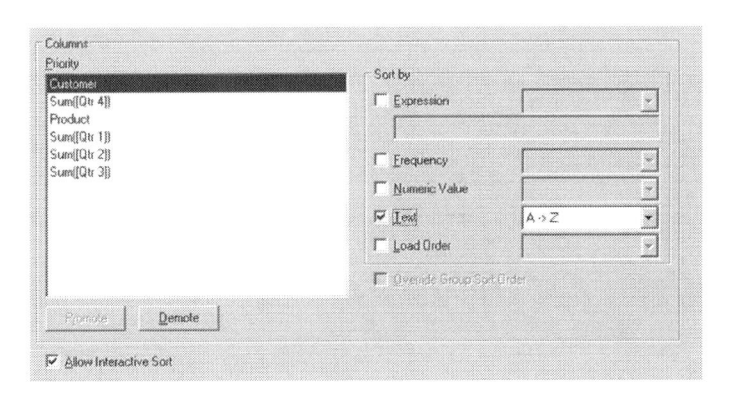

15. Click the Next button.

The Presentation screen.
16. One option to note is the 'Suppress Zero-Values'. Remove the tick from this option if you need to see zero values in your table\chart.
17. The Presentation screen is also where you set the Alignment of your data.
18. This is done by selecting the item from the Columns list and then setting what the alignment of the Label and Data should be (depending on whether it is numeric\text).

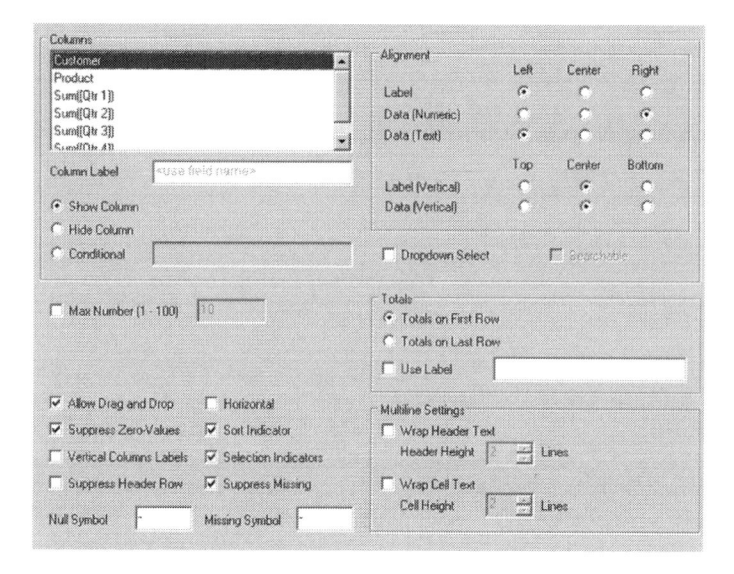

19. Click the Next button.

The Visual Cues screen
20. In this screen you can change the background color for example to Red if a value is below or greater than a certain value.
21. Click the Next button.

The Style screen
22. This screen is different from a normal chart. It is best to experiment with the different style options once the initial table has been created and you are happy with the data.
23. Click the Next button.

The Number screen
24. Use this screen to format your data.
    In this example click on each expression in turn and select the 'Money' option.
25. Check the Preview field to make sure the correct currency for your country is being displayed and change the Format Pattern if needed.

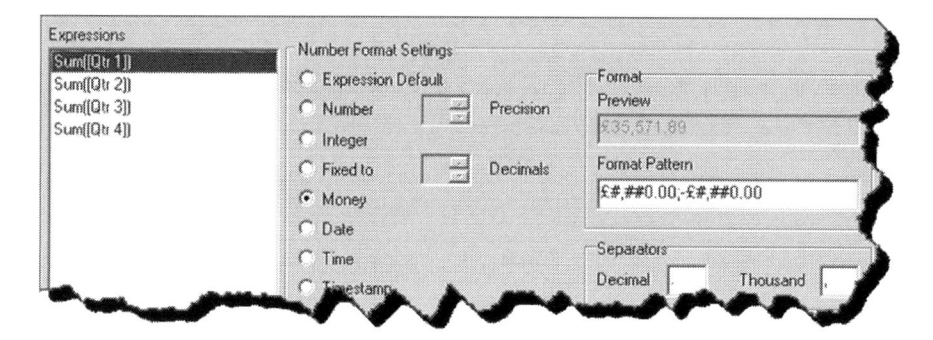

80 CHAPTER 6 - Charts and Tables

26. Click the Next button.

The Font screen.
27. Used to set default fonts or the font used in this chart object.
28. Click the Next button.

The Layout screen.
29. 'Apply Theme' - Allows you to select a QlikView Theme (qvt) file.
This is useful to save time and provide a consistent look and feel across the whole document. This will be covered later in the book.
30. Show – Always \ Conditional – You can set the object only to be displayed if some condition is true. For example you might want the Sales figures to be shown after a certain date. Click the Next button.

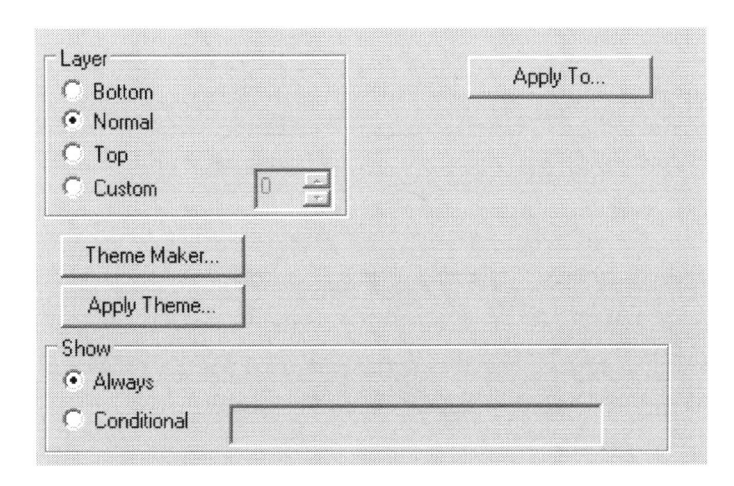

The Caption Screen
31. This screen allows you to set the Title.
32. Special Icons allow you to decide if the:
    - Data\image can be copied.
    - Table can be printed.
    - Data can be sent to Excel.
33. Select all Special icons so you can test each one.

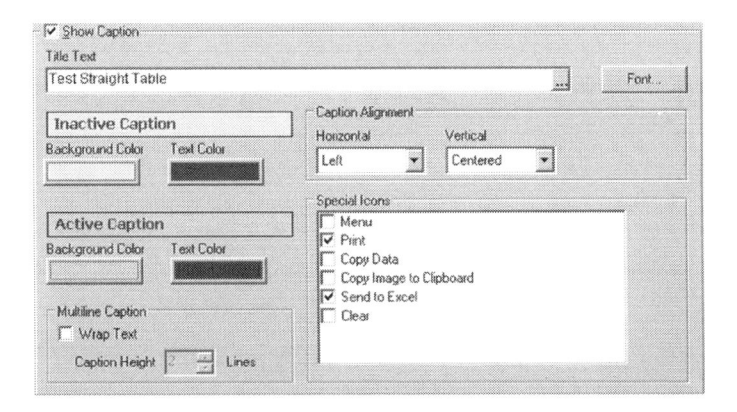

34. Click the Finish button.
35. Once you gain experience in creating sheet objects and charts in particular you will not have to step through all the screens.
36. But instead you can setup the dimensions and expressions within the first few screens of the of the chart setup wizard and make any further changes by going back to the chart properties and setting the options from there.
37. The next screenshot shows how your Straight Table should look.

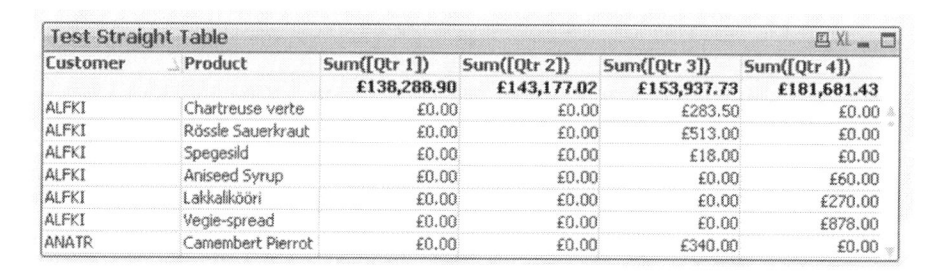

Customer	Product	Sum([Qtr 1])	Sum([Qtr 2])	Sum([Qtr 3])	Sum([Qtr 4])
		£138,288.90	**£143,177.02**	**£153,937.73**	**£181,681.43**
ALFKI	Chartreuse verte	£0.00	£0.00	£283.50	£0.00
ALFKI	Rössle Sauerkraut	£0.00	£0.00	£513.00	£0.00
ALFKI	Spegesild	£0.00	£0.00	£18.00	£0.00
ALFKI	Aniseed Syrup	£0.00	£0.00	£0.00	£60.00
ALFKI	Lakkalikööri	£0.00	£0.00	£0.00	£270.00
ALFKI	Vegie-spread	£0.00	£0.00	£0.00	£878.00
ANATR	Camembert Pierrot	£0.00	£0.00	£340.00	£0.00

38. Note the Totals in bold at the top of each column.
39. Select one customer such as 'ALFKI'.

40. The table will be filtered and the totals will change.
41. A green circle will appear in the column header for 'Customer' to show it is being used to filter the data.
42. Right click on the table and select 'Clear All Selections' or click in the 'Clear' button to return the table to its original state.

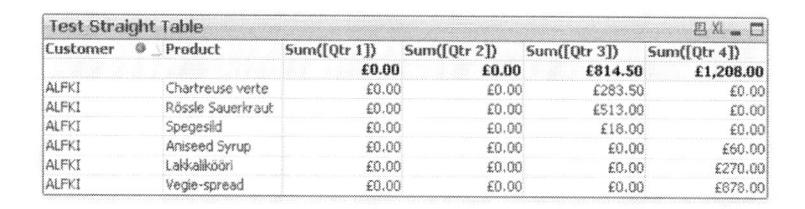

Customer	Product	Sum([Qtr 1])	Sum([Qtr 2])	Sum([Qtr 3])	Sum([Qtr 4])
		£0.00	**£0.00**	**£814.50**	**£1,208.00**
ALFKI	Chartreuse verte	£0.00	£0.00	£283.50	£0.00
ALFKI	Rössle Sauerkraut	£0.00	£0.00	£513.00	£0.00
ALFKI	Spegesild	£0.00	£0.00	£18.00	£0.00
ALFKI	Aniseed Syrup	£0.00	£0.00	£0.00	£60.00
ALFKI	Lakkalikööri	£0.00	£0.00	£0.00	£270.00
ALFKI	Vegie-spread	£0.00	£0.00	£0.00	£878.00

Other Chart Types

Bar Chart

Now that we have covered the Pivot\Straight Table and Bar chart we will move onto the more common chart types:

1. Select the Straight Table you created in the previous example and open the properties.
2. In the General Tab click the 'Bar Chart' type.
3. Go to the 'Dimension Limits' tab, in this tab we can reduce the data that is displayed. In this example we are restricting to the top 5 customers

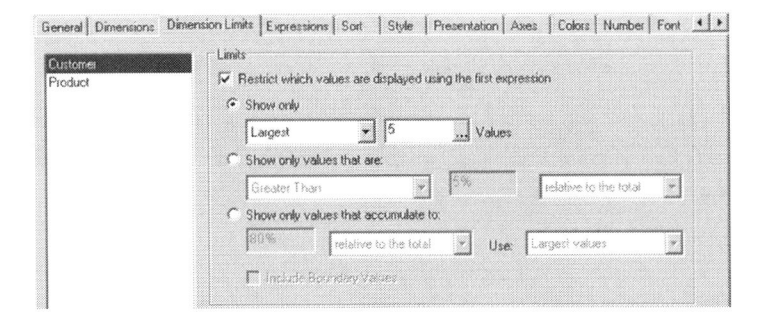

4. In the Dimension tab, remove the Product Dimension from the Used Dimensions list.

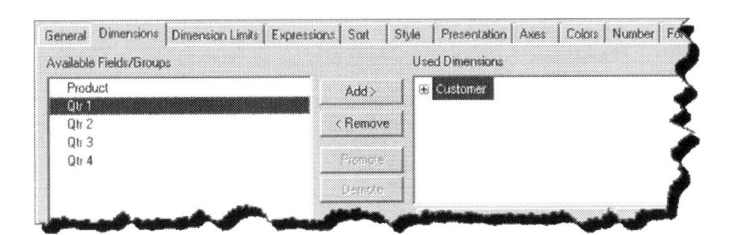

5. Remove all expressions except Q1 in the Expressions tab:

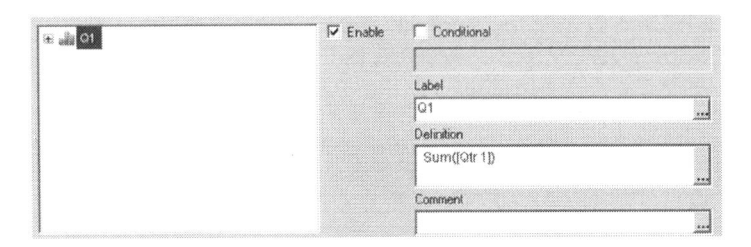

6. Click on the OK button and your chart should look like the next screenshot:

Charts and Tables - CHAPTER 6   83

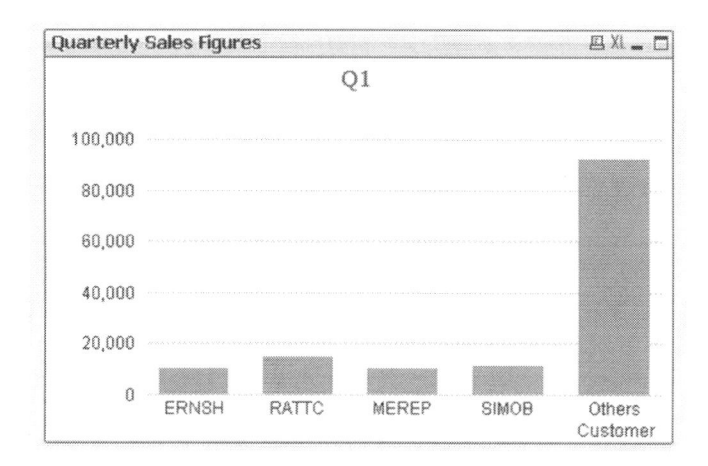

Line Chart

1. Once you have created one type of chart it is easy to change the chart type:
2. Right click on the chart object and select properties.
3. Go to the general tab and select the following icon from the 'Chart Type' section:

4. Click the apply button, you will see that in the Style tab the options have been updated for a Line Chart.
5. Click OK and now the chart will be displayed as a 'Line Chart'.

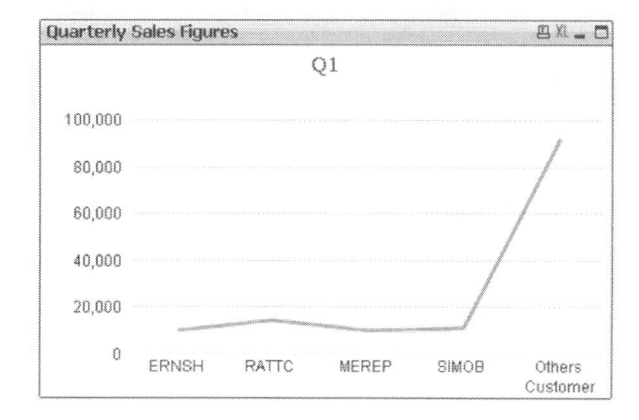

Pie Chart

1. Right click on the chart object and select properties.
2. Go to the general tab an select the following icon from the 'Chart Type' section:

84   CHAPTER 6 - Charts and Tables

3. Click the apply button, you will see that in the Style tab the options have been updated for a Pie Chart.
4. You should also notice that the Axes tab disappears, because there are no axes on a pie chart.
5. Click OK and now the chart will be displayed as a 'Pie Chart'.

Chart Expressions

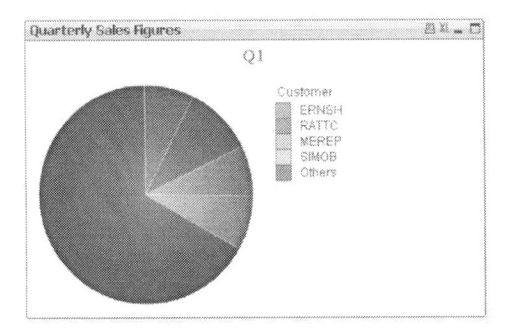

Chart Expressions are used to calculate the values plotted on the y-axis.

In previous examples we have already created expressions to Sum the total values for a quarter.

1. If you click on the '...' to the right of the definition field the Edit Expression screen will open.
2. Click on the Functions tab at the bottom.
3. There you will find a vast array of possible functions.
4. Delete your current expression.
5. Select the 'Aggregation' Function Category.
6. Select the 'Avg' Function name.
7. Highlight the 'sum' text in the current expression and press the Paste button.
8. The SUM function will be replaced with the AVG function.

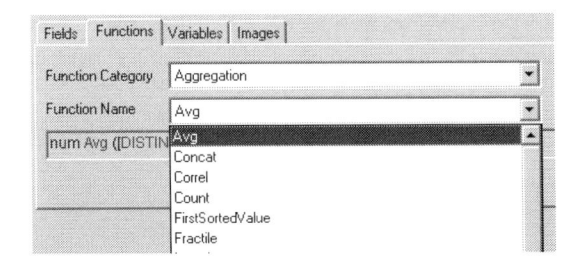

Charts and Tables - CHAPTER 6

9. Complete the expression so it now is:
   Avg([Qtr 1])

10. Click the OK button on the 2 open screens. The chart now displays the Average Sales for Q1 for the Top 5 Customers.

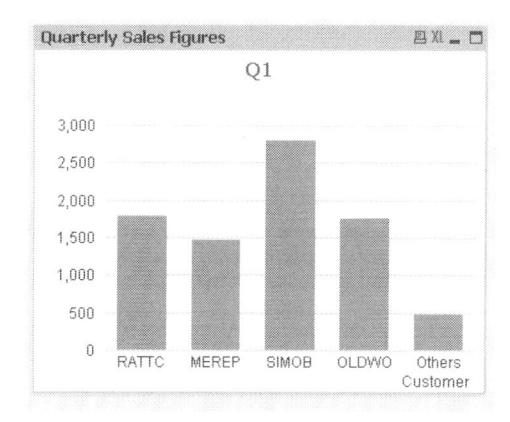

NOTE: When using logical functions in QlikView such as IsNum() , -1 is returned if the function is true and 0 for false.

Calculated Dimension
Calculated Dimensions allow the user to select dimensions based on an expression.

1. Open the Chart Properties.
2. Select the Dimension tab.
3. Click on the 'Add Calculated Dimension'.
4. The Edit Expression screen will open.
5. Here you can add an expression to calculate a dimension.
6. You cannot use Aggregation functions in the expression such as Sum() or Avg(). But you can use the aggr() function.
7. An simple example might be to put the dimension in lower case using the following expression:

   =Lower(Customer)

NOTE: If you click the 'Remove' button when selected a 'Calculated Dimension' in 'Used Dimension' list. The dimension is deleted rather being moved to the 'Available Fields\Groups list.

Synthetic Dimension Functions

In this example we are going to use the **ValueList** function to create a list of dimensions.

We are going to display the following dimensions:

2012-Q1 and 2012-Q2

These dimensions represent the sum of quarter 1 or quarter 2 sales for the year 2012.

NOTE: These dimensions do not exist in the data.

1. Open the Chart Properties.
2. From the Dimension tab remove all dimensions from the 'Used Dimensions' list.
3. Click 'Add Calculated Dimension' add the following expression:

    =ValueList('2012-Q1','2012-Q2')

4. Click the OK button.
5. Go to the Expressions tab.
6. Remove all expressions.
7. Click the Add button and enter the following expressions:

    if(ValueList('2012-Q1','2012-Q2')='2012-Q1',Sum([Qtr 1]),
    (
        if(ValueList('2012-Q1','2012-Q2')='2012-Q2',Sum([Qtr 2]))
)
)

8. The format of the IF statement is:

    IF(<test something>, <test is TRUE>,<test is FALSE>)

    In this example the test we are doing is if the dimension used is either '2012-Q1' or '2012-Q2'.

    The <test is TRUE> part of the first if statement totals the sales for Qtr 1.
    The second if statement is nested in the <test is FALSE> part of the first if statement.

9. Click on the OK button to close the Edit Expression screen.
10. Add a Label to the expression: 'Total Sales by Quarter'.
11. Click on the OK button.
12. Your chart should look like the next screenshot:

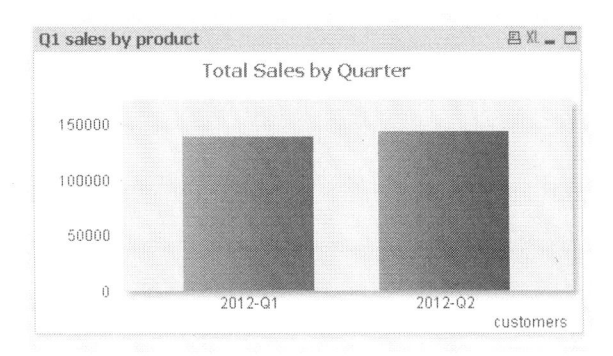

Charts and Tables - CHAPTER 6

Chart Groups

There are 2 different types of group:

Drill-down group
This enables you to drill down into the chart for example: Year->Month->Day

Cyclic group
This allows you to easily switch between graphs using different dimensions.
This type of group is useful for saving space.

1. Right Click on the chart used in the previous example.
2. Select Properties, go to the Dimensions tab.
3. Click the 'Edit Groups' button.

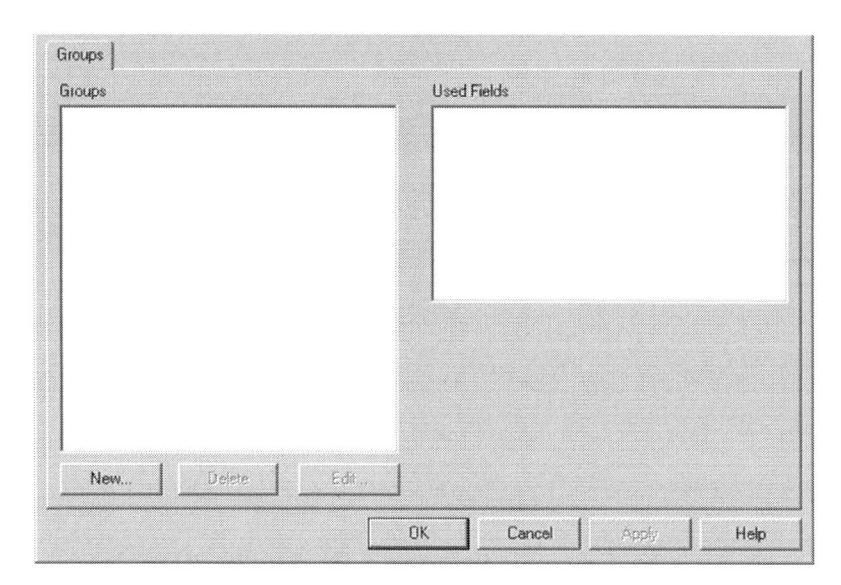

4. Click on the New... button.
5. With this option you can create a group of fields.

Cyclic Group

6. Set the Group Name to: customer-product
7. Move the Customer and Product fields to the 'Used Fields' list by selecting the field in the 'Available Fields' list and clicking the Add button or just double-clicking the field.
8. Select the 'Cyclic Group' radio button.

9. Click on the OK button
10. If you select the group you have just created you will see the list of fields contained within the group in the 'Used Fields' list. Click the OK button.
11. Remove all from 'Used Dimensions' list and add the 'customer-product' group.

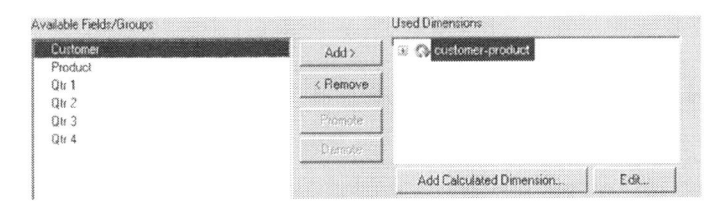

12. Go to the 'Dimension Limits' tab and restrict the Chart to use the 5 largest values, as shown in the next screenshot.

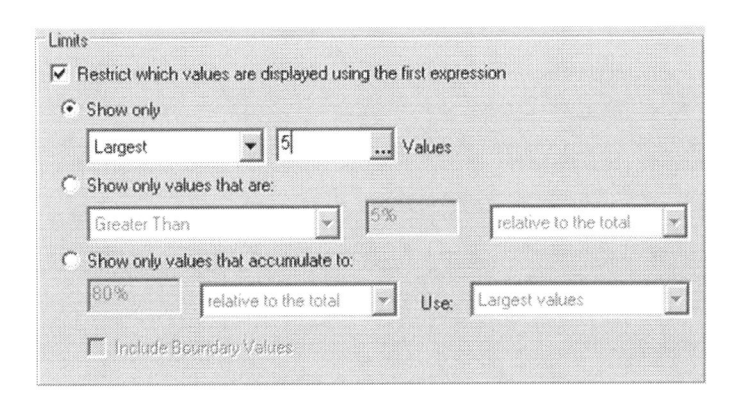

13. Click the OK button.
14. You will notice there is a new icon in the bottom right corner of the chart with the label 'Customer' to denote which field is being used. This is the cyclic group icon.
15. If you click on the cyclic group icon it will change the chart to use the Product field.

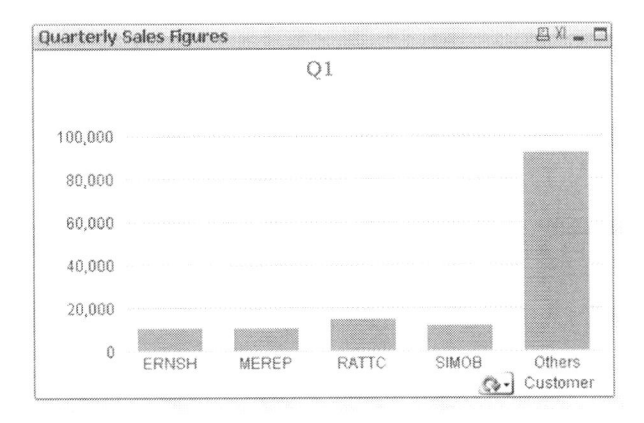

16. After you click on the cyclic group icon the chart will change to the next screenshot:

Charts and Tables - CHAPTER 6   89

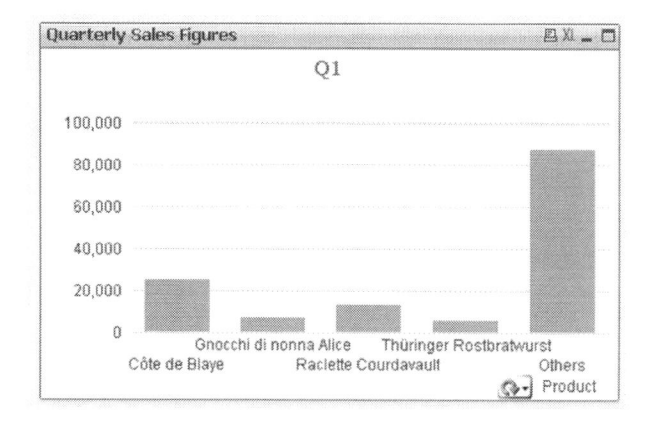

17. The cyclic group is very useful for saving space as you can have multiple charts taking only one area of the sheet.

Next we will look at drill-down groups.

Drill-down Group

1. You setup a drill-down group in the same way as a cyclic group described previously.
2. The only difference is that you need to select the 'drill-down' group rather than the cyclic group option.
3. To change the cyclic group to a drill-down group:
4. Open the Properties page of the Chart.
5. Go to the Dimensions tab and select the 'Edit Groups' button.
6. You will see the group you created in the previous example.
7. Click the Edit button, otherwise click the Add button if the group does not exist.
8. Make sure the drill-down option is selected.
9. Click the OK button on the 'Group Settings' and 'Document properties' screens.
10. You will notice that the icon for the drill-down groups is a downward pointing arrow.

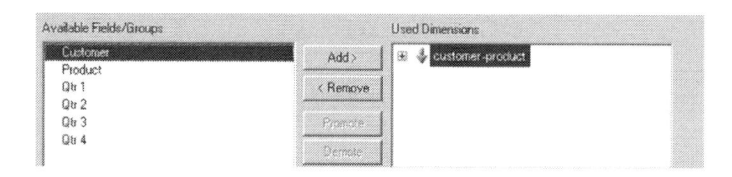

11. Click the OK button.
12. Your chart should look like the next screenshot.

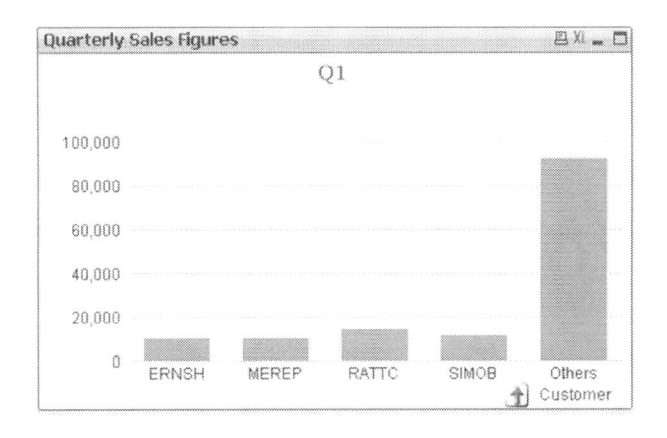

13. If you click on one customer it will drill down to the product chart for that customer.

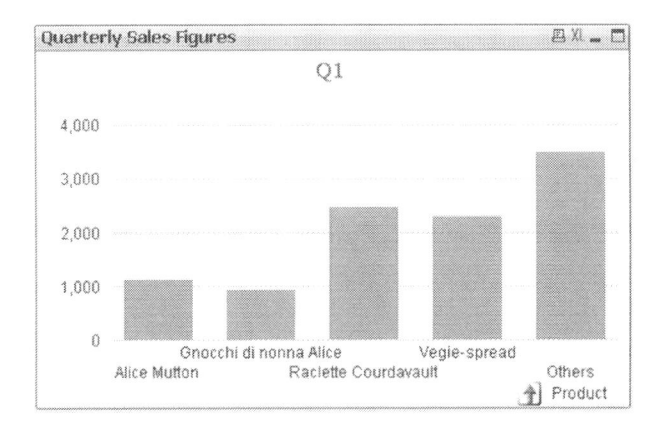

14. You can then click on the drill-down group icon to return to the chart of customers.

Chart Style

1. Right click on your Chart and select Properties.
2. Go to the Style tab.
3. Here you will find various aspects of the look and feel of the chart you can change.
4. For example by clicking on different icons in the 'Look' area of this tab you can give your chart a 3D effect.
5. A lot of these changes are down to personal preference.
6. The 'Plot Color Style' option of 'Light Gradient' is good option to start with.

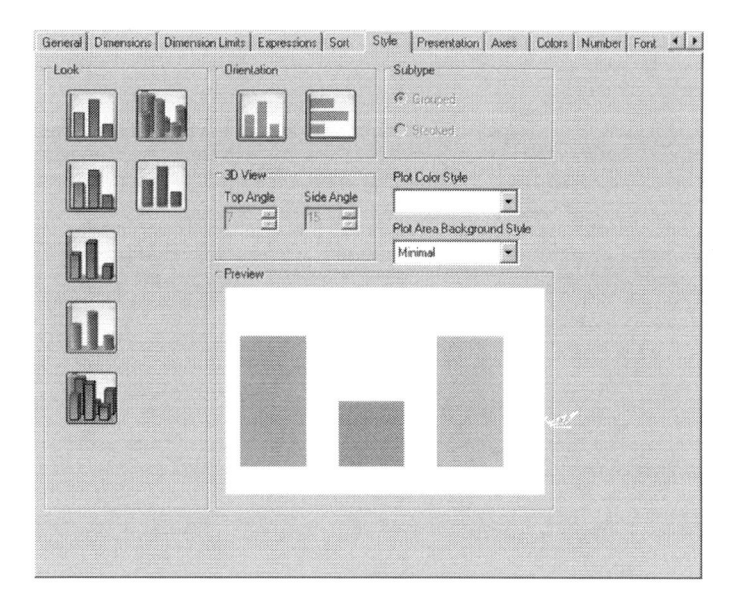

7. Go to the Colors tab. Tick the 'Multicolored' checkbox.

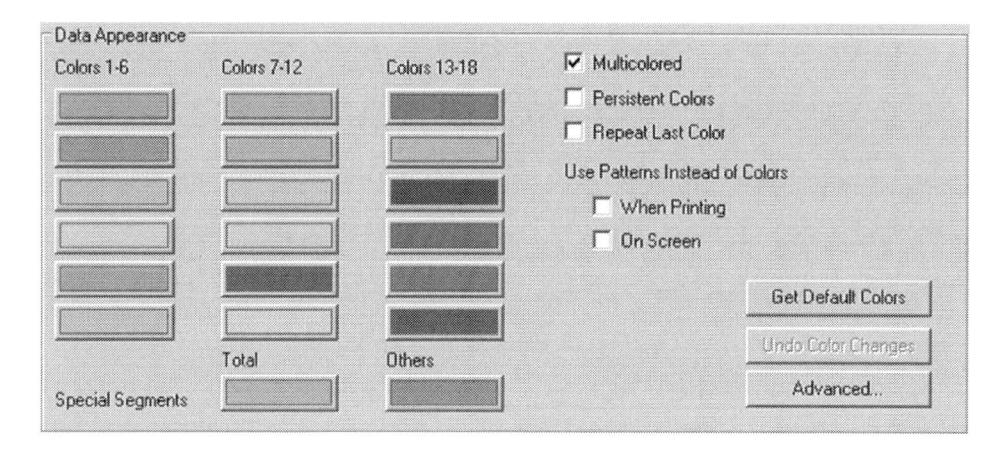

8. Click OK. You will see that each Customer in your chart is now assigned a different color (you will appreciate the colors\colours if you are following this example on your computer).

92 CHAPTER 6 - Charts and Tables

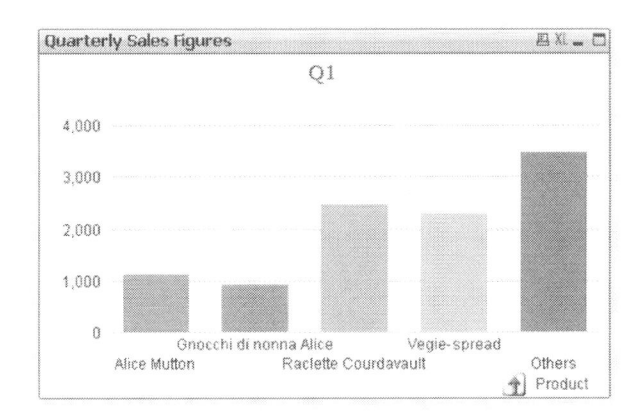

9. If you are not printing your charts to a color printer and wish for them to look the same on screen as when printed in black and white then tick both options below the 'Use Patterns Instead of colors':

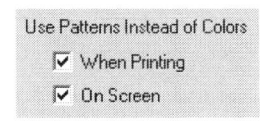

10. Click OK and you will see how your chart has been transformed.

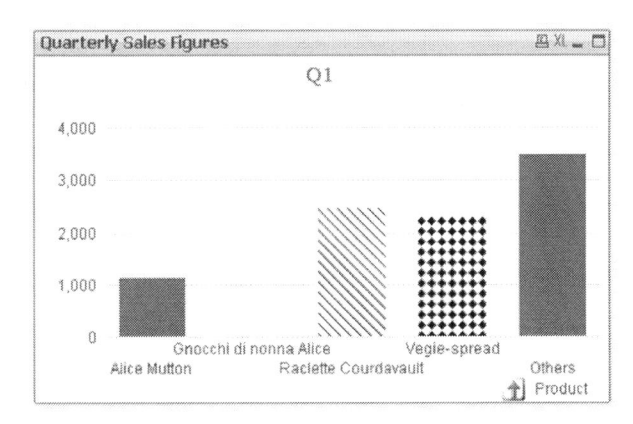

Charts and Tables - CHAPTER 6   93

Animate

You can make an animation of changes occurring in your chart.
This option is probably more useful for demonstration purposes rather than everyday use.

1. Right click on your Chart and select Properties.
2. Go to the Dimensions tab.
3. Click the Animate button at the bottom of the screen.

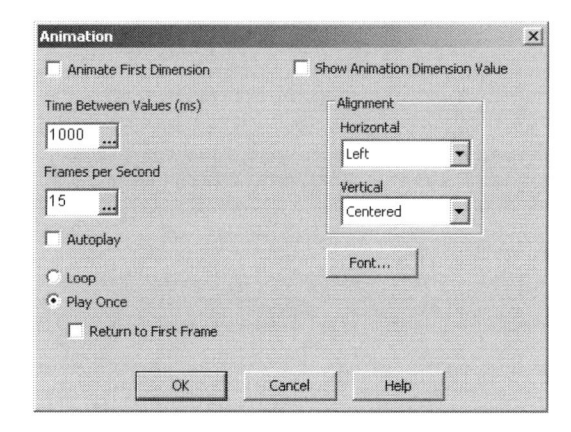

4. Click the 'Animate First Dimension' option and then click the OK button.
5. Click the OK button again to return to the chart.

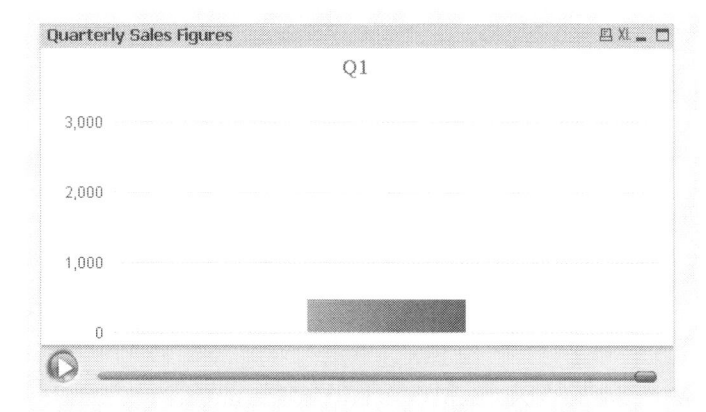

6. You will see that now there is a play button at the bottom left corner of the screen.
7. Click the play button and an animation will be created moving between the different Q1 sales figures for the top 5 customers.
8. From the next screenshot you will see the animation in progress.
9. The current customer name is displayed on the bottom of the chart.

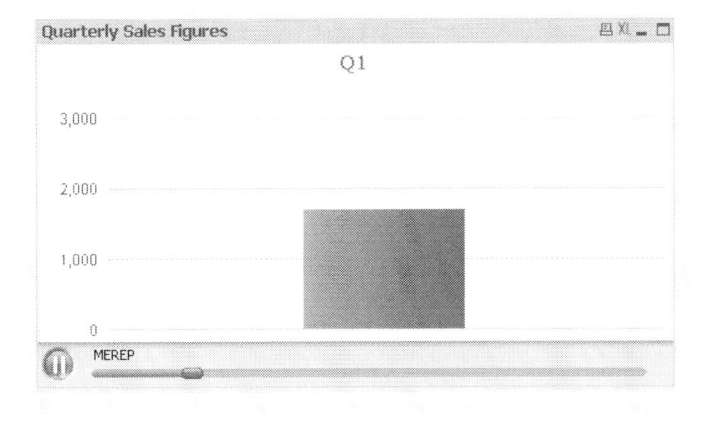

NOTE: You cannot animate a pie chart.

Trellis

The Trellis option will display each record within the dimension in a separate chart.
A scrollbar will be provided if the space taken up by the charts exceed the area allowed for the chart on the sheet.

1. Right click on your Chart and select Properties.
2. Go to the Dimensions tab.
3. If the Trellis button is greyed out click the Animate button at the bottom of the screen.
4. Turn the animation off by removing the tick from the 'Animate First Dimension' option.

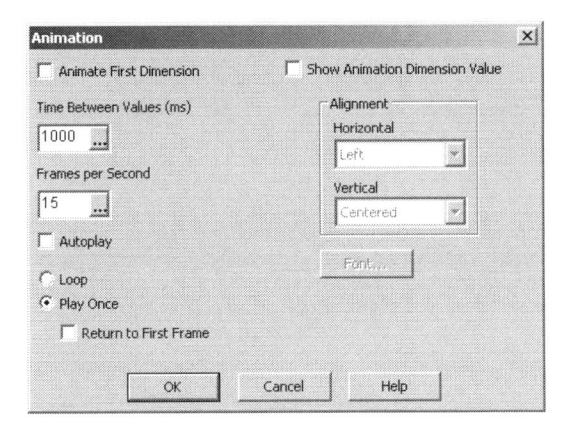

5. Click the OK button.
6. Click the Trellis button.
7. Select the checkbox 'Enable Trellis Chart'

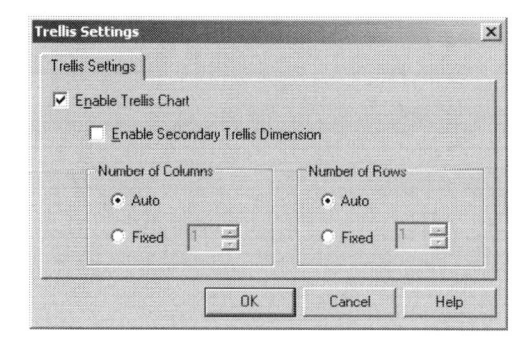

8. Click the OK button.
9. Notice that the Animate button is now greyed out.
10. Click the OK button again to close the Chart Properties.
11. The next shows an example of the Trellis, if you reduced the size of the chart area a scroll bar would appear.

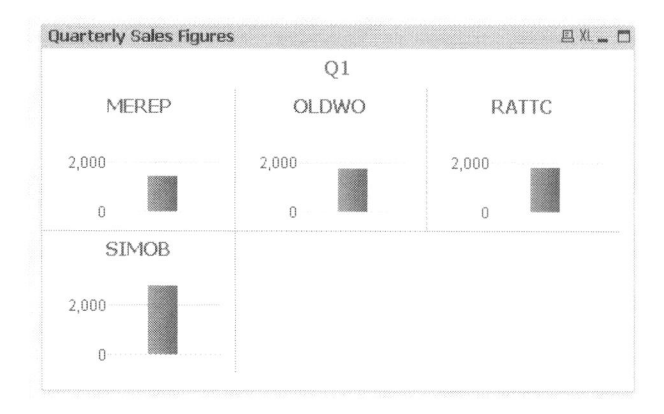

12. Go back to the Dimension tab of the Chart Properties and remove the tick from the 'Enable Trellis chart' checkbox.

Fast Type Change

This option allows you to easily switch between different types of charts.

The fast type change option is very useful when deciding which type of chart to use or if you have users with differing preferences.

1. Right click on your Chart and select Properties.
2. Go to the General tab.

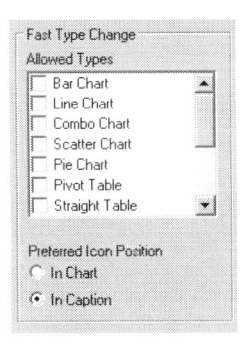

3. In the Allowed Types list select the following Types
   a. Bar Chart
   b. Line Chart
   c. Pie Chart

4. Click the OK button.
   There is now an extra icon in the top right corner of the chart.
5. Hovering over the fast change icon will display the label as shown in the next screenshot.
6. Click on the fast change icon to switch between the chart types you selected in the 'Allowed Types' list.

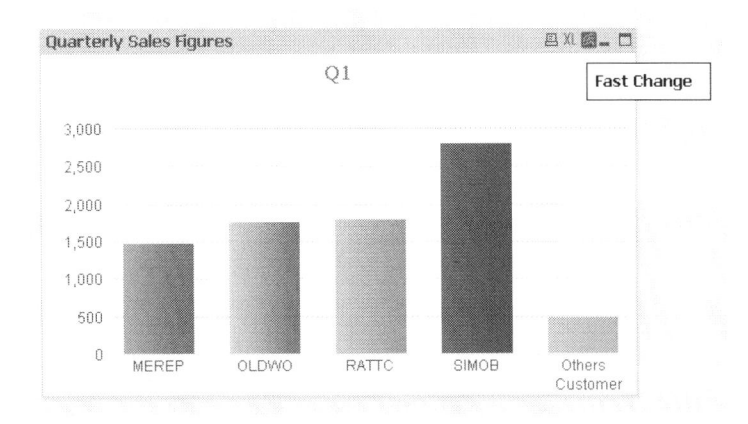

7. Right click on your Chart and select Properties.
8. Go to the General tab.

9. Change the preferred icon position to 'In Chart'.
10. Click the OK button.
11. You will now see that the fast change icon is in the chart just below the chart title.

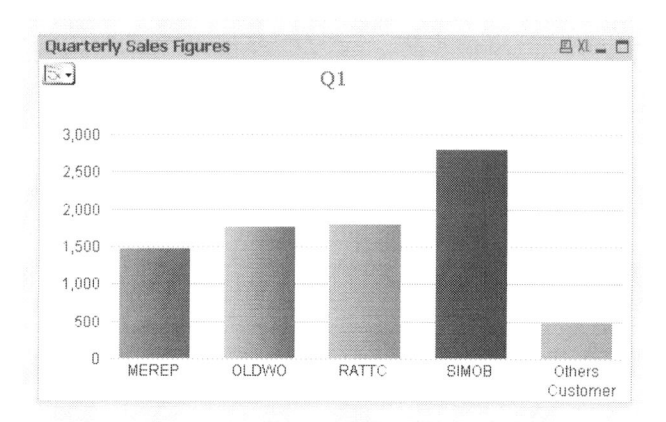

12. Click on the icon to change the chart to the next chart type or select the arrowhead on the fast change icon to pick which change you want from the 'Allowed Types' (As shown in the next screenshot)

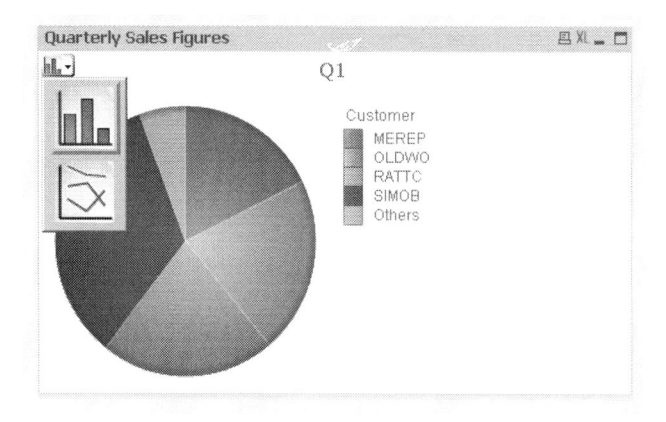

13. Next, we will discuss ways to make your life a little easier when developing QlikView documents by covering some development tips.

7. QlikView Development Tips

The following chapter will consist of a series of tips such as useful options and features of QlikView that can help with making the creation of the QlikView documents easier.

Wizards

There are wizards several within QlikView to guide the user through tasks such as the creation of a new QlikView document or a chart object. The "Getting Started Wizard" can be turned off in the Settings->User Preferences menu option in the General tab.

User Preferences

Useful options in the Settings->User Preferences menu option are:

Save Tab
Here we can set the autosave QlikView settings.

You can set QlikView to save a backup version of the QlikView document after you Reload the data, but to only keep 3 instances as shown in the next:

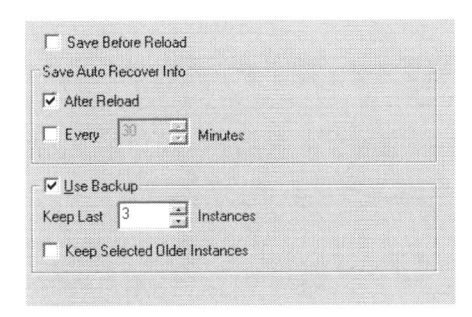

You can see how the autosave feature works from the files listed in the next screenshot.
The autosave files start from 'Version 1 of <original filename>'. In this example only the last 3 versions are kept. If all autosave versions of the file are deleted the filename will start from 'Version 1' again.

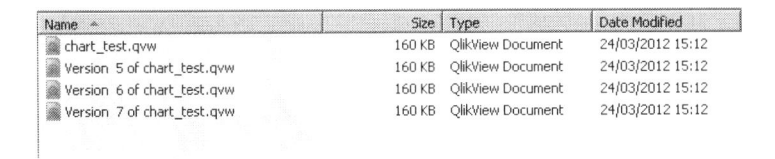

Printing Tab
The tick in the option 'Repeat Header Rows' means that the headers will be printed on every page. This the default setting.

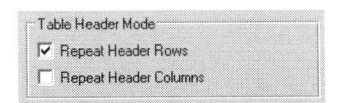

Themes

Themes are very useful in providing a consistent look and feel to your QlikView documents.

In the next example we will show how you can take properties from a Chart object and apply them to other objects such as the Text Object.

1. Set the Caption font for a chart to the style you would like to save to a theme that can be applied so other sheet objects.
2. Right click on the chart, select properties and go to the Caption tab.
3. Click on the font button and change the font type.
4. The screenshot next shows 'Times New Roman, Bold Italic and size 14'.

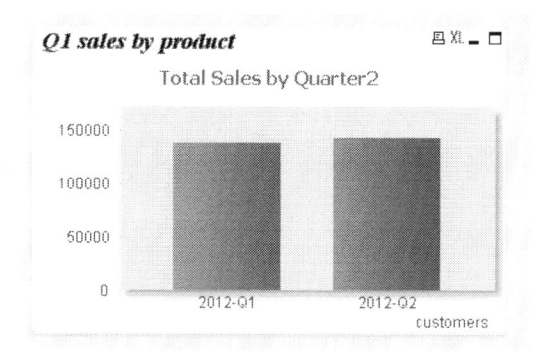

5. Click OK on the font screen and then properties screen to close them.
6. Select Tools->Theme Maker Wizard.
7. Click the Next button.

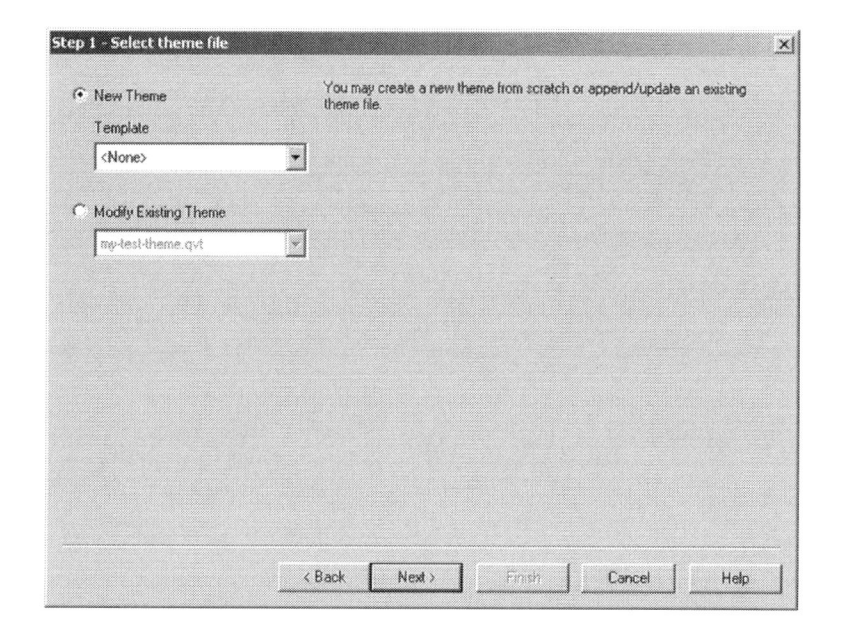

8. Click the Next button as this is the first theme we are creating.
9. Save the theme as 'my-test-theme'. The file will have a .qvt extension.
10. Click the Save button.

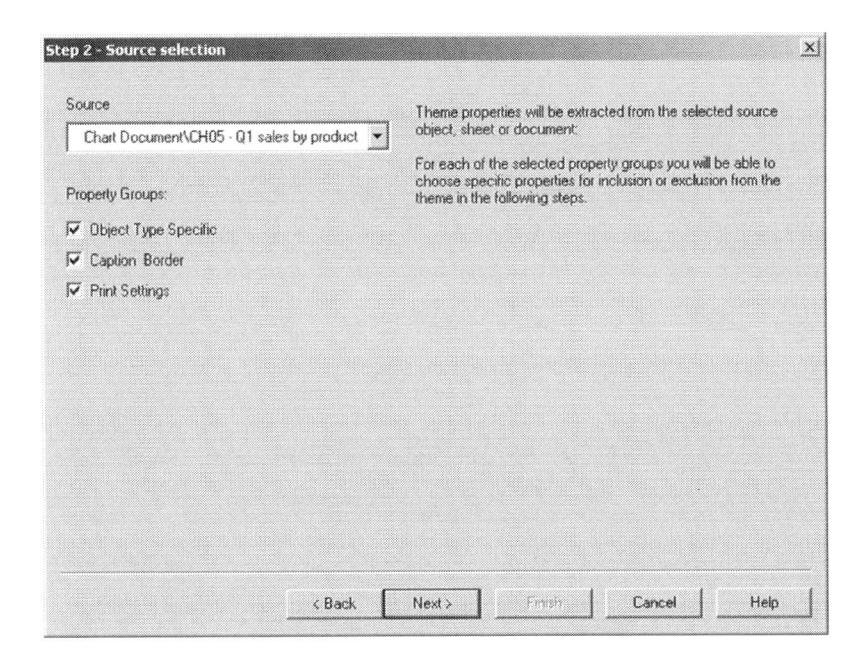

11. Select the source for the properties of this theme.
    Select all 3 Property Groups. We are selecting a chart object as the source.
12. Click the Next Button.

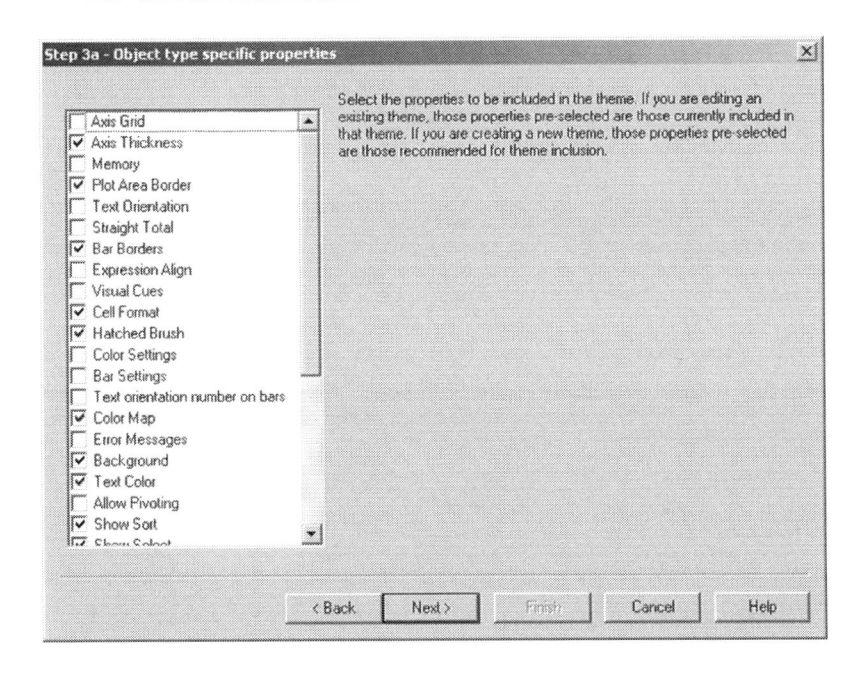

13. For this example keep the default selection of properties to add to the theme.

QlikView Development Tips - CHAPTER 7   **101**

14. Click the Next button.

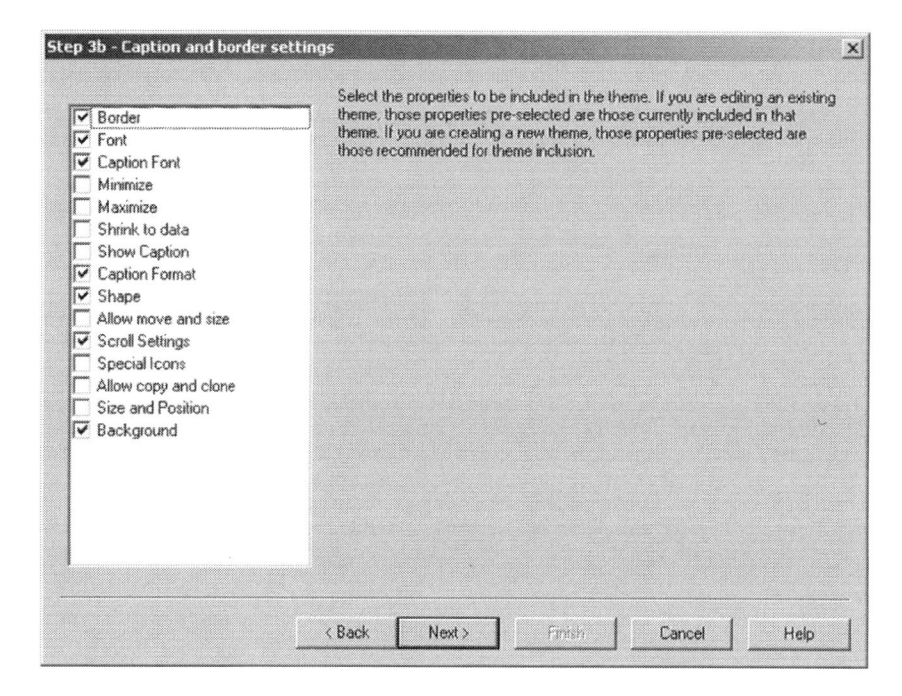

Step 3b - Caption and border settings

15. Keep the default properties.
16. Click the Next button.

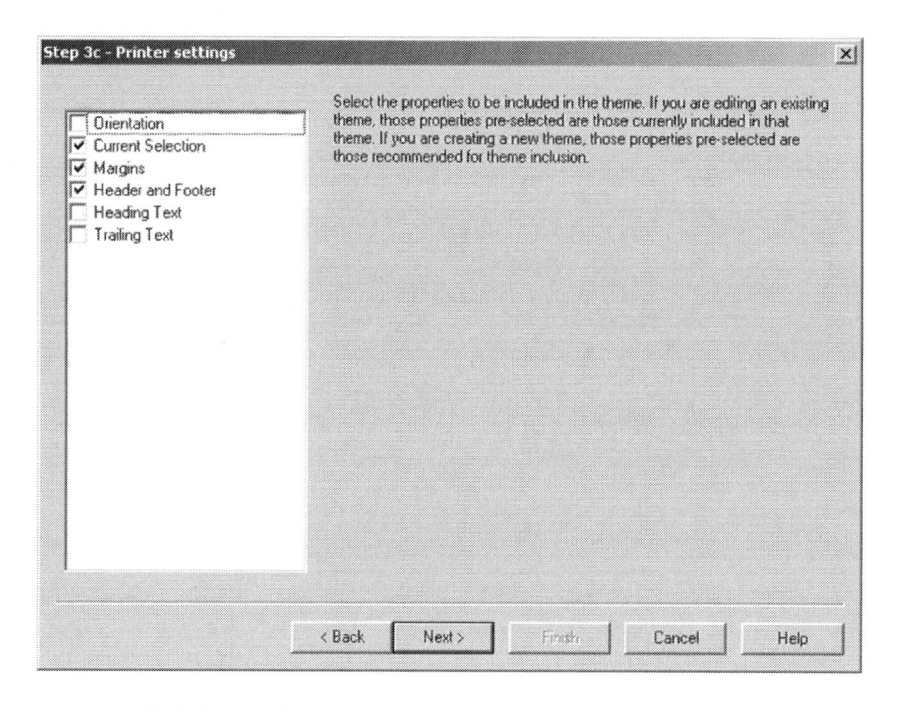

Step 3c - Printer settings

17. Click the Next button.

Object Spec. column
   18. Properties added to the same type of object as the source, in this case a Chart object.

Caption & Border \ Printing columns
   19. The properties from these property groups can be applied to any object type.
   20. In this example we are going to allow the Caption & Border be applied to 'Text Objects' as well as charts by ticking the 'Text Object' field in the 'Caption & Border' column.

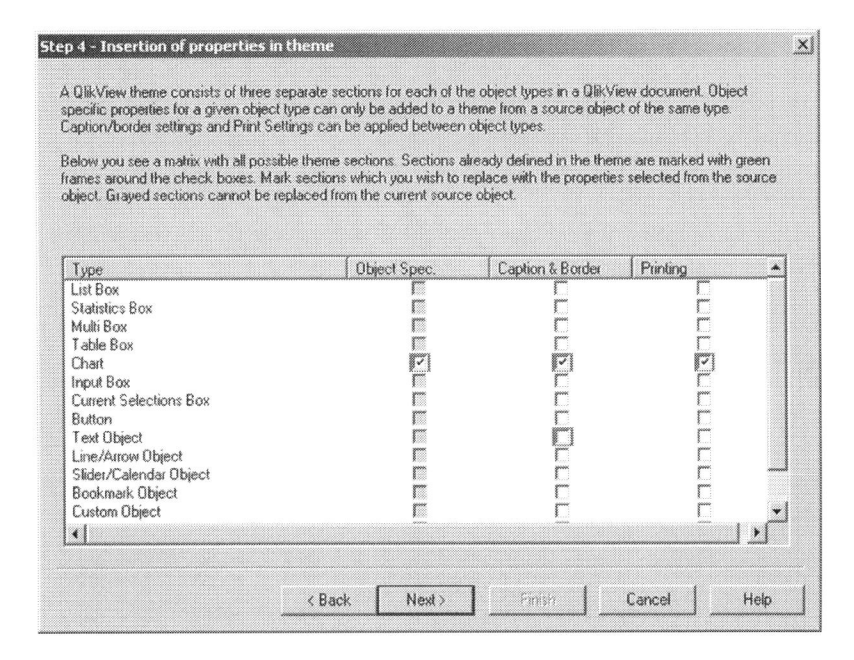

   21. Click the Next button.
   22. Remove the tick from 'Set as default theme for new documents.
   23. Add a tick to 'Set as default theme for this document.

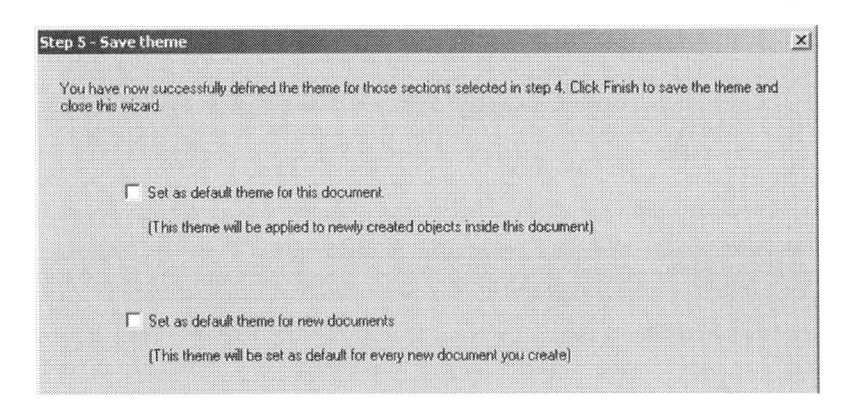

   24. Click the Finish button and save your document.
   25. Right click on the sheet, select 'New Sheet Object' then 'Text Object. Enter something in the 'Title text' field.
   26. Click on the OK button.

27. You will see that the Caption of your next Text Object has the same style as the Chart object that was used to create your theme.

my test textbox

28. If you wish to apply a theme to an object that already exists this can be done using the 'Apply theme' button from within the properties screen of the object in the Layout tab.

Sharing your QlikView Document

Because this is the Personal Edition of QlikView you cannot load your document into QlikView on another computer, only the computer on which is was created.
In order to do this you need to get a license from QilkTech.

What you can do is export the report to Excel\Image files\Html and other file types.
To export one sheet object Right click on the object and select the Export object.
Depending on the type of object you wish to export you will be given different options.

For example if you click on a pivot table and select export you will be able to save the export in any of the following formats:

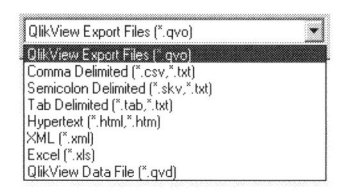

```
QlikView Export Files (*.qvo)
QlikView Export Files (*.qvo)
Comma Delimited (*.csv,*.txt)
Semicolon Delimited (*.skv,*.txt)
Tab Delimited (*.tab,*.txt)
Hypertext (*.html,*.htm)
XML (*.xml)
Excel (*.xls)
QlikView Data File (*.qvd)
```

Whereas for a Chart object you will have the following options.

To export the values from the Chart. Right click on the Chart object and select 'Send Values to Excel'.

Select File-Export->Export Sheet Image. This option will export an image of the current sheet.

104 CHAPTER 7 - QlikView Development Tips

Reports

1. Select the Reports->Edit Reports menu option.
2. Change the drop down list under 'Available Reports' to 'User Reports'

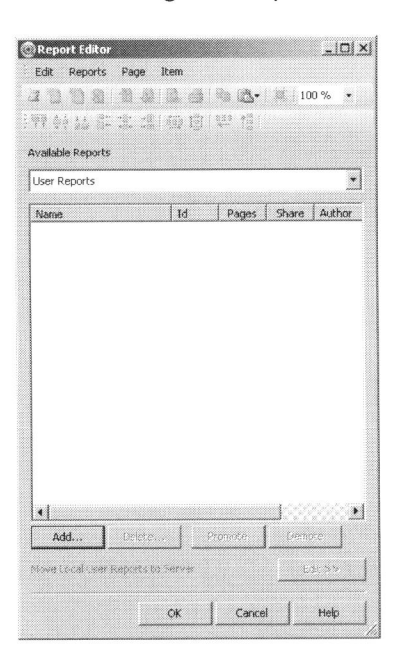

3. Click the Add button and give your report a name.
4. Click the OK button.

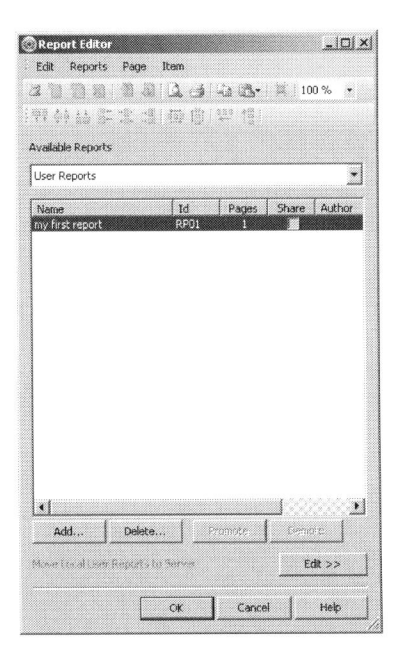

5. Click the Edit button. Now you have the first page of your report.
6. You can drag and drop objects from the sheet and add items such as text and images from the Item menu. Once done select Reports-Print to preview.

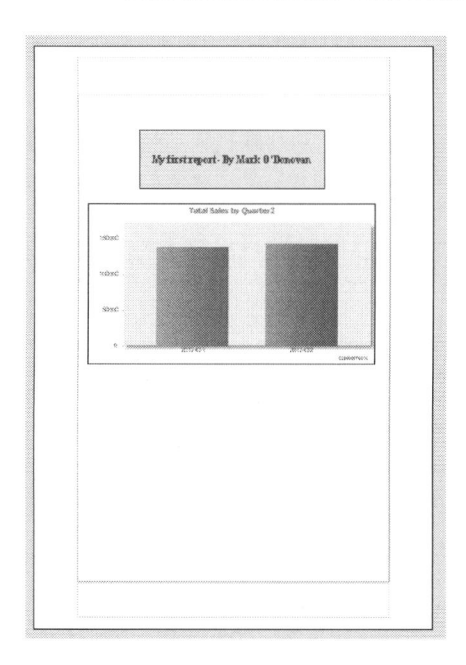

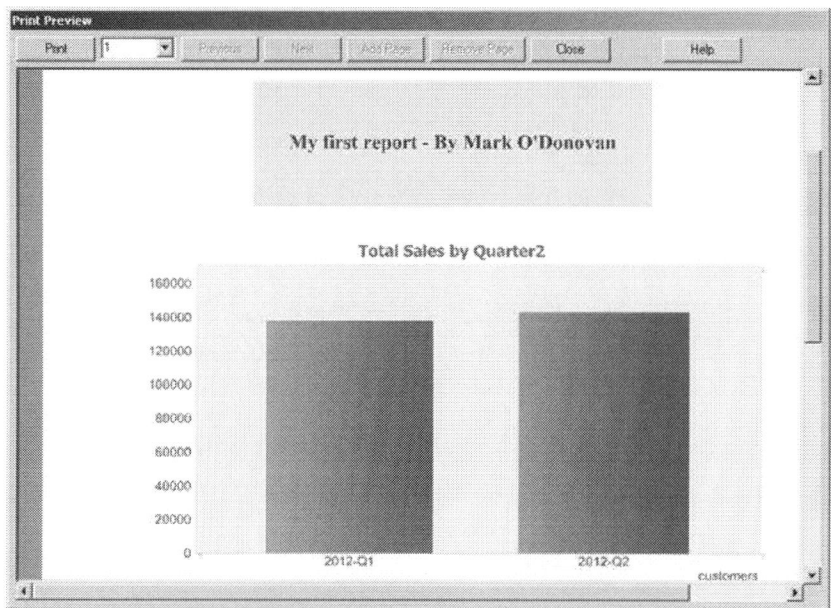

7. Click the Close button, then click the OK button of the Reports Editor and save your document. Now you will have an option from the reports menu to print the report you have just created.

Other Useful Options

Detach\Attach
If you right click on a chart you have the 'Detach' option.
The Detach option makes the Chart static so that any user selections do not affect the chart.

Clone

Select this option by right clicking on the chart\table.
This option makes a copy of the Chart and is useful when creating multiple objects that only have minor differences.

Menu options

Layout Menu – Multiple Sheets and Multiple Load script Tabs.
Add Sheet – This option allows you to create multiple sheets to organise the objects so the sheet doesn't become too cluttered.

You can use multiple tabs in the load script to separate your data sources \ tables your are loading into QlikView.

If you select the File -> Edit Script option, then the Tab->Add Tab , then give the new tab a name and click the OK button. Tabs are used to organize your load script into manageable chunks.

Section Summary

This is the end of Section 1.

Hopefully you are still reading the book and feel more confident that you know what QlikView can do, you have ideas on how QlikView might be able to help you and are keen to start creating your own QlikView documents from scratch.

To help you start creating your own QlikView documents the next section covers several practical examples of QlikView documents you can create.

One reason for creating these example QlikView documents is to cover how the data is obtained and connected to and how to analyse the data once loaded.

The idea is that you will take something away from each of these examples that will assist you in creating your own QlikView documents or give you hints on the different ways in which creating QlikView documents can help you.

Section 2: Practical Examples

Section 2: Overview

In this section of the book we will cover various practical applications of QlikView.

The following examples are grouped into the following chapters

- Everyone
- Personal computer
- Database
- Websites

As the examples in the rest of the book have been focused on Sales related information these next examples will be based on different areas such as tracking your spending and analyzing the performance of your own computer to tracking aspects of a sql server database or when people are accessing your website.

1. Everyone

In this chapter we will create simple examples using data from day to day life.
Later examples in this chapter will be focused on computer performance.

Track your spending

See the downloads page on http://practical-qlikview.com for sample data.

As budgets tighten it is important to keep a track of where you are spending your money.
In this example I have setup some sample data in an Excel spreadsheet.

Date	Food	Petrol	Coffee	Clothes
01/01/2012		40	2.5	
02/01/2012			2.5	
03/01/2012			2.5	
04/01/2012			2.5	
05/01/2012			2.5	
06/01/2012	30		2.5	
07/01/2012			2.5	
08/01/2012			2.5	
09/01/2012			2.5	
10/01/2012			2.5	
11/01/2012		40	2.5	
12/01/2012			2.5	

The names of the worksheets are Jan, Feb and Mar for each month we will be analyzing.

The headers represent the different categories which I have been spending money each day.

1. Start a new QlikView document using the "Getting Started Wizard", select the excel spreadsheet with your spending data in it.
2. Click the Next Button.

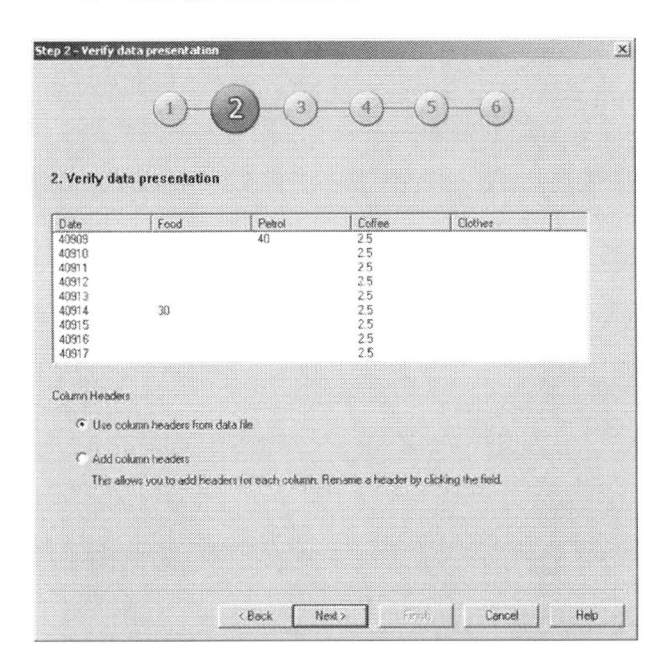

3. Click the Next button and save your QlikView document.
4. Select the straight table option and click the Next button.

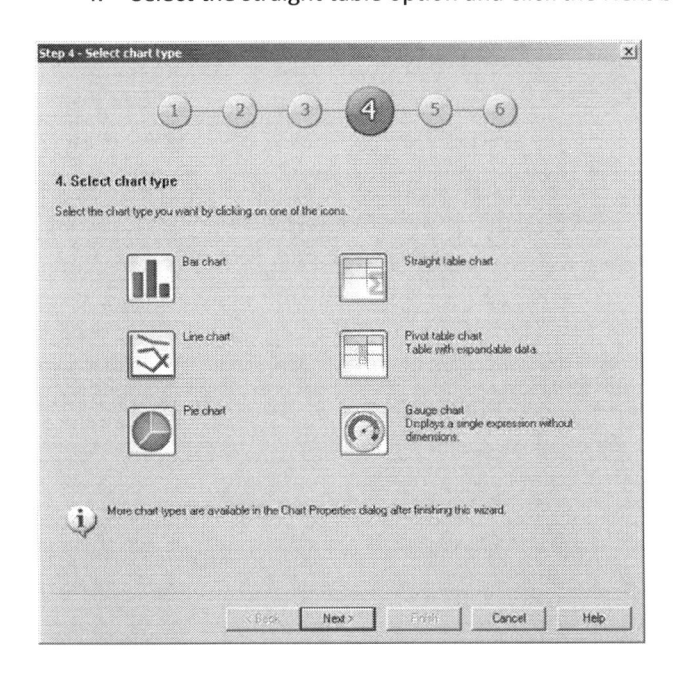

5. Click the Next button.
6. Sum the values of the Coffee column.

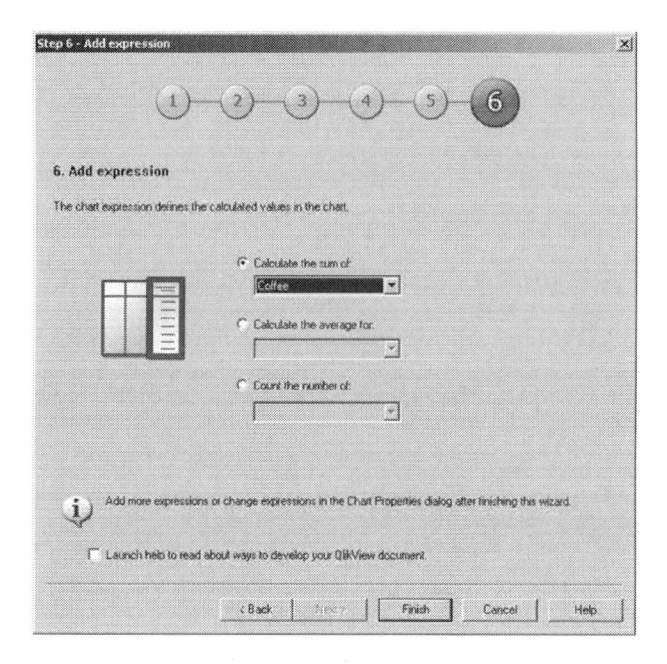

7. Click the Next button.
8. Select the Date field as the first dimension.

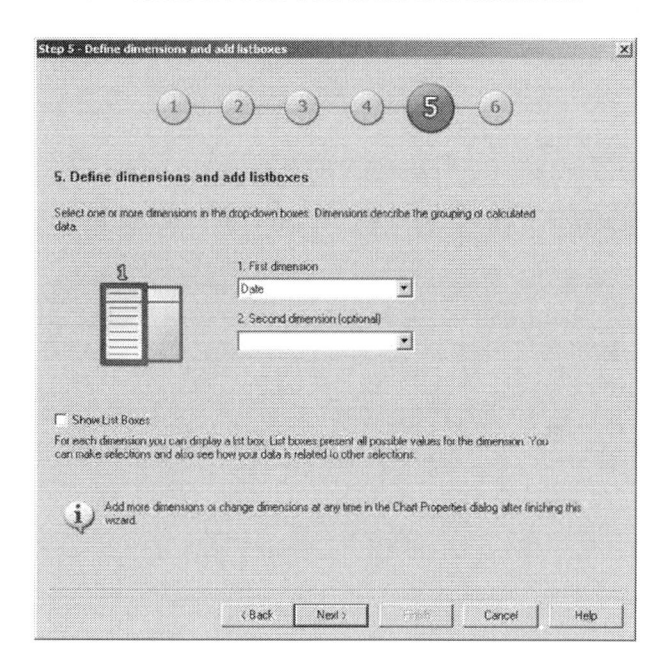

9. Click the Next button, click the finish button.
10. The table displayed will only have the Coffee values for January as shown next.

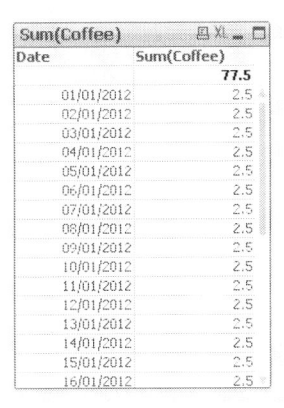

11. Next, we are going to use the **CROSSTABLE** feature to read in all the values for January.
12. Select File->Edit Script
13. Select the LOAD statement and Right click and select comment.
14. Click the Table files button and select your spending spreadsheet.

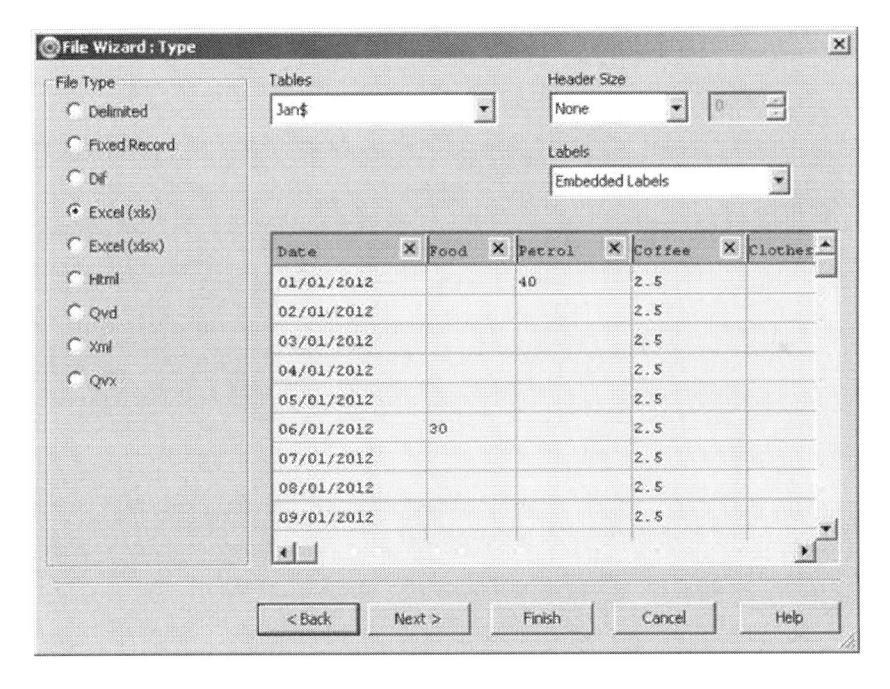

15. Click the Next button.
16. Click the Next button.

Practical Example - Everyone - SECTION 2 CHAPTER 1   **111**

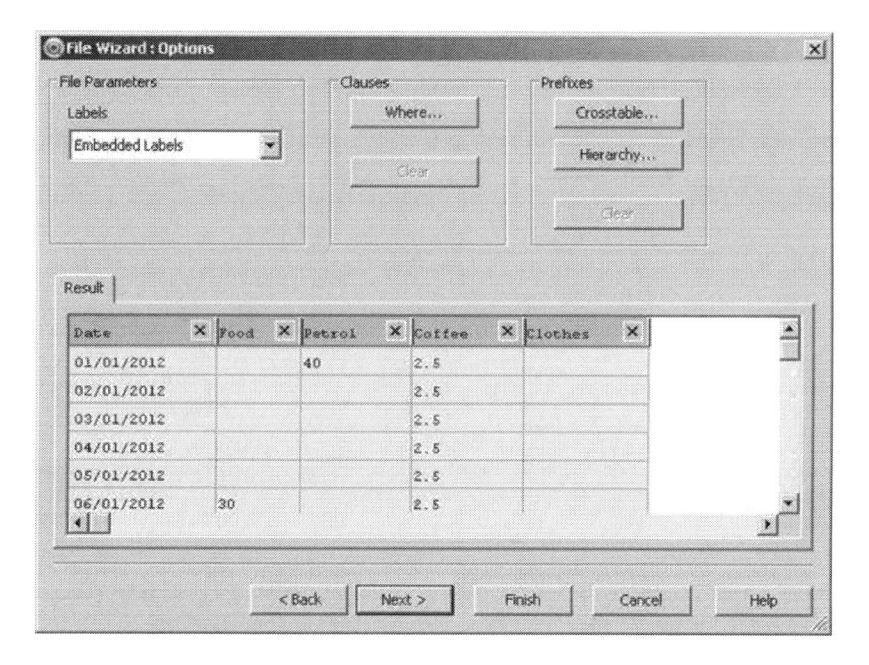

17. Click the **Crosstable** button.
18. The **Attribute** field is set to the column header that will contain one of the categories the money was spent on eg: food, petrol etc..
19. The **Data** field is the column header for the amount that was spent.
20. The **Qualifier** field is the number of fields before the categories, the columns in pink will be read in the normal way.
21. In this case there is only one qualifier field which is the date field.
22. If you increase the number of Qualifier fields you will see the pink section of the preview increase .

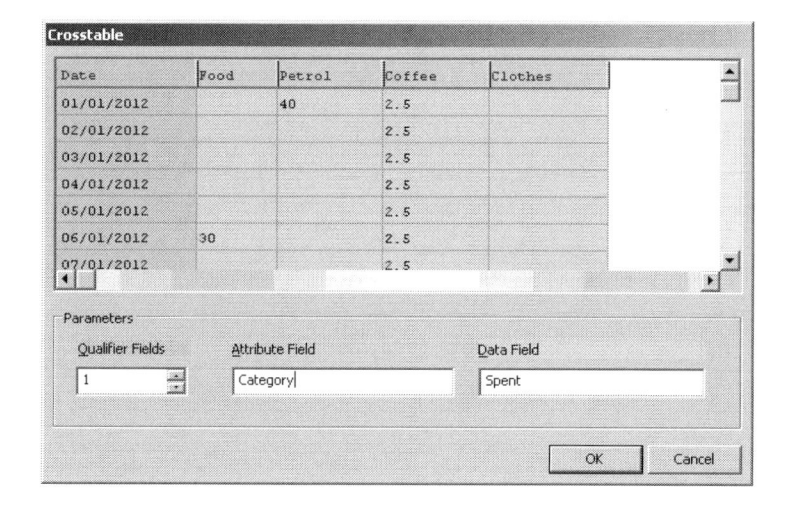

23. Click the OK button and you will see that the preview of the data to be load has been changed:

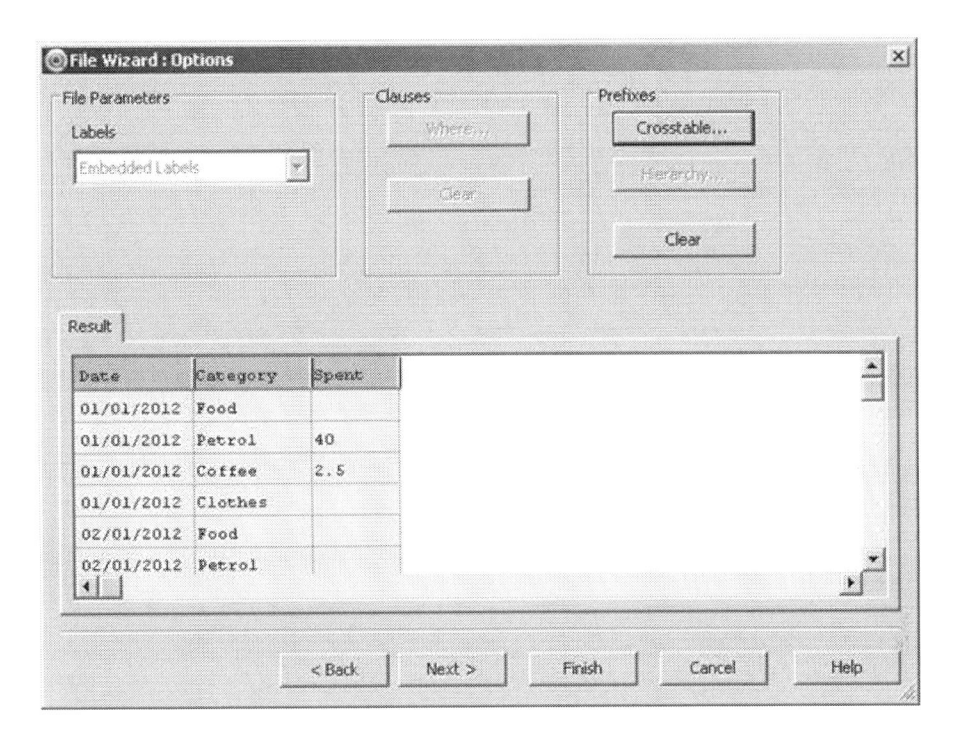

24. Click the Next button.

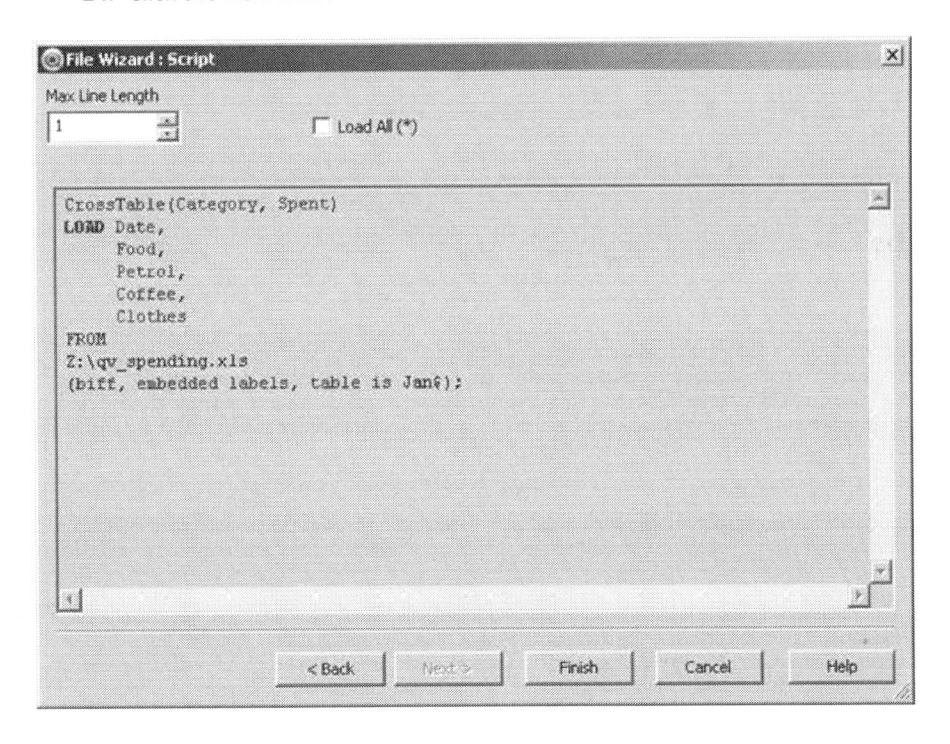

25. Finally click the Finish button.
26. Add a name for the Crosstable and save your document.
27. This is the script I have used with the table name above the Crosstable statement.

Practical Example - Everyone - SECTION 2 CHAPTER 1   113

```
January_spending:
CrossTable(Category, Spent)
LOAD Date,
        Food,
        Petrol,
        Coffee,
        Clothes
FROM
Z:\qv_spending.xls
(biff, embedded labels, table is Jan$);
```

Create a table of spending data for January:
28. Right click on the sheet and select 'New sheet object'->Chart
29. Enter a Window Title: January Spending
30. Chart Type: Straight Table
31. Click the Next button.
32. Select a Dimension: Category.
33. Click the Next button.
34. Enter the following expression:

Sum(Spent)

35. Click the OK button.
36. Click the Finish button.
37. Your table should look like the next screenshot:

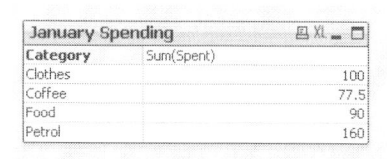

January Spending	
Category	Sum(Spent)
Clothes	100
Coffee	77.5
Food	90
Petrol	160

38. One way to combine several sheets is to have several cross table statements one after the other as in the example below.
39. I have changed the table name as it is no longer just data from January.

```
track_spending:
CrossTable(Category, Spent)
LOAD Date,
    Food,
    Petrol,
    Coffee,
    Clothes
FROM
Z:\qv_spending.xls
(biff, embedded labels, table is Jan$);
```

```
CrossTable(Category, Spent)
LOAD Date,
     Food,
     Petrol,
     Coffee,
     Clothes
FROM
Z:\qv_spending.xls
(biff, embedded labels, table is Feb$);

CrossTable(Category, Spent)
LOAD Date,
     Food,
     Petrol,
     Coffee,
     Clothes
FROM
Z:\qv_spending.xls
(biff, embedded labels, table is Mar$);
```

40. Go back the table and change the dimensions to be: Category, then Month(Date).

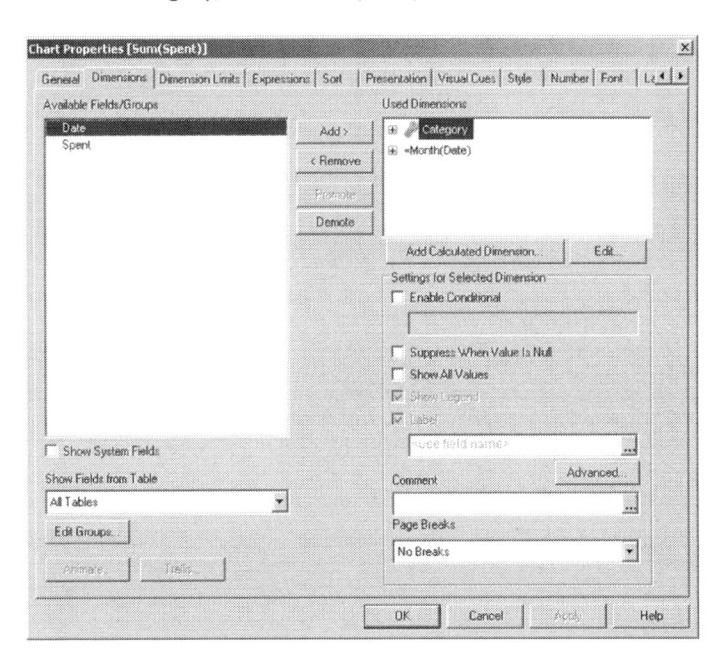

41. Change the expressions to be Sum(Spent) , then click the OK button.

Practical Example - Everyone - SECTION 2 CHAPTER 1   **115**

Category	=Month(Date)	Sum(Spent)
		1105.69
Coffee	Jan	77.5
Food	Jan	90
Clothes	Jan	100
Petrol	Jan	160
Clothes	Feb	50
Coffee	Feb	58.2
Food	Feb	90
Petrol	Feb	160
Clothes	Mar	19.99
Coffee	Mar	60
Food	Mar	100
Petrol	Mar	140

42. Right click on the chart and select Clone.
43. Go to the properties and change the Chart Type in the General Tab to 'Bar chart' and enter a title of 'Spending By Category' then click the OK button.
44. Your new chart should look like this:

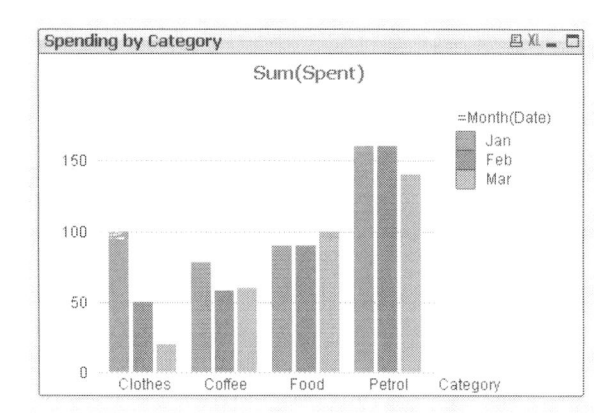

45. The only worrying thing is the amount of money I am spending on coffee compared with food.
46. Some banks allow you to download your statements in Excel\csv format which would make a good start for tracking your spending using QlikView.
47. If we go back to the properties on the chart and remove the Category Dimension and click the OK button we can see the total amount spent on a monthly basis.

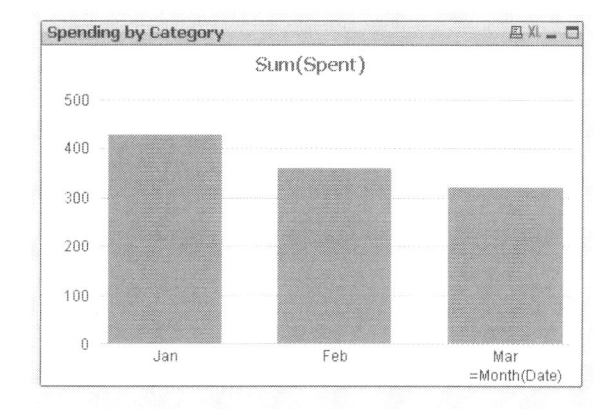

48. If you change the dimension to Week(date) the result is your spending on a week by week basis.

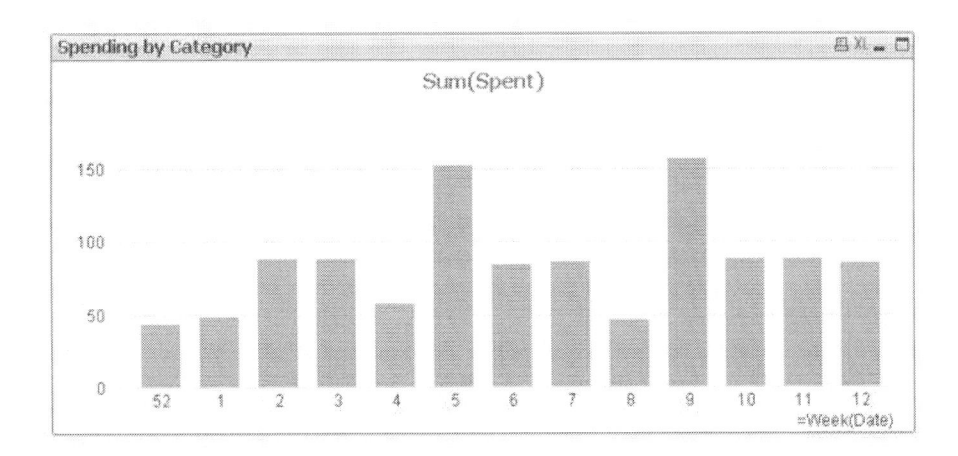

Loops in Load script

The current load script is fine for 3 months. But as the months\years increase the script will begin to become awkward to manage very quickly. Next is an example of an updated load script.

1. You can comment out current load script and replace it will one using a loop.

    for Each Sheetname in 'Jan$','Feb$','Mar$'

    track_spending:
    CrossTable(Category, Spent)
    LOAD Date,
         Food,
         Petrol,
         Coffee,
         Clothes
    FROM
    Z:\qv_spending.xls
    (biff, embedded labels, table is $(Sheetname));
    Next

2. The first line starting 'For Each' followed by Sheetname.
3. Sheetname is the name of the variable that will contain a list of the Excel sheets to load.
4. Where we had the worksheet name of the Excel spreadsheet such as Jan$ we have replaced it with $(Sheetname).
5. Each time the load scripts goes around the loop it updates the $(Sheetname) variable with the next item from the list.
6. This loop makes the load script shorter and easy to manage.
7. You could even try loading the list of Sheetnames from a textfile\Excel so that you don't have to update your load script each month.

Football Scores

1. Select File->New to create a new QlikView document.
2. Press escape
3. Select File->Save to save your document.
4. Go the File-Edit script menu option
5. Click the 'Table files' button.
6. Select the spreadsheet with the sample football results.
7. From the Tables drop down list select the Results$ sheet.
8. Set 'Header Size' to 2 lines and the Labels to 'Embedded Labels'.
9. Click the X on the F3 column to remove from the load as this column is not needed.

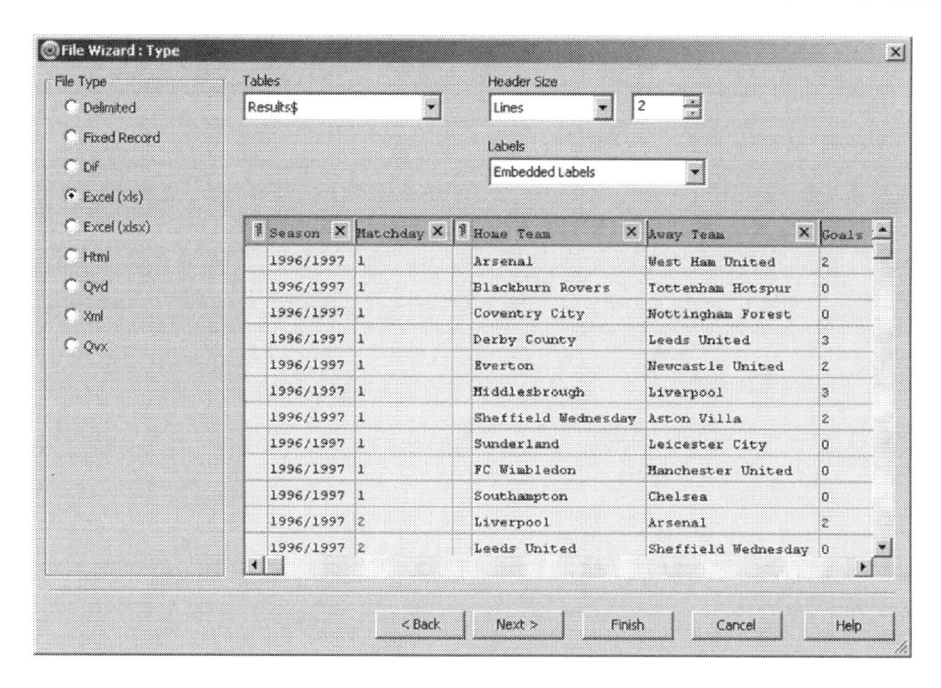

10. Click the Next button.
11. Transform screen: Click the Next button.
12. Options screen: Click the Next button.
13. Add a table name of premier_results before the load statement.
14. You script should look as follows:

Directory;
premier_results:
LOAD Season,
   Matchday,
   [Home Team],
   [Away Team],
   [Goals Home],
   [Goals Away]

FROM
premier_league_2011.xls
(biff, embedded labels, header is 2 lines, table is Results$);

15. Click the Finish button.
16. You will return to the Edit Script.
17. Click the Reload button in the toolbar.
18. Click the OK button on the Sheet properties.
19. Make sure you save your document.
20. The following script reads the Results$ sheet from the Excel spreadsheet.
    a. We have added a table name of 'premier_results'.
    b. We have created a field using the Rec() for a row number called 'recordno'.
    c. We have used the QUALIFY\UNQUALIFY statements so that the table can only link to other tables using certain fields.
21. The only field that can be linked to another table is the 'recordno'.

Directory;
QUALIFY *;
UNQUALIFY recordno;
premier_results:
LOAD
RecNo() as recordno,
Season,
    Matchday,
    [Home Team],
    [Away Team],
    [Goals Home],
    [Goals Away]
FROM
premier_league_2011.xls
(biff, embedded labels, header is 2 lines, table is Results$);

22. Once you have made these changes Reload the script and save the document.
23. Add the following script to your Load script.
    (Add after the premier_results table)

    Directory;
    QUALIFY *;
    UNQUALIFY Team,recordno;
    Linktogames:
    LOAD
    [premier_results.Home Team] as Team,
    recordno
    resident premier_results;

    Directory;
    QUALIFY *;
    UNQUALIFY Team,recordno;

LOAD
[premier_results.Away Team] as Team,
recordno
resident premier_results;

24. This script uses QUALIFY\UNQUALIFY statements to only allow links using the Team, recordno fields and the table uses the RESIDENT statement to use the already loaded premier_results table:
25. If you look at the File->Table Viewer option you will see that the 2 tables are linked together using the recordno field.

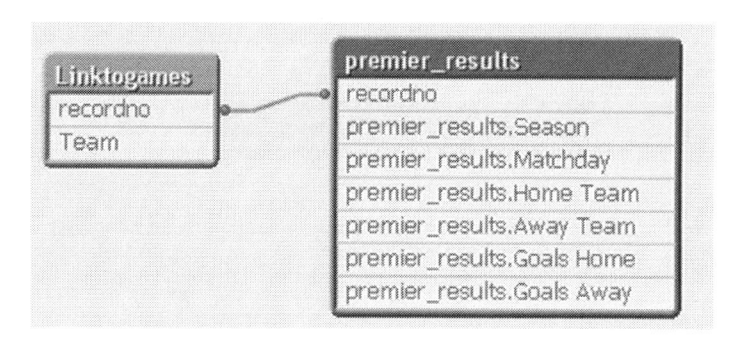

26. Now we have the data loaded into our QlikView document we can add objects to our sheet to display the data.
    Next we will show how to display all games played in a table for a selected Team:
27. Right click on the Sheet select 'New Sheet Object'->Multi Box.
28. Set the Title to : 'Select Season\Team'
29. Select the 'Home Team' field as change the Label to 'Team' as show in the next screenshot.

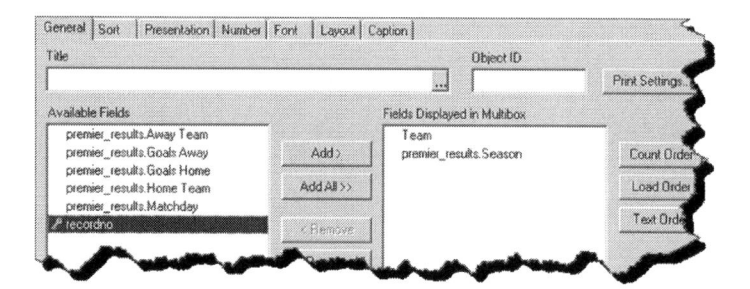

30. Click the OK button and position the object in the top left corner of the sheet.

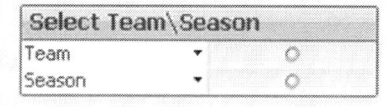

31. Next we will create a straight table to list the games that have been played for the selected team\season.
32. Right click on the Sheet select 'New Sheet Object'->Table Box.
33. Set the Title field to: 'Matches played'
34. Add all fields except Team as displayed in the next screenshot.

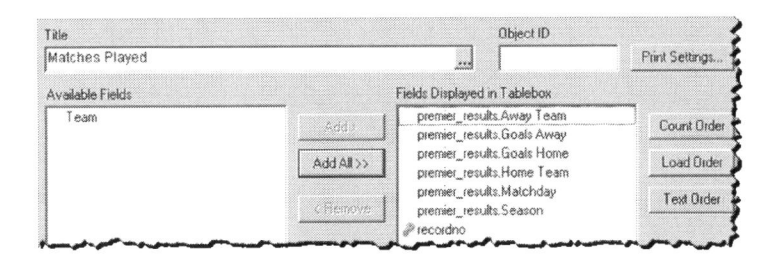

35. Click on each field in the 'Fields Displayed in Tablebox' and set the label to be the name of the Field without the tablename ie: premier_results.Matchday becomes just Matchday.
36. Click on the Sort tab. Notice that QlikView has identified Season as a Text field and Matchday as a Numeric. This is because the Season has the '/' character in the field to separate the years.
37. Click on the OK button and your table should look like the following screenshot:
38. If the columns are too wide right click on the table and select 'Fit Columns to Data'.

Calculation condition

1. In the general tab of the Table Box properties you can add a 'Calculation Condition'.
2. Set the Calculation Condition to:
   premier_results.Season='2003/2004'

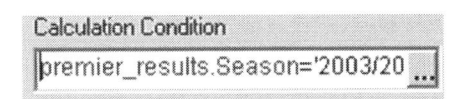

3. If the 'Calculation Condition' is not met the message 'Calculation condition unfulfilled' is displayed in the text box. If you select a Season of '2003/2004' results will be displayed.

2. Personal Computer

What is happening on your computer: Events

When something happens on your computer such as when you logon or install some software information about what happened is stored in Event Logs.

The information in Event logs can contain different types of events that refer to errors, warnings or information about what an application is doing.

In this example we are going to save the event log data from your computer into a csv file.

Then using QlikView we are going to analyse the events occurring on your computer and the source of the events.

1. Go to the Event view on your computer.
2. The event viewer can be found in:

    XP Users: Control panel, then Administrative tools.
    Vista users: Control panel, then System and Maintenance, then 'Administrative tools'.

3. Right click on the Application log and select Export List ... (For vista: Save Events As...)

4. Save the log file as a csv file.
5. Open QlikView and select File->New to create a new document.
6. If the "Getting Started Wizard" start click the Cancel button.
7. Select the File->Edit Script option.
8. Click the Table files button and select the application event log you saved.
9. QlikView will detect the format and the embedded headers.

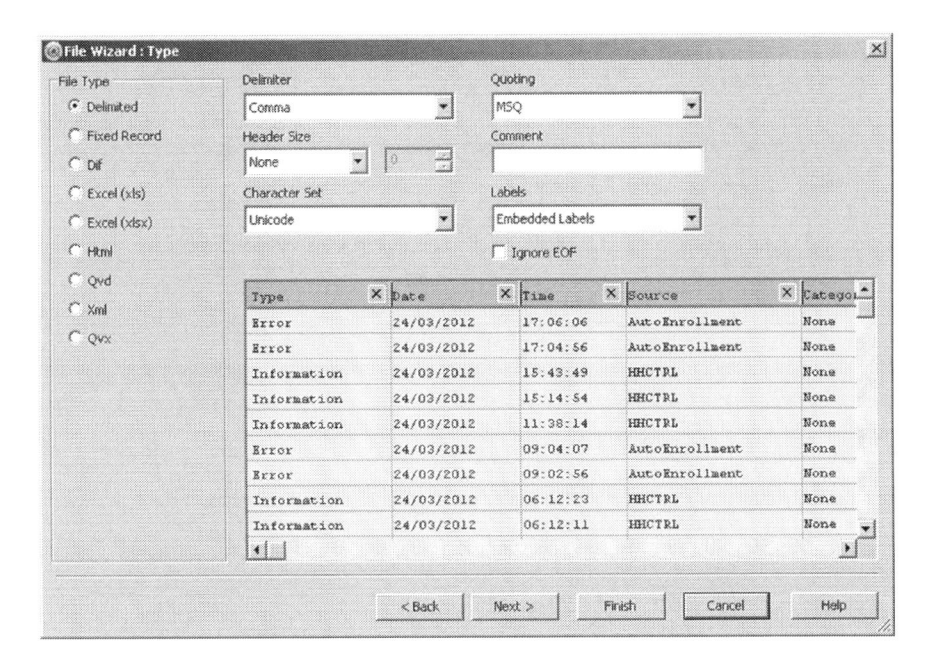

10. Click the Finish Button.
11. Select File->Save Entire Document to save your new QlikView document.
12. Click the Reload button in the toolbar.
13. If there were no problems the Sheet properties screen should be displayed
14. Click the OK button.
15. Right click on the sheet and select 'New Sheet Object', then Chart.
16. **Window Title**: Event Type Count by Month
17. Chart Type: Bar Chart
18. Click Next.
19. **Used Dimensions**: Add Calculated Dimension of Month(Date),then the Type dimension.

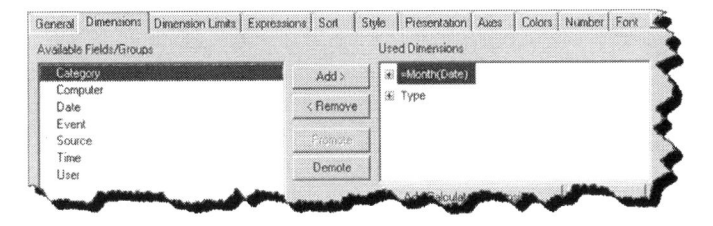

20. Click Next. Add the following expression to count the type of events we are getting on our computer.

    Count(Type)
21. Click OK.

Practical Example - Personal Computer - SECTION 2 CHAPTER 2   **123**

[Event Type Count by Month chart]

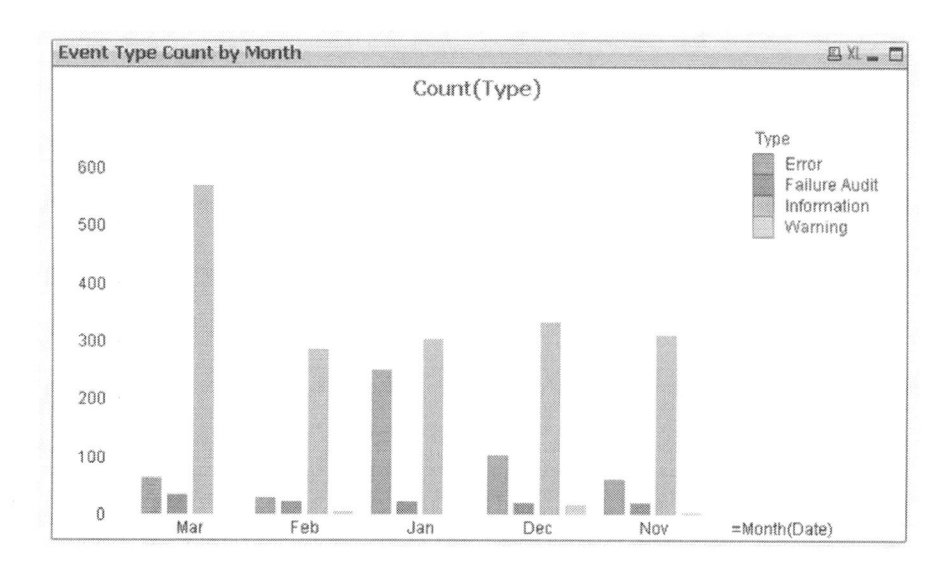

22. As you can see from this graph I might want to look into what caused all the Error Events in January (The Error Events are the first column to the left).
23. If you replace the Type Dimension with a Category Dimension, change the Window Title and change the expression to: Count(Category)

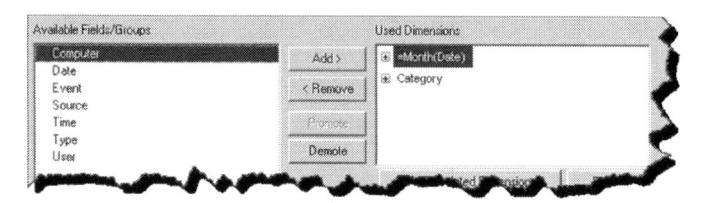

[Dimensions dialog screenshot]

24. Click OK and you will see a chart of the Event categories by Month as shown in the next screenshot.

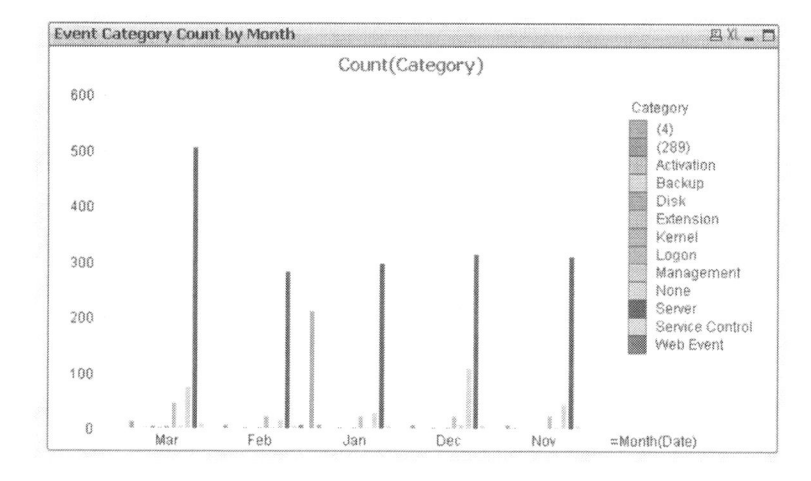

[Event Category Count by Month chart]

25. As you can see there are many Server category events which are mainly from SQL Server running on the machine.

How well is my computer running: Computer Performance

In this example we will show you how to find out how well your computer is performing.

This can help you answer questions like: Do I need more memory for my computer?

(**NOTE**: The examples for collecting the performance data are based on Windows XP and will be different for other versions of Windows)

1. Select Start->Run and type the command 'Perfmon'.
2. The Performance screen will be displayed.
3. Select the 'Performance Logs and Alerts' option.

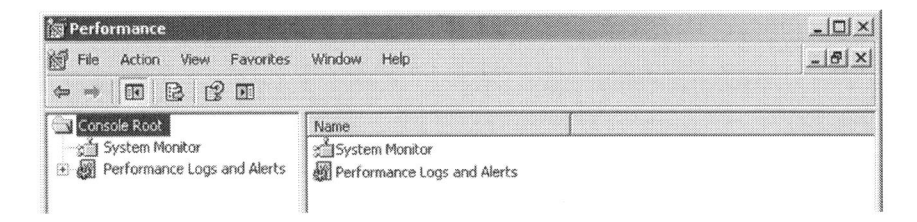

4. Click on the 'Counter Logs' option.
5. Right click on the right hand side of the screen and select the option
6. 'New Log Settings...'

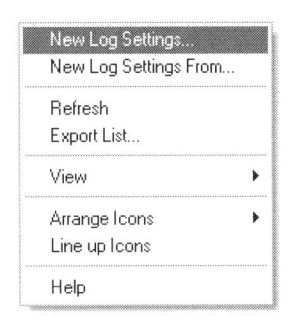

7. Enter a name for your log settings.
8. Click on the option 'Add Counters...'.

Practical Example - Personal Computer - SECTION 2 CHAPTER 2

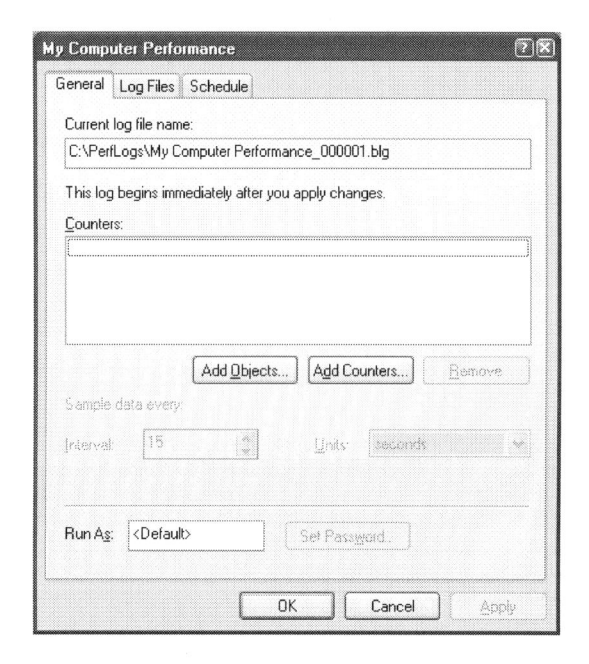

9. Select the following counters and click the add button for each one :

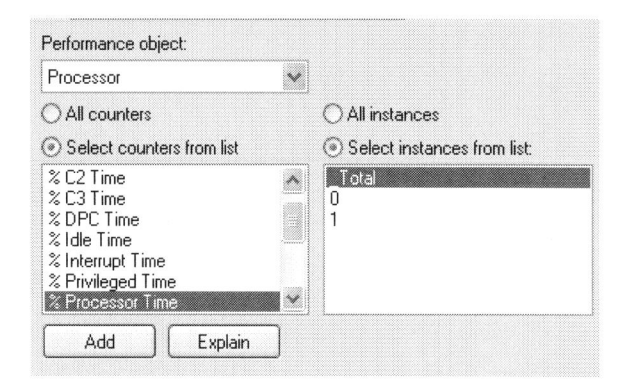

% Processor Time
10. This counter tells you how much of the time the processor is busy.
11. It is normal for the processor to busy when starting a new program.
12. If the values are 70% or more this could need more investigation.

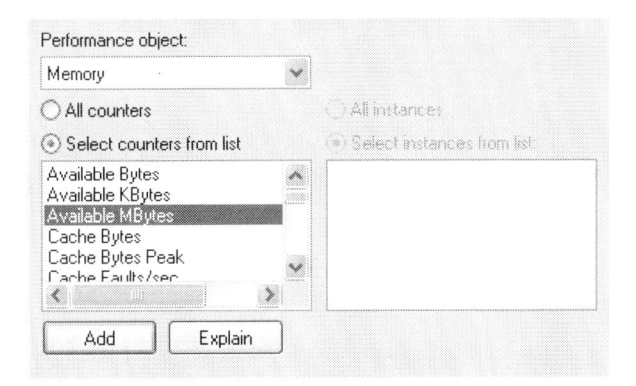

Available Mbytes
13. This will tell you how much Memory (RAM) you have free when using your computer.
14. This is useful to know if you are thinking of upgrading the memory on your computer.
15. Click the Close button.

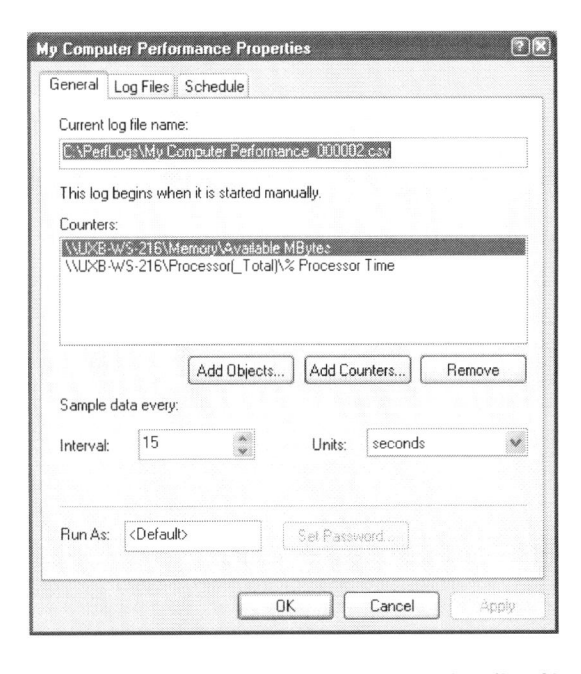

16. Click on the log files tab and select 'log file type' of 'Text File (Comma delimited)'.
17. Add a comment to describe the performance data you are gathering.

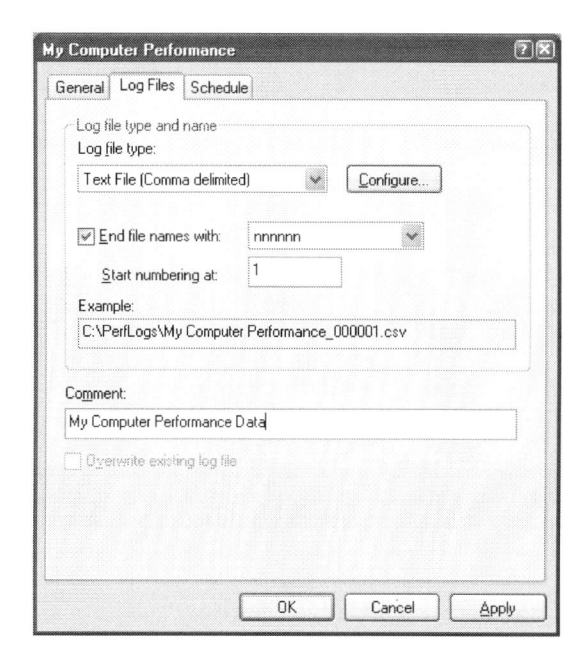

18. You can change the location of the file if you click on the configure button.
19. Click OK.

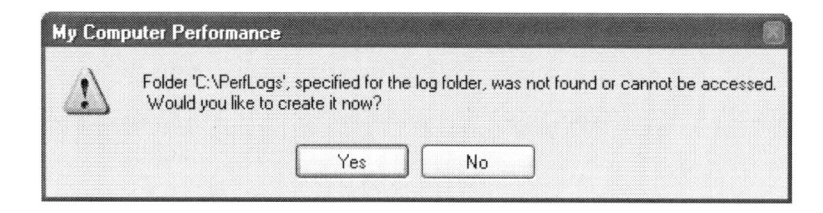

20. Click Yes.

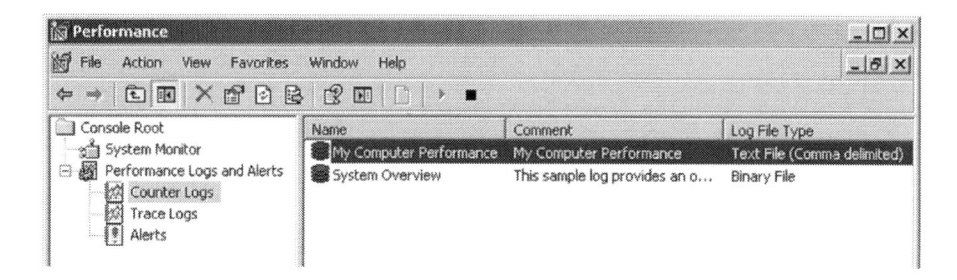

21. If you do not use your computer while you are gathering the performance data you will not get an accurate picture of the amount of memory\processor that is being used.
22. Leave the performance monitor to gather data for a few minutes\hours while you use your computer.
23. Then right click on the name 'My Computer Performance' and select stop.

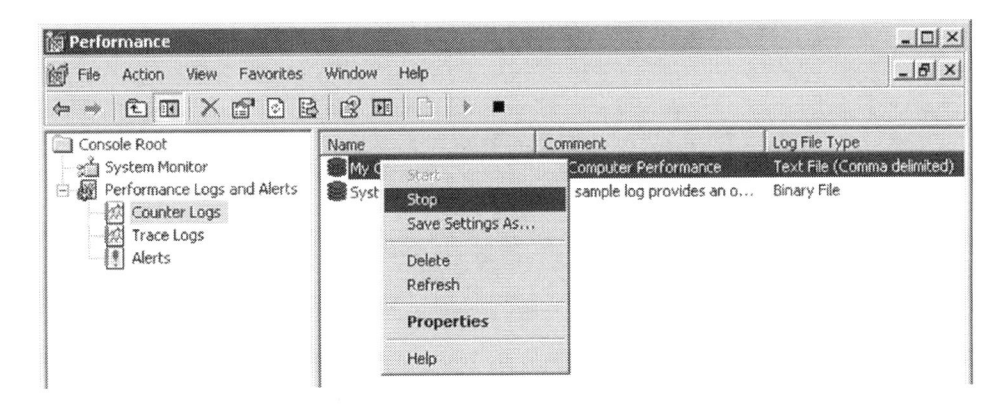

24. Close the Performance screen by selecting File->Exit.
25. Now that you have created the data to be analysed you can open QlikView.
26. Select the File->New option to create a new QlikView document.
27. Cancel the "Getting Started Wizard".
28. Open the Load script by selecting File-Edit Script.
29. Click the 'Table Files' button and select the CSV file that contains your performance data.

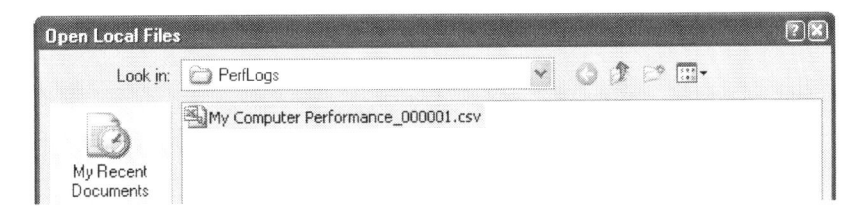

30. Click Open
31. QlikView will have detected that this is a csv file.
32. Change the Labels field to: Embedded Labels (as shown in the next screenshot).

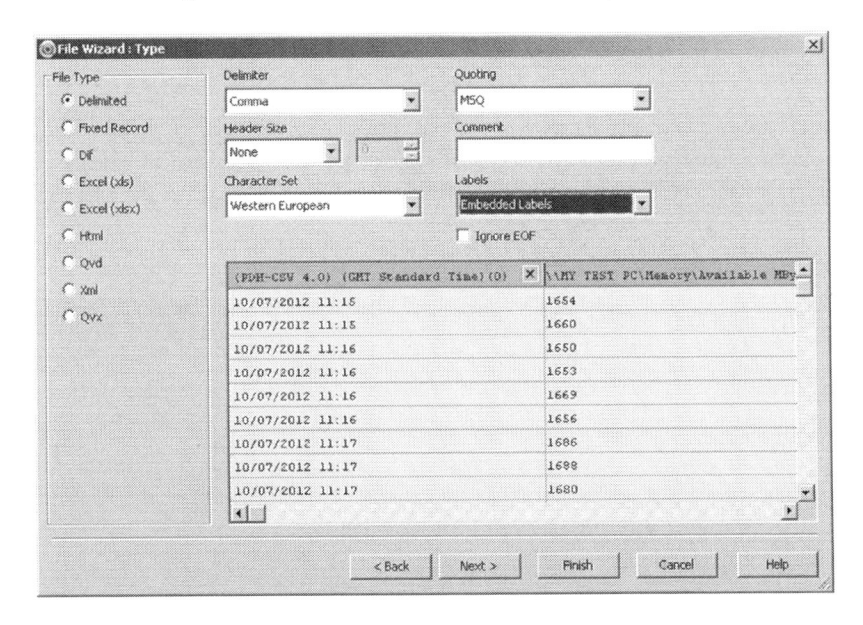

33. Click Next.
34. Click Next on the 'File Wizard: Transform' screen.
35. Click Next on the 'File Wizard: Options' screen.
36. Click Finish. You will see the script added to your load script as shown.
37. Add the following expression as the field Minutes:

    Minute(Right((((PDH-CSV 4.0) (GMT Standard Time)(0)]),5)) as Minutes

    This expression simply gets the time and extracts the minute value.
38. If you have more data you might want to change this to use the Hour() function instead.
39. Click File-Save Entire Document.
40. Click the Reload button in the toolbar.
41. If there are no errors you will see the following 'Sheet Properties' screen:
42. Click the 'Add All' button.
43. All the 'Available Fields' will be moved to the 'Fields Displayed in Listboxes' list.
44. Go to the General tab and change the Title to 'My Computer Performance'.
45. Click the OK button. You should now see a listbox for each field on your sheet.
46. From the layout menu, select the option 'Rearrange Sheet Objects'.
47. Now you can view the data you have loaded into your QlikView document.

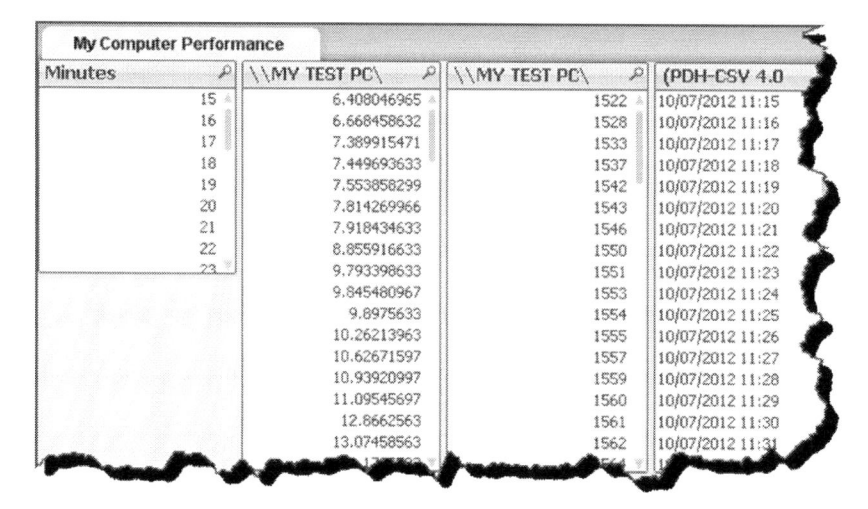

48. Select File->Edit Script to open your load script.
49. Add a name to the table by added the table name followed by a colon (:)
50. Before the load statement. In the next script I have called the table PerfData.
51. Click the Reload button.

PerfData:
LOAD
    Minute(Right((((PDH-CSV 4.0) (GMT Standard Time)(0)]),5)) as Minutes,
    [(PDH-CSV 4.0) (GMT Standard Time)(0)],
    [\\MY TEST PC\Memory\Available MBytes],
    [\\MY TEST PC\Processor(_Total)\% Processor Time],
    [My Computer Performance Data]

FROM
[Z:\My Computer Performance_000001.csv]
(txt, codepage is 1252, embedded labels, delimiter is ',', msq);

With this chart we will show the different performance counters by the minute.

1. Create a new Sheet by selecting the Layout->Add Sheet menu option.
2. Change to the new sheet by clicking the sheet tab.
3. Right click on the blank sheet, select 'New Sheet Object', then 'Chart...'.
4. If you have more performance data you can change this to by the hour.
5. Add a 'Window Title' of 'Performance By Minute'. Click Next
6. Add the following Dimension: 'Minutes'.

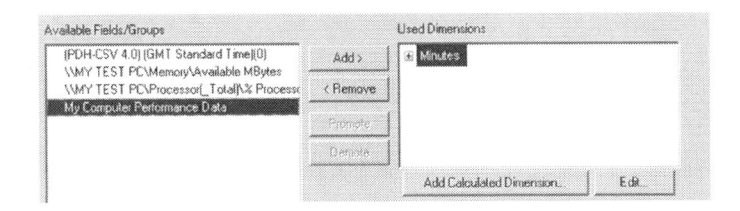

7. Click Next.
8. Add the following expression: Avg([\\MYTESTPC\Memory\Available MBytes])
   Click OK.
9. Click Finish. Your chart should look like the following screenshot:

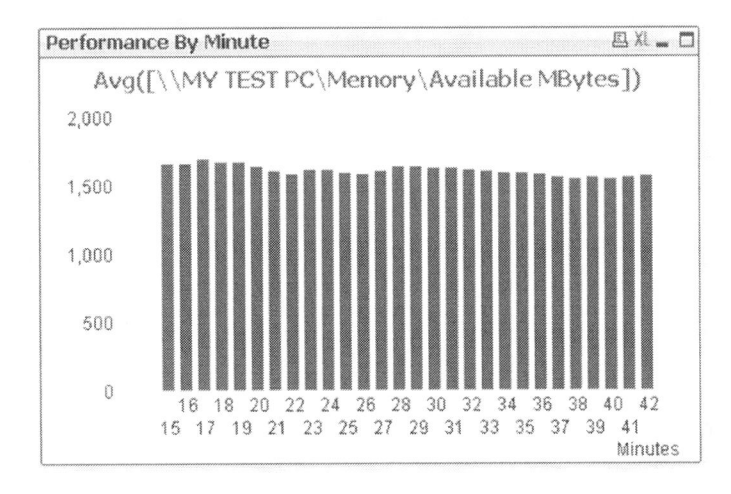

10. As you can see the memory usage is fairly even which is a good sign.
11. Next we will add the processor usage to this chart.
12. Right click on the Chart and select Properties.
13. Select the Expressions tab , click the Add button and add the following expression:

    Avg([\\MYTESTPC\Processor(_Total)\% Processor Time])

NOTE: When adding expressions just type AVG(), move the cursor between the brackets, select the field you require in the fields tab (such as Processor Time) and click the paste button.

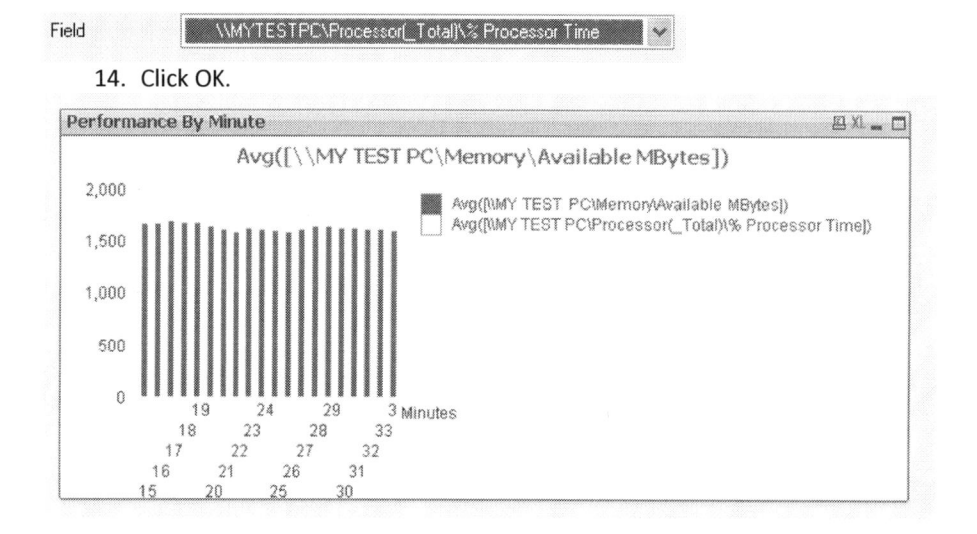

Field \\MYTESTPC\Processor(_Total)\% Processor Time

14. Click OK.

15. As you can see because the values that need to be plotted for Memory and Processor are very different it is difficult to see what values are being plotted for the Processor Time value.
16. You can try hovering over each bar and it will tell you the value.

Group Chart Expressions

To resolve this problem, go to the chart properties, then Expressions tab.
1. Select the bottom expression as shown in the next screenshot and you will see you have the Group button:

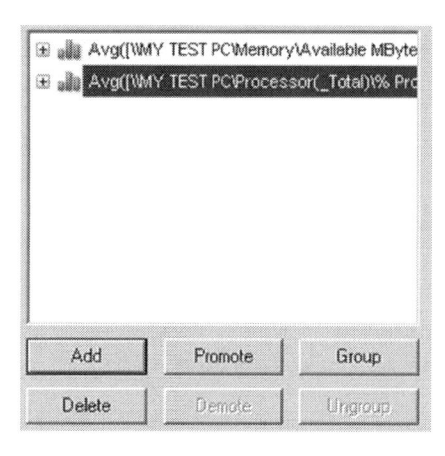

2. Click the Group button. The two expressions will be grouped together.
3. Click OK.
4. Now in a similar way to 'Cyclic groups' for dimensions you can switch between charts for the 2 expressions.

5. The group icon for expressions is in the bottom left corner of the screen.

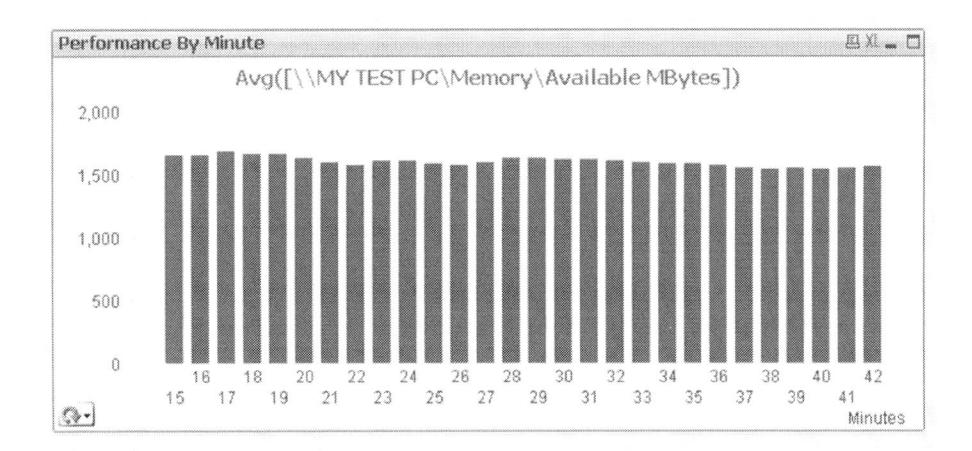

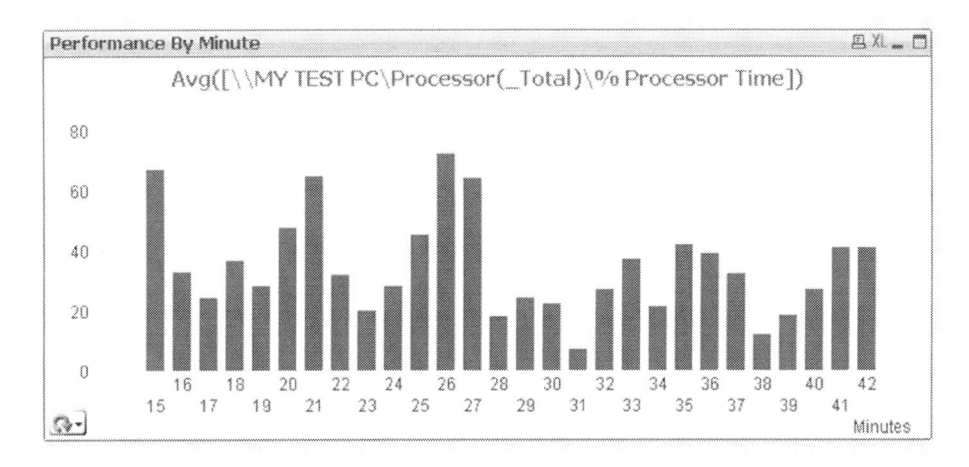

6. Problem solved. You can see the %Processor time changes much more than the amount of memory used.

Practical Example - Personal Computer - SECTION 2 CHAPTER 2   133

3. Database

Sql Server Reporting Services (SSRS)

Sql Server Reporting Services (SSRS) is a tool that comes with Sql Server that enables the user to run reports on data from many different sources such as OLE DB, ODBC, SAP, XML or Oracle.

In this example we will produce a QlikView document to analyse the SSRS reports database. The SSRS reports database is normally called 'reportserver' and contains data such as what reports have been run, by which user and how long it took to produce the report.

The queries that this document will answer are:

- Which reports take the longest to run?
- Which are the largest reports?
- What reports are the selected user running?
- Are there any reports that are causing errors?

To answer these questions we will load the data from the ExecutionLog3 view of the ReportServer database.

Next is the script you will use to get the data from the database.

```
OLEDB CONNECT TO <your connectionstring>
LOAD
    ItemPath as ReportName,
    UserName,
    TimeStart,
    TimeDataRetrieval + TimeProcessing + TimeRendering as TotalTime,
    Status,
    ByteCount;
SQL SELECT *
FROM ReportServer.dbo.ExecutionLog3;
```

If you are running this on a large database it is best to click the Debug button in the toolbar and only read a limited number of records:

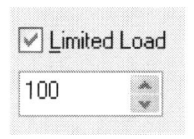

(Another way to restrict the number of records read is using a WHERE clause in your SELECT statement)

1. Click the Run button from the debug screen.

2. Once the records have been read the Sheet Properties screen will be displayed.
3. Select New Sheet Object -> Multi Box.
4. Add the following Fields to the 'Fields Displayed in Multibox' list.

   UserName
   ReportName
   Status

This will give you the following selection options:

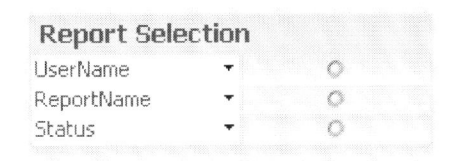

5. Next we will create some charts\tables to answer our queries:
   Which reports take the longest to run?
6. Right click on the sheet and select New Sheet Object ->Chart. We will create a Bar chart displaying the top 5 longest running reports.
7. Set Window Title: Longest running reports
8. Bar chart is the default. Click Next.
9. Add the Dimension of 'ReportName'.
10. Set the Expression: Sum(TotalTime)

Dimension Limits tab:
11. Select the 'Restrict which values are displayed using the first expression' option and set to show only the 5 largest values as shown in the next screenshot.
12. Click OK. My test server displays a chart as shown in the next screenshot:
13. This value is in milliseconds.

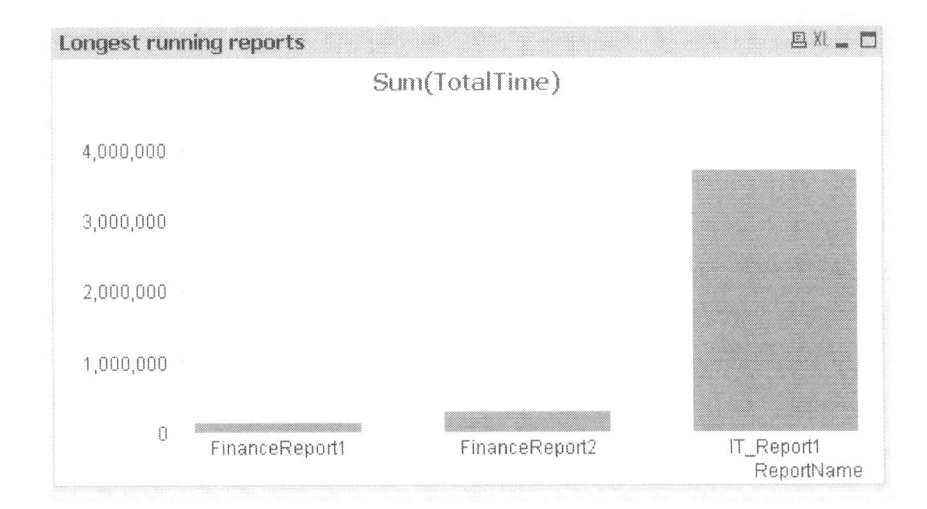

14. If we change the expression used to: Avg(TotalTime)/1000
    We can see the Average time for each report in seconds:

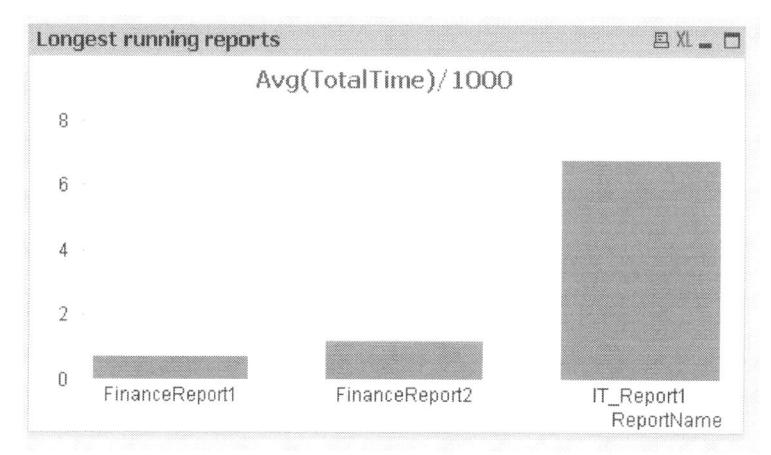

[Chart: Longest running reports - Avg(TotalTime)/1000, showing bars for FinanceReport1, FinanceReport2, and IT_Report1]

15. As you can see the report IT_Report1 is the report that takes the longest time to run on average.

Next query: **Which are the largest reports?**

1. For this query we will alter our current report to use a cyclic group.
2. Open the Chart properties and click the Dimensions tab.
3. Click the Edit Groups button.
4. Click New to create a New group.
5. Add the following fields to the 'Used Fields' list.
   a. Status
   b. ReportName - change label to 'Report'.
   c. UserName - change label to 'User'.
6. Select the 'Cyclic Group' option and give the group a name:SSRS_Report
7. Click OK.

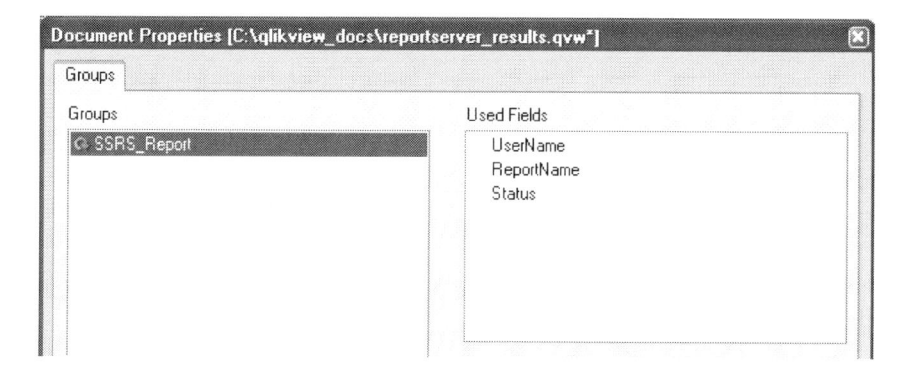

[Screenshot: Document Properties dialog showing Groups tab with SSRS_Report group and Used Fields: UserName, ReportName, Status]

8. Click OK again.
9. Replace the 'Used Dimension' of 'ReportName' with the group 'SSRS_Report'.

10. From the General Tab, change the name of the chart to 'SSRS Reports'.
11. Click OK.
12. Now you will able to switch between the different Dimensions using the group icon.
13. As you can see TestUser4 is the one who is running the reports that are taking the longest time.

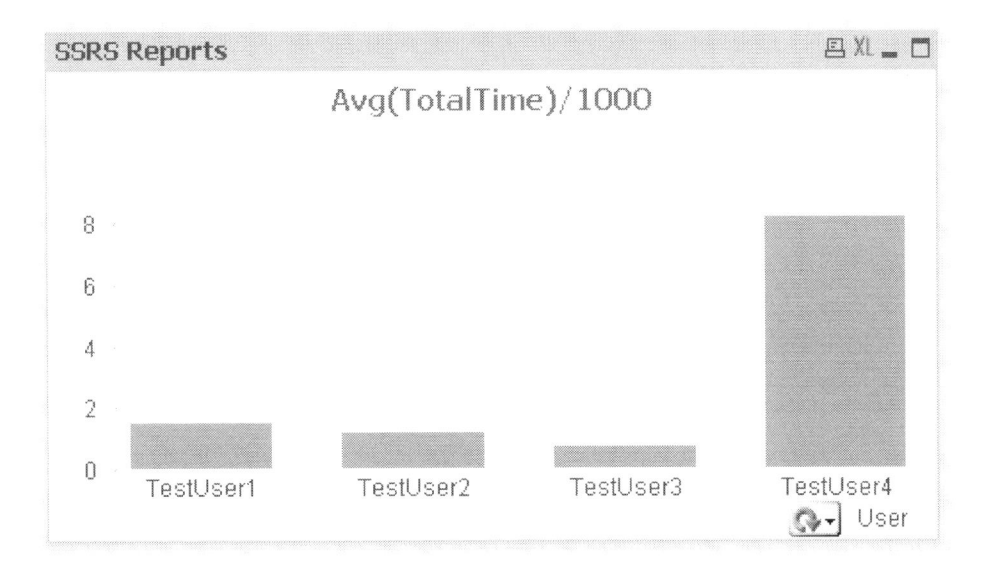

This chart can be used for 3 queries:
- Which users are running reports that are taking the longest time to complete?
- Which reports are taking the longest time to complete ?
- What is the Status of the reports that are being run? ie: Are you getting a lot of errors.

You can then use the 'Report Selection' object to answer specific queries.

The next screenshot shows the query:
For Reports that completed successfully what where the longest running reports and how long did they take to complete in seconds.

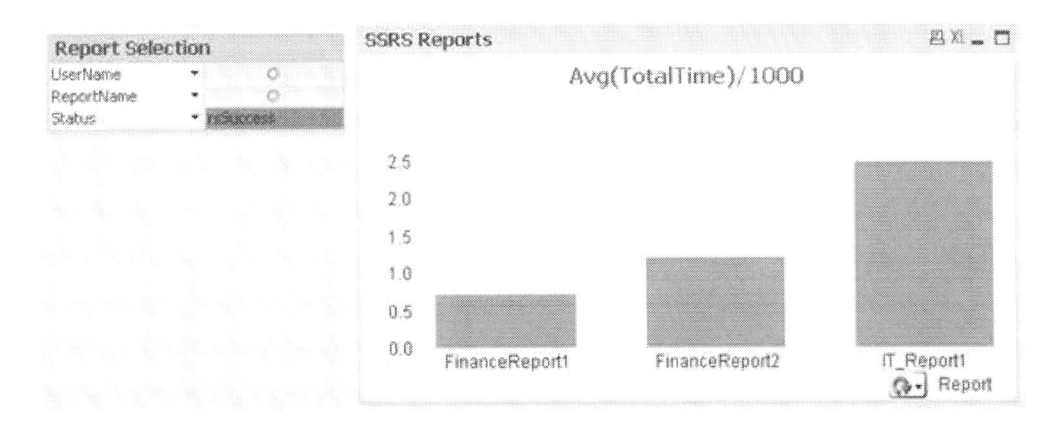

Practical Example - Database - SECTION 2 CHAPTER 3

TIP: When using the UserName field which is in the format of: DOMAIN\User

You can remove the domain portion of the username by using the following expression:

=Right(UserName,len(UserName)-index(UserName,'\'))

This expression finds portion where the '\' is location in the string, and substracts that value from the total length of the field.

It then uses the Right() function which returns the remaining characters from the right side of the string. For example:

MYDOMAIN\Joe

Len(UserName) would return 12.
Index(UserName,'\') would return 9.

12-9=3, therefore it would only return 3 characters from the right side of the string which should be 'Joe'.

SQL SERVER – database versions

This next example is one that uses SQL SERVER.

In particular these commands are useful to sql server dba\developers but the commands used and the concepts can be applied to anyone that needs to get data from a SQL SERVER database.

1. Create a new QlikView document (File->New) and cancel the "Getting Started Wizard".
2. Open the Load script (File->Edit Script or CTRL+E).
3. Create and OLE DB connection to your sql database.
4. Change the Database dropdownlist to OLE DB.
5. Click the Connect button.
6. Select 'SQL Server Native Client 10.0'.
7. Click Next. Enter your connection information:

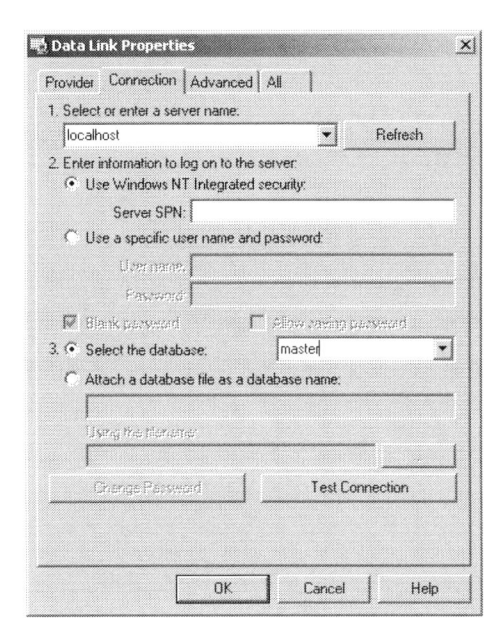

In my example the server is on the local machine.

I am connecting to the SQL Server with the username\password I am logged onto the machine with using 'Windows NT Integrated Security'.
The initial database I am connecting to is the master database.

8. Click the 'Test Connection' button to make sure you do not have any problems connecting to the server.
9. Click OK to return to the load script
10. Directly after the OLEDB CONNECT command type the following script

```
SQL
SELECT
Name as database_name,
dbid as database_id,
cmptlevel as compatibility_level
from master..sysdatabases
```

This sql select statement will return the database name, database id and database compatibility level of each database on your server.

Database compatibility level

This level tells you which version of SQL Server the database is compatible with:

80 = SQL Server 2000
90 = SQL Server 2005
100 = SQL Server 2008 and SQL Server 2008 R2
110 = SQL Server 2012

The reason why this is important for sql server users is that there are certain commands that can only be run on databases with a certain compatibility level.

Mapping – ApplyMap function

In order to convert the compatibility level code into the description we are going to use the mapping load and applymap commands.

Next is the full script to run the tsql command and convert the compatibility level code into the description.

Map_compat_level:
mapping load
*
INLINE [
cmptlevel,Desc
80 ,2000
90 , 2005
100 , 2008 or 2008 R2
110 , 2012
];

db_info:
LOAD
database_name,
database_id,
cmptlevel,
ApplyMap('Map_compat_level',cmptlevel) as compat_desc;

SQL
SELECT
Name as database_name,
dbid as database_id,
cmptlevel
from master..sysdatabases;

First we setup the mapping table called **Map_compat_level**.
The **Map_compat_level** table is an inline table with 2 columns.

The **db_info** table is loading the results from a SQL SELECT command into our QlikView document.
The last field of the LOAD statement uses the **ApplyMap** function.
The **ApplyMap** function takes 2\3 parameters in this example:

The first parameter is the name of the mapping table ie: **Map_compat_level**.
The second parameter is the field that will be used to lookup the value in the first column of the mapping table and return the corresponding value from the second column.

You can also add a third parameter if you wish for instances where no match in the first column of the mapping table is found.

For example, if we removed the row with a cmptlevel = 80.
Then we add a third parameter of 'Unknown' (as shown below)

ApplyMap('Map_compat_level',cmptlevel,'Unknown') as compat_desc;

Any databases we a cmptlevel = 80 would have a compat_desc of 'Unknown'.

Next we will create a simple chart to display this data.

1. Right click on the Sheet and select 'New Sheet Object'->Chart.
2. Set the Window Title: DB Count by Compatibility level. Click Next
3. Move compat_desc to the 'Used Dimensions' list and set the label to 'Compatibility level'. Click Next.
4. Set the expression to : count(database_name)
5. Click OK.
6. Click Next
7. **Sort**: Remove the tick from Numeric.
8. Tick the Expression checkbox and add an expression of 'cmptlevel'.
9. The reason for this is so that the database versions of Sql Server will appear in chronological order with 2000 on the far left.
10. Click Finish. The next screenshot shows what your chart should look like:

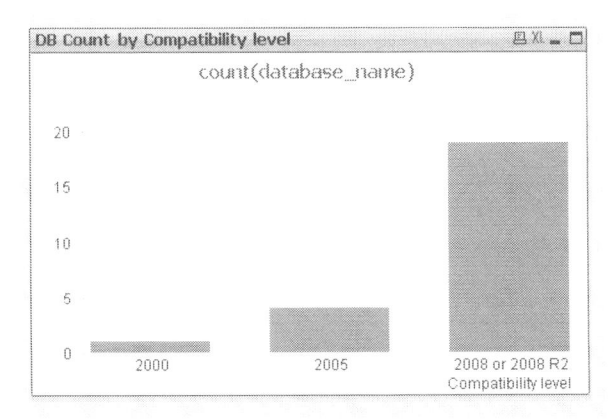

Practical Example - Database - SECTION 2 CHAPTER 3   141

Load Data from SQL Stored Procedures

After your OLEDB CONNECT TO... command to can call stored procedures to load data from a sql server database.

For example :

SQL EXECUTE testdb.dbo.getsomedetails

Sometimes it will be faster to create stored procedures on your sql server than to manipulate in Qlikview

4. Websites

Google Analytics – website data

This example will show you how you can use QlikView to analyse data exported from Google Analytics.

Google Analytics is used my many owners of websites to monitor who is visiting their website and when.

Although it is useful to have your own historical record of users accessing your website.
Google Analytics have their own graphs which make a good comparison to your QlikView documents to check there are setup correctly.

So why would you want to create your own charts ?

If you wish to store the data for your website on your own computer.
If you wish to do some analysis of the data that is not covered by Google for example you have data of changes that you made to your website in an Excel spreadsheet and you want to see if the changes affected the number of visitors to your site.

The data used in this example is taken from a small website over the period of amount 1 month.

1. Once you have logged into your Google Analytics account go to the overview page.
2. Set the metrics to the following:

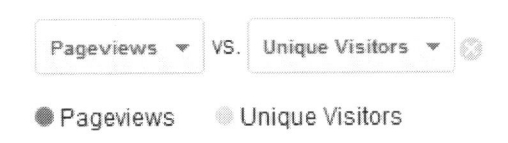

3. Select Export->CSV and save the file.

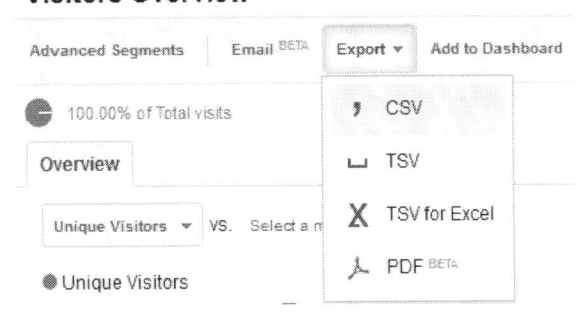

4. Open QlikView, create a new document (Ctrl+N).
5. Go to the load script (Ctrl+E).

6. Select Table files.
7. Set the Header Size to 6 lines and the Labels to 'Embedded Labels'.

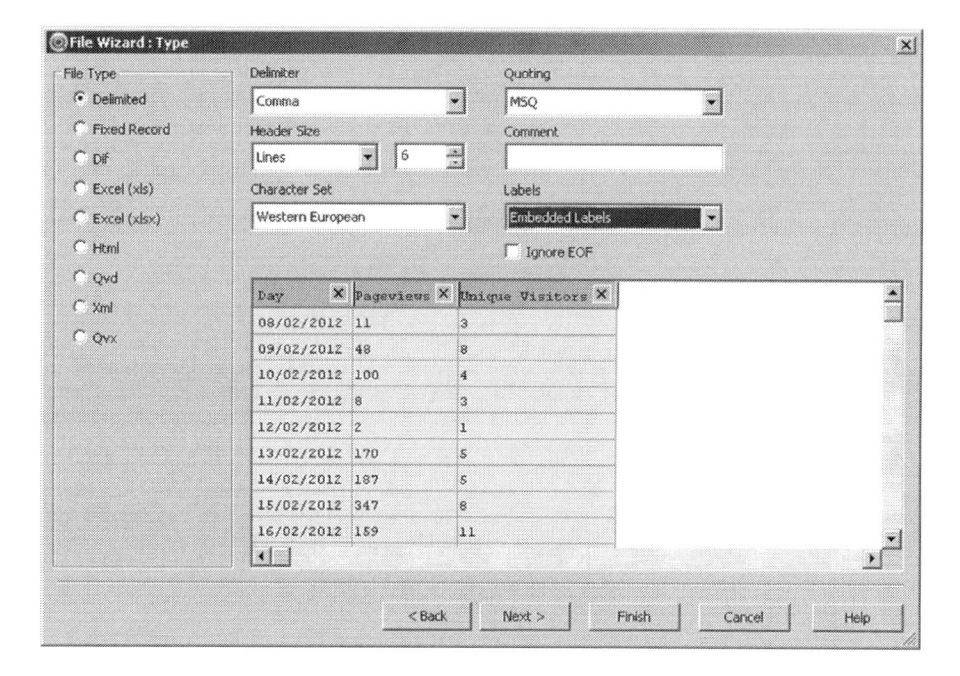

8. Click Finish.
9. Select Save->Save Entire Document.
10. Click the Reload button in the toolbar.
11. Right click on the sheet and select 'New Sheet Object'->Chart.
12. The aim is to replicate the Chart in Google Analytics.

General:
13. Set **Window Title**: 'Pageviews Vs Unique Visitors'
14. **Chart Type**: Line Chart
15. Click Next on the General screen.
16. Add a 'Used Dimension' of Day. Click Next.
17. Add expression: Pageviews. Click OK
18. Click Add and enter another expression: [Unique Visitors]
19. Click OK.

The expressions page should now look like the following screenshot:

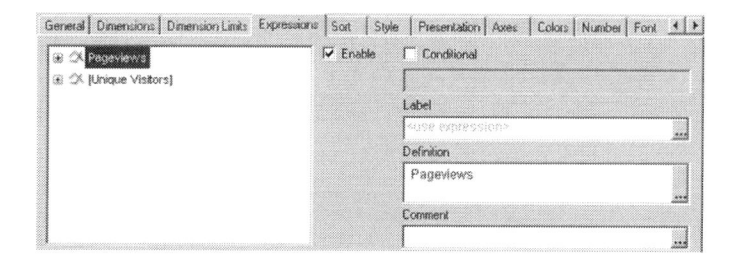

20. Click OK

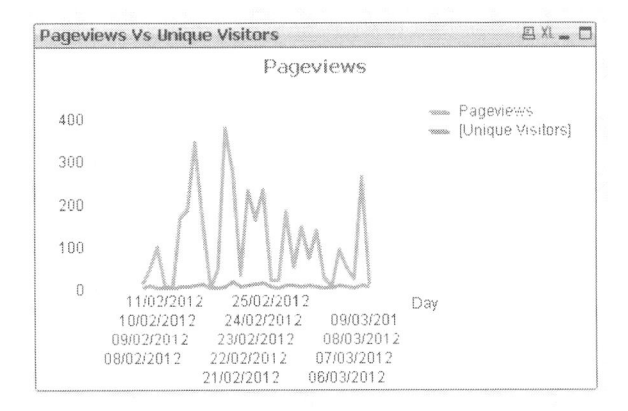

The Chart doesn't look great because each expression is sharing the same axes. One solution is using Multiple Axes.

Multiple Axes

1. Go to the Chart properties , then the axes tab.
2. In the Expressions list select Pageview.
3. In the position box select Right(Top).

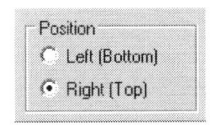

4. Click OK. Now as the next screenshot shows you have one axes for each expression.

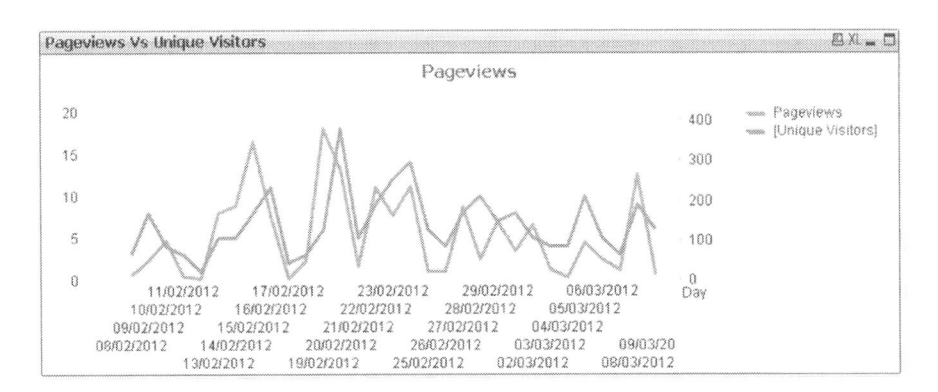

5. To tidy up the dates you could remove the year from the dimension by editing the Dimension and changing it to the following expression to just display the day/month (if the data is within 1 year). Set the dimension to '=Left(Day,5)'.

Section 3: Advanced Topics

Once you are happy with the chapters in sections 1 and 2 it is worth looking at the advanced topics we will cover next.

1. Partial Reload - for large amounts of data

Partial reload is important when you are using large data sources.

To use the partial reload prefix your load \ select\'map using' statement with ADD or REPLACE. In these examples we will focus on the load\select statements.

ADD LOAD\ADD SELECT:
The table with the same table name as the add load or add select statement will have its results appended to.

It is best practice to add a WHERE clause to your ADD LOAD\ADD SELECT statement so that you don't get duplicate rows in your table.

For example you might store the row number or date of the last row read from the current table.

If you add the ONLY option to your statement eg: **ADD ONLY** …. Then the partial reload will not be used when run the normal reload.

A good example of using this would be to use the 'track your spending' example.

Obviously as the months progress it might be an idea to only load the last month of spending and add it to the table for the rest of the months (especially if you do a lot of spending).

To refresh your memory, below is the current script to read the data:

```
for Each Sheetname in 'Jan$','Feb$','Mar$'

track_spending:
CrossTable(Category, Spent)
LOAD Date,
    Food,
    Petrol,
    Coffee,
    Clothes
FROM
Z:\qv_spending.xls
(biff, embedded labels, table is $(Sheetname));
Next
```

Next we copy this script, change the Sheetname string to be just the Apr sheet for our April spending.
Then we prefix the load statement with 'ADD ONLY' and our script looks like the one below:

for Each Sheetname in 'Apr$'

track_spending:
CrossTable(Category, Spent)
ADD ONLY LOAD Date,
    Food,
    Petrol,
    Coffee,
    Clothes
FROM
Z:\qv_spending.xls
(biff, embedded labels, table is $(Sheetname));
Next

1. Save your QlikView document.
2. To test this we first do a normal reload.
3. If we change the dimension and expression of current chart to:
   Dimension: Month(Date)
   Expression: Sum(Spent)

4. We will get the following chart (please see section 2, chapter 1 for the full 'track your spending' example)

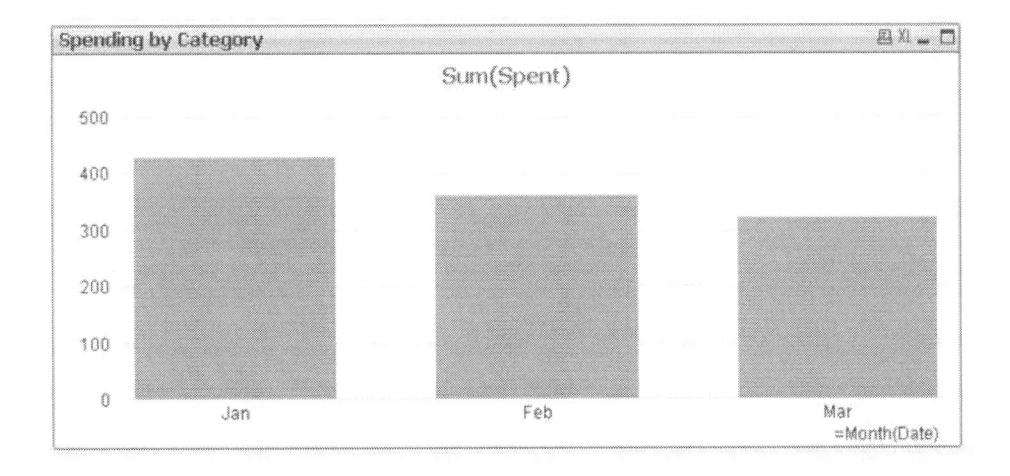

5. Now if we do a file->partial reload
6. We will get the following error message if we have not created the Excel Worksheet yet:

Advanced Topics - Partial Reload - SECTION 3 CHAPTER 1   147

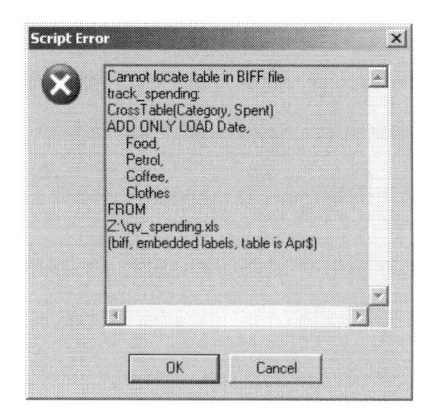

[Script Error dialog showing:]
```
Cannot locate table in BIFF file
track_spending:
CrossTable(Category, Spent)
ADD ONLY LOAD Date,
    Food,
    Petrol,
    Coffee,
    Clothes
FROM
Z:\qv_spending.xls
(biff, embedded labels, table is Apr$)
```

7. Create the Excel Worksheet called Apr.
8. Select File->Partial Reload again
9. Now the chart is automatically updated to include the next month.

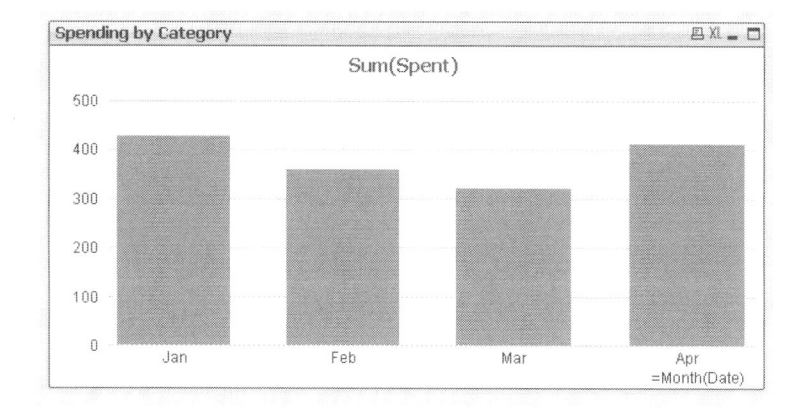

[Bar chart: Spending by Category, Sum(Spent) by Month(Date) showing Jan, Feb, Mar, Apr]

This is not a problem when looking at small sets of data but a real boost to performance when trying to analyze large amounts of data.

NOTE:
If you run the 'ADD ONLY' partial reload option more than once it will just keep adding the same records to the table again and again.

You should notice this as the total for your spending in April will suddenly double when you do this first.

2. Set analysis

In this chapter we are going to briefly cover the subject of set analysis.

So far you have seen that you can do quite a lot with QlikView without ever having to think about set analysis.

So why and where would you use set analysis?

Set analysis is used with aggregation functions ie: functions do something to a set of fields.

For example a function might add up the total of a set of numbers, this would be the sum() function.

Currently QlikView has been using the current selection to decide what is included in this set of numbers when you use the sum() function but you can change the set using set analysis.

We will continue to use the 'tracking your spending' example to demonstrate how you can use set analysis.

A set is defined in curly brackets {}

$ = the current selection in this example this could be one month.

So the sum(Spent) expression = Sum({$} Spent)

1. If we select the month March our table\chart displays the following information.

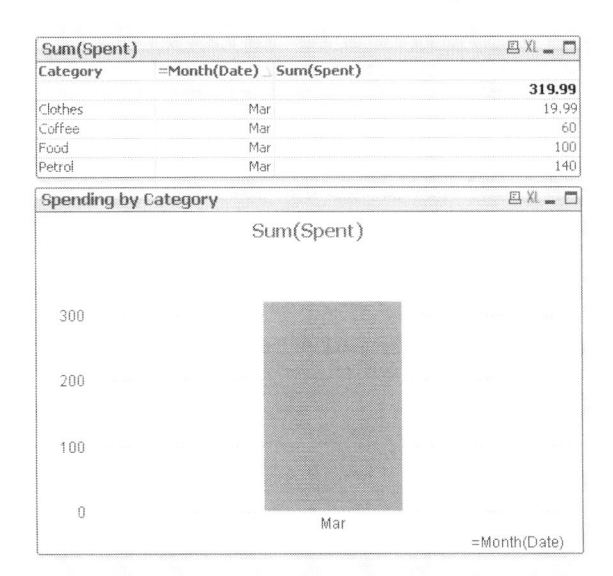

Category	=Month(Date)	Sum(Spent)
		319.99
Clothes	Mar	19.99
Coffee	Mar	60
Food	Mar	100
Petrol	Mar	140

2. To display just the data for category 'Food' in the chart we would add the expression:

Sum({ $<Category={Food}> } Spent)

To make this expression easier to understand it helps to break it into parts:

There is the **Sum({$} Spent)** part:
This tells us that based on our selections all the Spent fields are going to be totaled.

There is the **< Category={Food}>** part:
This is called the set modifier, and changes the current selection to only include Spent records where the Category record is equal to Food (and ignore the rest).

3. Next is the screenshot of the Chart Properties , Expressions tab with our expression using set analysis added.

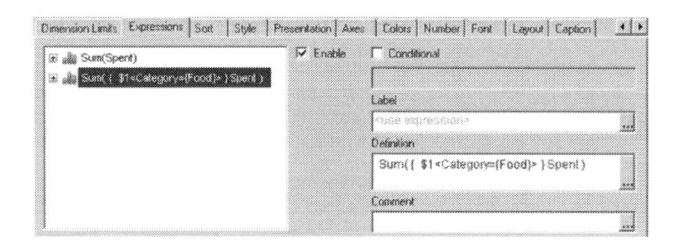

4. Now the chart should show both the total for all categories and one for just the food category as the next screenshot shows:

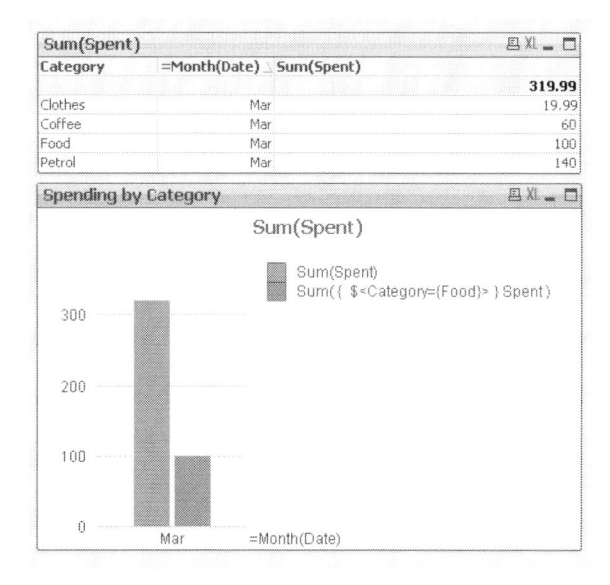

5. If you replaced the $ with a 1 in our expression it would ignore the current selection

Sum({ 1<Category={Food}> } Spent)

6. Therefore for this expression it would display the values across all months:

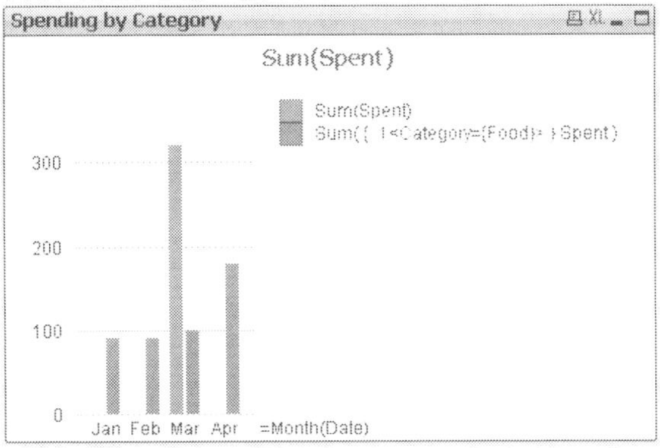
Spending by Category
Sum(Spent)
Sum(Spent)
Sum({ 1<Category={Food}> } Spent)
300
200
100
0
Jan Feb Mar Apr
=Month(Date)

7. Finally replacing $ with a $1 would change the expression to return the result for the previous selection:

Sum({ $1<Category={Food}> } Spent)

The purpose of this chapter was to give you an introduction to set analysis using some examples.

The QlikView help (F1 from the application) is a good source of information if you wish to look at Set Analysis in more depth.

3. Dual Function

The dual command associates a number with a string.

For example:

1. Place the load dual command at the top of the script

    load dual (string,compat_desc) as compatibility_desc inline

    [string, compat_desc
    SQL2000,80

    SQL2005,90

    SQL2008,100

    SQL2012,110

    ];

2. Then the following load command after you have loaded the table with the resident table in it.

    (See section 2, chapter 3 for information on the rest of this script)
    The cmptlevel will return values of 80,90,100 or 110).

    Load
     cmptlevel as compatibility_desc
    resident db_info

3. An issue with QlikView that the dual function solves is when you read multiple strings into a field that have numeric representations they will share the first strings representation that is read.
4. The dual function creates the first string representation.
5. This example will display the text as SQL2000,SQL2005 etc... but store the numeric which can be used for sorting.

4. Calendar Tables

Often when analyzing data you want to have a table of dates that you can use to link to the data you are importing.

1. To generate such as table you can add the following script to your load script:

   Calendar:
   LOAD *
   ,Month(Date) as Month
   ,year(Date) as Year;

   LOAD date(makedate(2012)+recno()-1) as Date
   AUTOGENERATE 366;

2. The makedate() function returns the date calculated from the Year, Month and Date in the following format:

   Makedate(YYYY,MM,DD)

The only parameter that is required in the makedate() function is YYYY.

- If MM is omitted then it uses the 1st January.
- If DD is omitted then the 1st of the month is used.

3. In our expression for the Date field we only use the year (in this case 2012) so the dates start from the 1st January 2012.
4. We then add 1 substracted from the current row number to the date.
5. Therefore the first date will be 1st January because the row number function recno() starts from 1 so you will be adding nothing to the function makedate(2012).

   LOAD date(makedate(2012)+recno()-1)

6. As the row number generated by recno() increases so will be date generated by the date() function.
7. The AUTOGENERATE command repeats the command. In this case it will generate dates for the whole of the year 2012.

If you go to the table viewer you will see that the Calendar table has been created:

Calendar
Date
Month
Year

5. Powershell and QlikView

In this final chapter of this section we will cover how to run QlikView from the command line.

I will also conclude with an example of how you can use powershell to automate some tasks.

The powershell commands that will be used to automate the QlikView tasks can be applied to any windows application and therefore are very useful to learn.

QlikView command line

Why use QlikView command line options?

The best reason is that you want to automate reloading your data on a scheduled task so that when you go into QlikView you immediately have up-to-date data to look at.

Reloading a QlikView document

& "C:\Program Files\QlikView\qv.exe" "C:\qlikview_docs\track-my-spending.qvw" /R

This is the command to run from Powershell to reload the data for the track-my-spending.qvw QlikView document.

/R = Reload the data.

OR

/RP = Partial Reload the data.

You can set variables in QlikView using the option /v.
To set the variable MyVar to 3 add the following command to the command line:

/vMyVar=3

Automate Tasks in QlikView

The following script example uses a great little snapin for powershell called wasp.
You can get it from:

http://wasp.codeplex.com

The wasp snapin allows you to automate key strokes in any windows application.

1. To use this will Powershell download the snapin and extract to a folder.
   Within Powershell change to the folder where you extracted WASP.

2. To find out the version of Powershell use are running type the following command and read the value of the version field: **host**

   For Powershell version 1.0:
   Run the following command from the WASP folder:
   .\Install.ps1

   For Powershell version 2.0:
   From within the folder that contains the WASP.dll file run the following command:

3. Add-PSSnapin WASP
4. Now you are ready to run your script using WASP commands. See the commented example below:

#Start the QlikView document and give is a few seconds to start using Start-Sleep

& "C:\Program Files\QlikView\qv.exe" "C:\qlikview_docs\track-my-spending.qvw"
Start-Sleep 5

#Set a variable to the current date and time
$filename_timestamp = Get-Date -format yyyyMMddHHmmss

#Select the Window that is running QlikView and send some keystrokes to the QlikView window

Select-Window Qv | Select -First 1 | Send-Keys
"%FX{DOWN}{ENTER}Myname#$filename_timestamp%s%{F4}%n"

The keystrokes broken down are:
%FX - this is Alt+F then X = This takes you to the Export option of the File menu in QlikView.

{DOWN} – press the down arrow key once = To 'Export Sheet image' option.
{ENTER} – Select the 'Export Sheet image' option.

Myname#$filename_timestamp – set the filename.

%s – Alt+S to save the image file

%{F4} – Alt+F4 to close QlikView
%n – incase it asks to save send Alt+n

As you can see you could combine the reloading of the QlikView document with this script to export an image of the document after the data was reloaded.

NOTE: If you plan on using this snapin with a scheduled task you will have to add the snapin to your Powershell Profile.

Section 4: Going Further with QlikView

In this section we will discuss what you can expect if you decide to go further than using the personal edition of QlikView (QVPE).

1. Business Intelligence (BI) - What is it?

Business Intelligence can be summed up as analyzing data in order to gain insights into the data that were not evident before the analysis occurred.

This analysis often takes the form of summarizing the data in some way such finding averages or totaling values.

The analyzed data is displayed in charts as well as tables especially for large sets of data just 'pretty pictures for business' as I call them.

The purpose of all the analysis and creation of charts is to make better informed decisions that will help you in your goals.

In business that goal might be to make more profit, whereas for the personal user that goal might be to find where they are spending all their money or find out why their computer is running slower.

2. Microsoft Business Intelligence

Microsoft has its own business intelligence software that comes with Sql Server. Because of this in the world of work more people seem to be using Microsoft Business Intelligence software than other BI packages.

You can easily see this point if you search for the names of different BI packages on job websites.

Naturally any new Business Intelligence package will be compared to Microsoft.

The advantage Microsoft has in the business world is that it comes with your database server.

The advantage QlikView has is that it has a shorter learning curve than Microsoft BI. Also in QlikView it is easier to merge data from different sources.

I have seen QlikView give developers that 'zero to hero' moment once a useful QlikView document is deployed. The reason for this is that it seems easier to explore the data in QlikView than in Microsoft BI.

Please note that as of writing this book I have not used the Microsoft BI part of Sql Server 2012 in any depth to give a comparison with QlikView.

3. Employment and QlikView

Employment is a topic quite frequently on my mind especially in these economic trying times.

Questions that I am frequently asking myself are:

Is this application I am using going to help me gain employment in another job if I need\want to find another job?

Today (sometime in March 2012) I did the following searches for roles that are looking for QlikView skills:

>Dice.com (USA)

>137 for QlikView.
>722 for Microsoft BI – SSAS.

>Jobserve.com (UK)

>37 QlikView
>129 SSAS

There are less jobs requiring QlikView than Microsoft SSAS but still a reasonable number in comparison.

From my searches QlikView is more popular that other BI packages.

Another good site to track is http://itjobswatch.co.uk

This a great site to find out the locations where particular jobs are popular.

For example some jobs might only be available in London.

Also the itjobswatch.co.uk site shows you what related technologies employers are looking for.

4. Is QlikView just for IT\geeky people?

I would say no.

Firstly, I feel mostly everyone would gain from using the 'track your spending' example.

Secondly, it is a valuable skill that could be useful for your company whether you work in the Marketing, IT, Sales or especially the Finance department.

5. Link QlikView and Microsoft Office documents

With QlikView you can drag and drop sheet objects to Microsoft Office documents.

For example the next screenshot shows an Excel document where I am dragged and dropped a table from the QlikView Document I had created for the 'Football scores' example into an Excel document.

I can still use the table in Excel to filter the data.

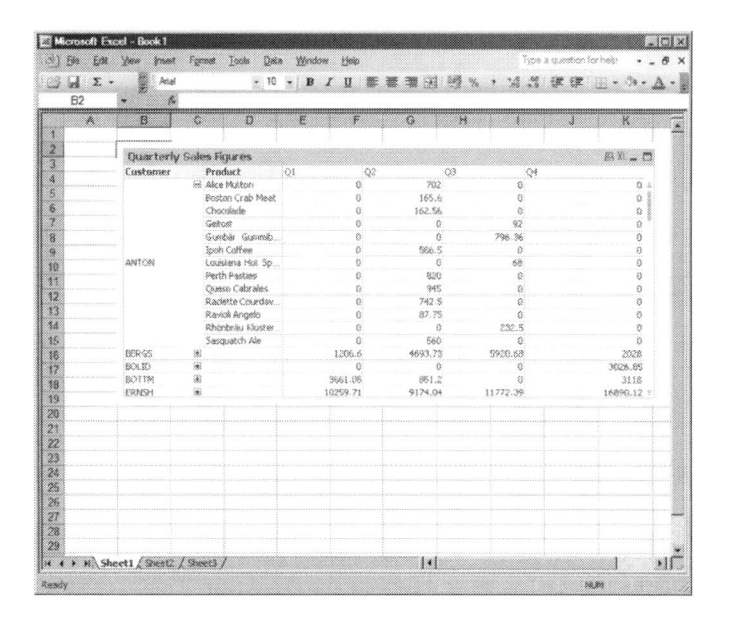

This feature to drag and drop to Microsoft Office documents is available from the QlikView Desktop as well through the browser.

The QlikView IE plugin needs to be on the document where the Office documents are used. The QlikView plugin uses ActiveX and its purpose is to provide a very similar look and feel to the sheet you developed in the QlikView Desktop.

From the QlikView Desktop select View->'Turn on/off WebView'. This option allows you to see how your QlikView app would look like when accessd by users without the IE plugin.

This sounds similar to a new feature in Microsoft Sql Server 2012 which allows users to insert BI documents linked to live data into their PowerPoint documents.

6. What else has QlikTech to offer?

There is more to QlikTech that just the QlikView Personal Edition (QVPE).

If you decide to take this further and use in your current business
you will need to obtain a license from QlikTech.

Other products supplied to use with QlikView are:

QlikView Desktop
This is the application which you have used in this book. The only difference is that to use it with the rest of the QlikView products and share documents the application has been licensed.

QlikView Server
AccessPoint - This is a portal to the QlikView Apps. Accesspoint allows users to search for apps.
This is to make QlikView documents accessible to users from desktops or mobile devices.
This product contains its own web server or you can use Microsoft IIS.

QlikView Publisher
 Addon to QlikView server
This is used to reload data and distribute the documents.

There are also product specific connectors for applications such as SalesForce, Informatica and SAP Netweaver. These connectors make it easier to use data from these applications within your QlikView app.

If your company is focussed on Microsoft products QlikTech has an offering of QlikView webparts for Microsoft Sharepoint.

There is also a plugin for Microsoft Visual Studio called QlikView Workbench. This plugin can be used to created QlikView web apps using Visual Studio.

Collaboration
With QlikView server you can also collaborate with other users and work on the same document.

Examples of business areas where QlikView documents can be used to gain insight:

- Finance - for Invoicing\Revenue reports.

- Sales - For Customer Relationship information from a CRM application.

- Marketing - To understand the relationship between changes to the company website and changes in the number\types of visitors accessing the website.

Appendix
Appendix A: Terms Used

QlikView Document
This is the document that will contain the layout and loaded data that you will learn how to create in this book.
This saved file has a .qvw extension.(see the QlikView file definition).
This document is sometimes also called the QlikView application or QlikView App.

Data Source
The data source is the location of the information you want to analyse with QlikView.
There are a variety of data sources that can be used with QlikView.
Because you can connect to so many different data sources it means that business users will be able to load data from a variety of systems.

Qlikview file (.qvw)
This is the saved is a binary file of your Qlikview document.
It has an extension of .qvw.

QVD file
This is a binary data file with one data table.
A QVD file can be used to load data into your QlikView document faster.

Appendix B: Other QlikView Sheet Objects

In this appendix I will review some of the Sheet objects that I did not cover in the rest of the book.

You can access each of these sheet objects by right clicking on the sheet and selecting 'New Sheet Object'.

Input Box
Input Box - DESCRIPTION

Use the Input Box object when you need to get some input from the user.

Input Box - REASON TO USE

Use this object when you cannot get the input from the user by presenting the possible values in a table\chart.

You store the input from the object into a variable so it can be retrieve later.

Input Box - EXAMPLE

1. Right click on the sheet and select 'New Sheet Object'->'Input Box'.
2. Click the 'New Variable' button, enter the name of the variable and click OK.

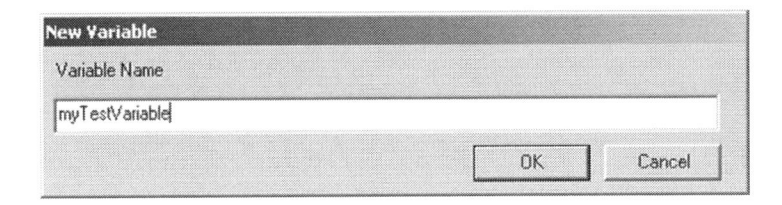

3. The variable will be added to the 'Displayed Variables' list as shown in the next screenshot. Add a title to your 'Input Box'.

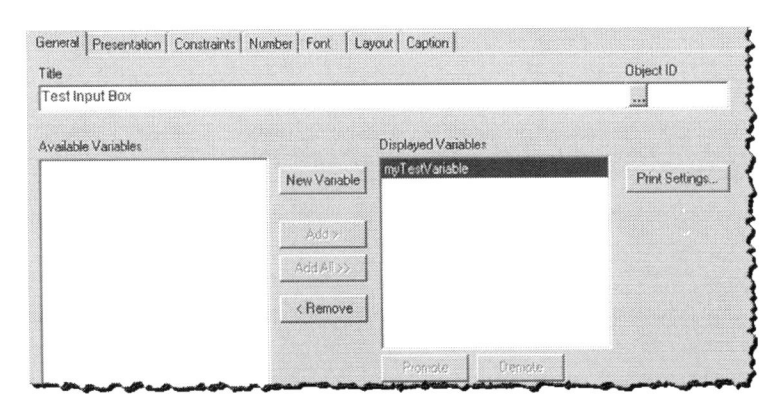

4. Click the Constraints tab, from this tab you can restrict what the user can enter.
5. For example for only positive numbers you would select 'Standard' in the 'Input Constraints' area and then change the dropdownlist to 'Positive Integer' as shown:

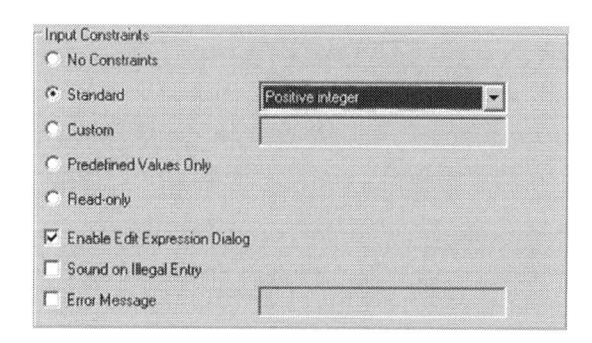

6. Click OK and the following input box is added to your sheet:

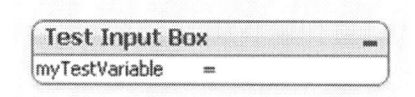

7. To test your new variable: Right click on the Sheet, select 'New Sheet Object'->Text Object...
8. Click the '...' on the right hand side of the Text field and enter your variable name for the expression:

9. Click OK.
10. Go to the Actions Tab:
11. Set the Action to 'Open URL'.

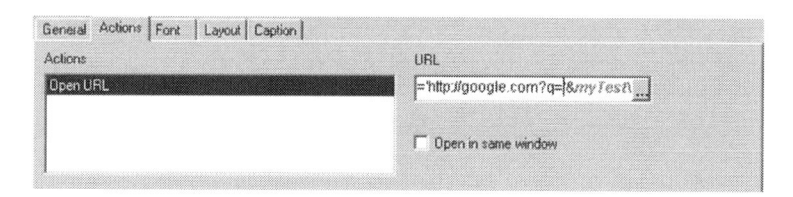

12. Add the URL as :
    ='http://google.com/?q='& *myTestVariable*

13. Go back the properties for the 'Input box' and remove any constraints.
14. Now if you enter a something into your 'Input Box' and click the Text field QlikView will update the text field and ask if it can open the URL.

Test Input Box
myTestVariable = 444

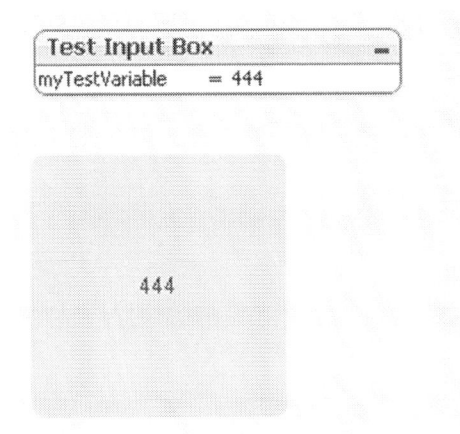

444

15. If you click ok the default browser will open with the google website:

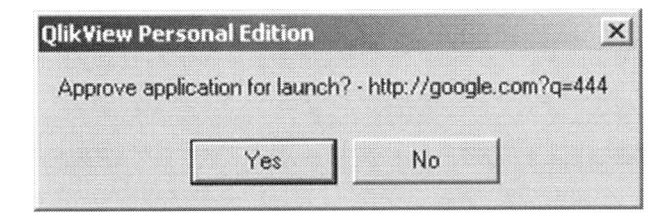

QlikView Personal Edition
Approve application for launch? - http://google.com?q=444
Yes   No

Statistics Box

Statistics Box - DESCRIPTION

The statistics box allows you to display various statistics about a particular field for example: count, min, max and average.

Statistics Box - REASON TO USE

You would like to find out more information about the data in a particular field.
But you are not interested in displaying all the rows of data in that field.

Statistics Box - EXAMPLE

1. Enter a title for your Statistics box.

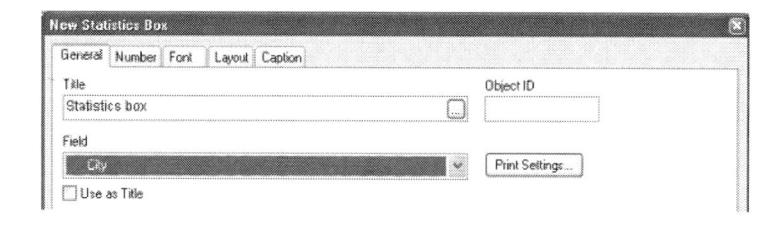

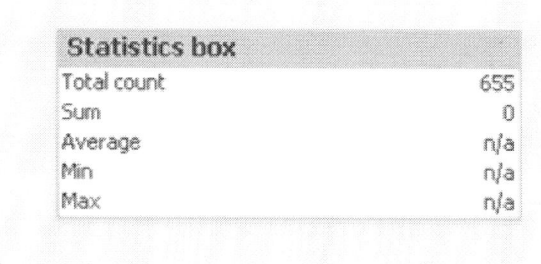

2. The example above shows a count of the number of cities.
3. In this example functions such as the Average, Min and Max are set to n/a because it does not make sense to calculate them.
4. The functions are recalculated when a record from the field selected in the Field list box is selected.
5. In this example it would be when a City is selected.
6. Otherwise all values are used in the calculated of the 'Displayed Functions'.

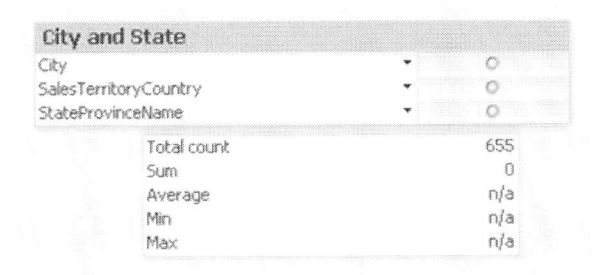

City and State		
City	▼	○
SalesTerritoryCountry	▼	○
StateProvinceName	▼	○
Total count		655
Sum		0
Average		n/a
Min		n/a
Max		n/a

7. When we select the SalesTerritoryCountry of Canada the statistics box recalculates it values.

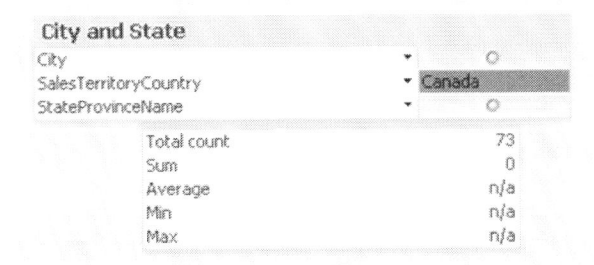

City and State		
City	▼	○
SalesTerritoryCountry	▼	Canada
StateProvinceName	▼	○
Total count		73
Sum		0
Average		n/a
Min		n/a
Max		n/a

Bookmark Object

Bookmark Object – DESCRIPTION

The bookmark object allows you to save the selection state of a QlikView document and return to the state.

Bookmark Object – REASON TO USE

You have setup a complex selection that you wish to save.

Bookmark Object – EXAMPLE

1. Right click on the sheet.
2. Select the Bookmark object from the 'New Sheet Object' menu.
3. Enter a title for your bookmarks and Click OK.

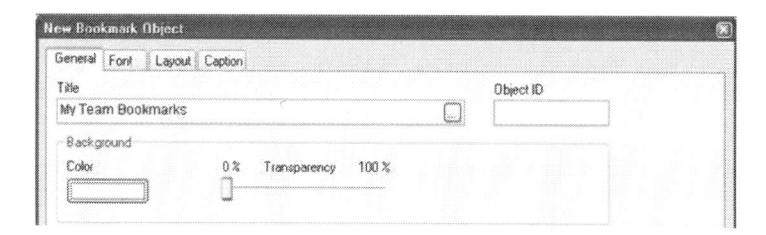

4. The following object will be added to your sheet:

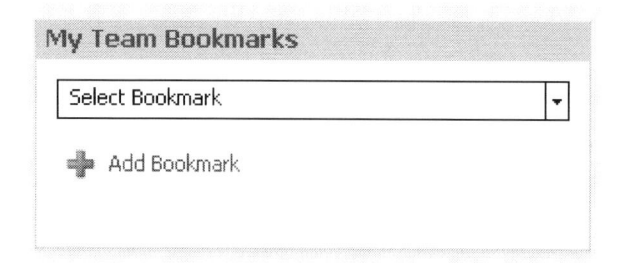

5. Get a selection on your sheet that you would like to keep.

166 Appendix B - Other QlikView Sheet Objects

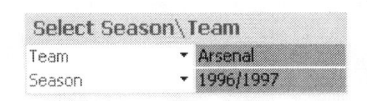

[Screenshot: Select Season\Team filter showing Team = Arsenal, Season = 1996/1997, and a "Matches played" table listing matches with columns recordno, MatchDay, Season, Home Team, Away Team, Goals Home, Goals Away.]

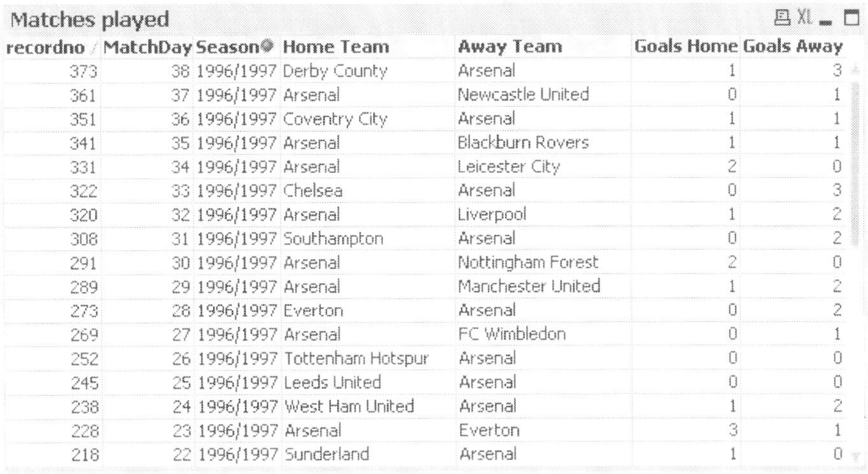

6. Click the Add Bookmark option on the bookmark object:
7. The following screen will appear.
8. I have entered a bookmark name of :Arsenal 1996.

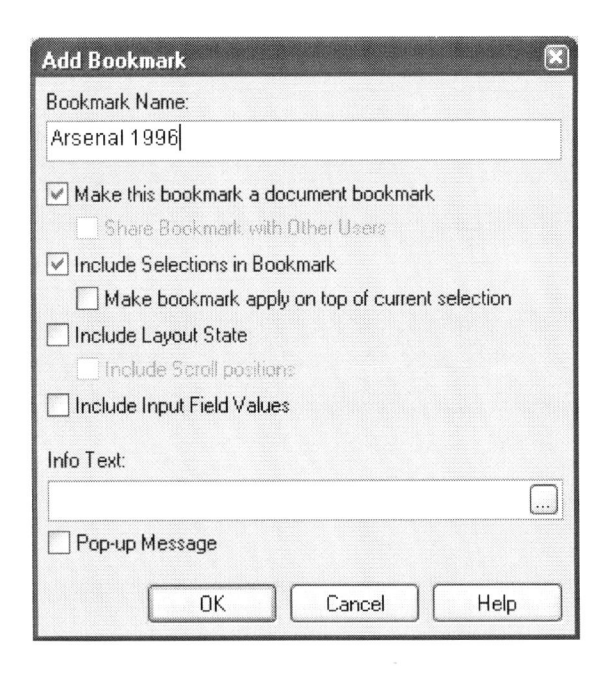

[Screenshot: Add Bookmark dialog with Bookmark Name "Arsenal 1996", checkboxes for "Make this bookmark a document bookmark", "Include Selections in Bookmark", and other options, with OK, Cancel, Help buttons.]

9. Click Ok.
10. You will now see the Bookmark option in the toolbar.

Other QlikView Sheet Objects - Appendix B **167**

11. And it will be added to your bookmark object:

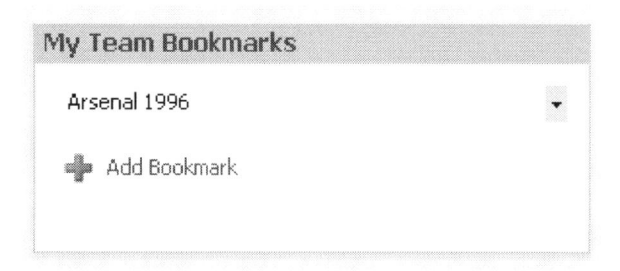

12. Change your selection on the sheet or just clear the selections using the clear button in the toolbar.
13. The bookmark object will then change to the following:

14. Click the dropdownlist on the bookmark object and select the option 'Arsenal 1996'.
15. You will see that the selections on the sheet will change to the settings that were on the sheet when you saved the bookmark.

Button

Button – DESCRIPTION

The button can be used for a variety of actions for layout, printing, opening urls and printing.

Button – REASON TO USE

The reason to use the button object is to make your QlikView document easier to use and save you time.

Button – EXAMPLE

1. In this example we will create a button to reload your data.
2. Right click on the sheet and select 'New Sheet Object', then 'Button…'.Add a title

3. Select the Actions tab and choose the following action to reload data.

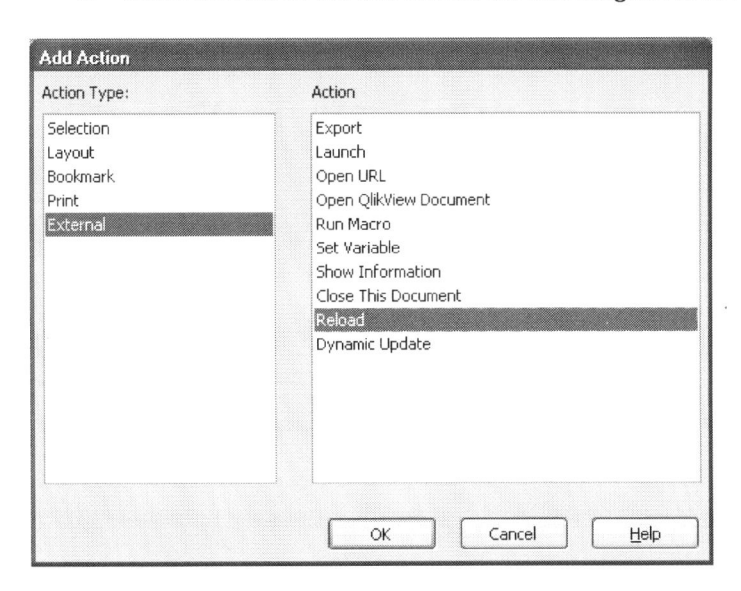

4. Click OK to close the Action screen and click OK again to close the Button screen.
5. The following button will be displayed on your sheet. Click the button to test it.

Other QlikView Sheet Objects - Appendix B

Current Selections Box

Current Selections Box – DESCRIPTION

This object displays all selections you have made for any charts\tables in your QlikView sheets.

Current Selections Box - REASON TO USE

The real advantage of this object is evident when you have several sheets that you are working with. A selection made on any of the sheets will appear in the 'current selections box' object.

Current Selections Box – EXAMPLE

1. Right click on the sheet and select 'New Sheet Object', then 'Current Selections Box'.
2. Click OK. The object that is added to your sheet will be blank at first.

3. When you start making selections they will be added to the list.

4. You can then use the 'Current Selections box' object to change the selected field (as shown next) by click the down arrow next to each selection. Clear selection by clicking the eraser icon.

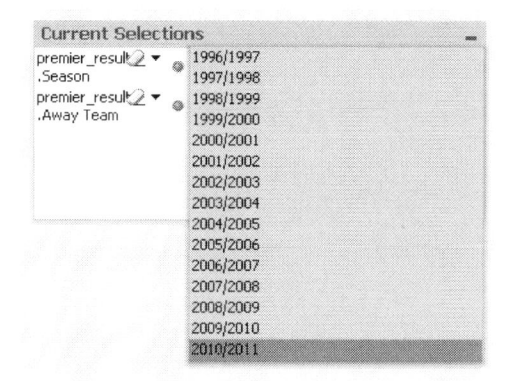

Appendix B - Other QlikView Sheet Objects

Search Object

Search Object - DESCRIPTION

The search object is easy to setup and allows you to search all the fields or just a selection of fields.

Search Object - REASON TO USE

Use this object to help you find data you have loaded into your QlikView document easily and very quickly.

Search Object - EXAMPLE

1. Right click on the sheet and select 'New Sheet Object', then 'Search Object'.
2. Click OK to use all fields.
3. The search object will be added to your sheet.

4. Click the input to the search object and start typing.
5. The results of the search will be displayed in a dropdownlist that you can select from.

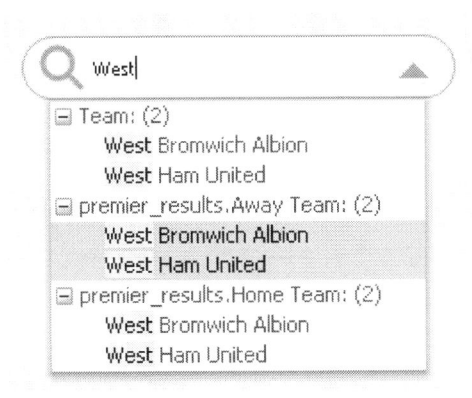

6. You can go back to the Search object properties and restrict the search by selecting which fields should be searched.
7. In the search properties you can also select different types of searches:

Other QlikView Sheet Objects - Appendix B   **171**

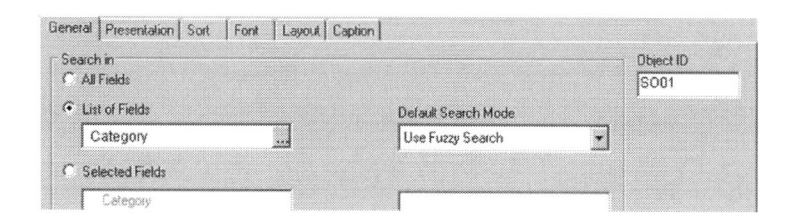

8. The previous screenshot shows a Fuzzy Search using just the Category field from our 'track your spending' example.
9. When start to use a Fuzzy search a ~ appears at the start of the string.
10. This is a best match search, so it will list items that are similar to the string being searched.

11. Whereas if you used the Normal search you could only get the results for 'Coffee' as shown next:

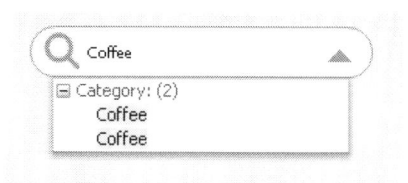

12. The wildcard search puts a * either side of the searchstring you are typing.
13. This search will find all values that contain the searchstring as we see in the next example 'f' is contained within Coffee and is displayed in the results.

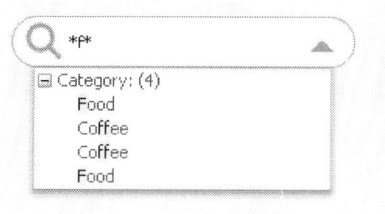

14. If the search of 'f' was done with a normal search the result would be food because this is the only Category that starts with 'F'.

Slider calendar object

Slider/Calendar object - DESCRIPTION

This object allows the user to select values

Slider/Calendar object - REASON TO USE

To give the user an easy way to select values from a list or dates from calendar.

Slider/Calendar object – EXAMPLE

1. Right click on the sheet and select 'New Sheet Object', then 'Slider/Calendar object'.
2. Select the Input Style: Slider and Field: Category

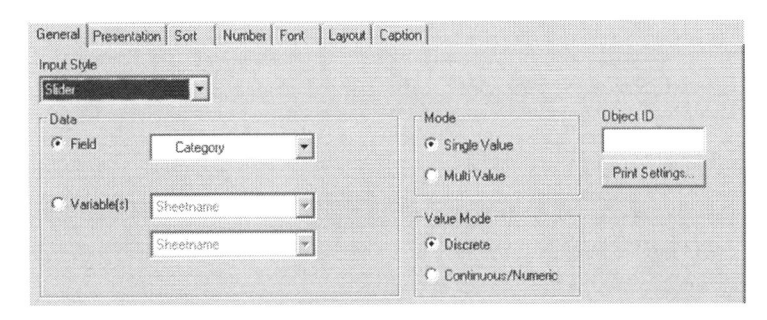

3. Click OK. The next screenshot shows the slider object that is added to your sheet:

4. Open the Properties for the 'Slider/Calendar' object.
5. Select the Input Style: Calendar
6. Field: set to Date (this field contains the date you spent the money – see the 'track your spending' example in section 2 for more information on the data used).

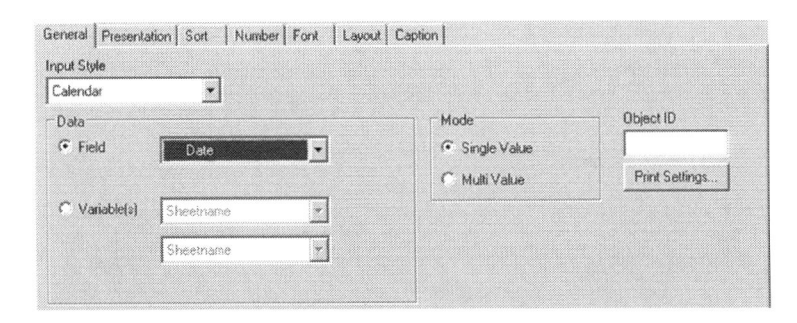

7. Click OK.

8. The object is changed on the sheet to look like the next screenshot:

16/01/2012

9. If you click on the calendar icon to the right of the dropdownlist a calendar appears so you can select the date (as shown).

10. You can also select the date from the drop down list(as shown next).

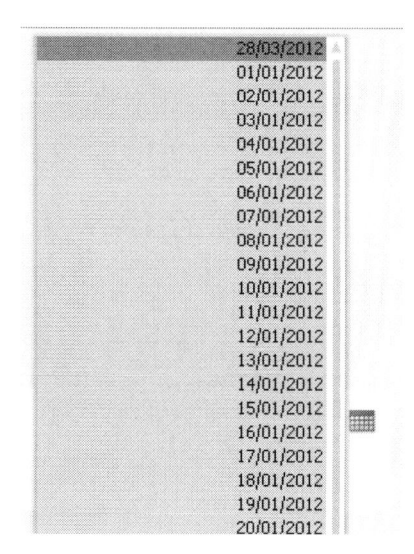

Line arrow object

Line arrow object – DESCRIPTION

This object allows you to create a line on the sheet (with or without an arrowhead).
You can also associate an action with the object in the same way you can with a button object.
This object can also overlap other objects.

Line arrow object - REASON TO USE

Use this object when you need to focus the attention of the user on a particular object on the sheet.

Line arrow object - EXAMPLE

1. Right click on the sheet and select 'New Sheet Object', then select Orientation of 'Diagonal (Climbing) and the Style as set in the next screenshot.

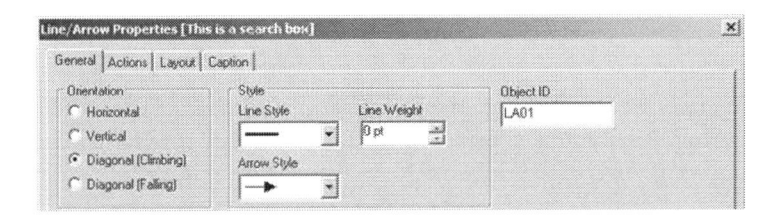

2. Go to the Actions tab. Click Add and select the following Reload action from the External 'Action Type'.

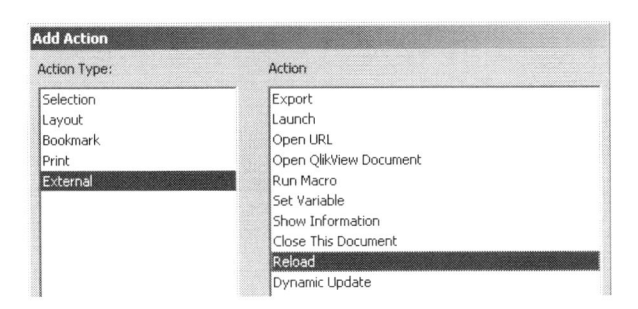

3. Click OK twice to close the Action and properties screens.
4. You should now have an arrow object on your sheet which looks like :

5. You can now arrange the arrow to point at an object.
6. If the arrow object is clicked the action is run, in this example it will reload the data.

Container

Container - DESCRIPTION

The container object allows you to groups objects together so they can be easier to manage.

Container - REASON TO USE

You can give objects within a single container common properties for font, layout and captions.

A container can also save space on your sheet as multiple objects can use the same space if you set the 'Container type' to 'Single Object' as you will see in the next example.

Container - EXAMPLE

1. Right click on the sheet and select 'New Sheet Object', then Container Object
2. In this example we are going to group the arrow object and the search box.
3. We select the objects from the 'Existing Objects' list and click 'Add' to move them to the 'Objects Displayed in Container' list.
4. Click OK.

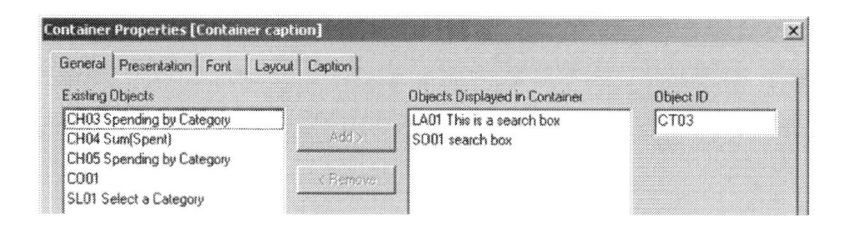

5. Caption Tab, Set the Title Text to: Container caption.

6. Presentation tab: Select Container Type: Grid.

7. Click OK.
8. The Container will look like the next screenshot:

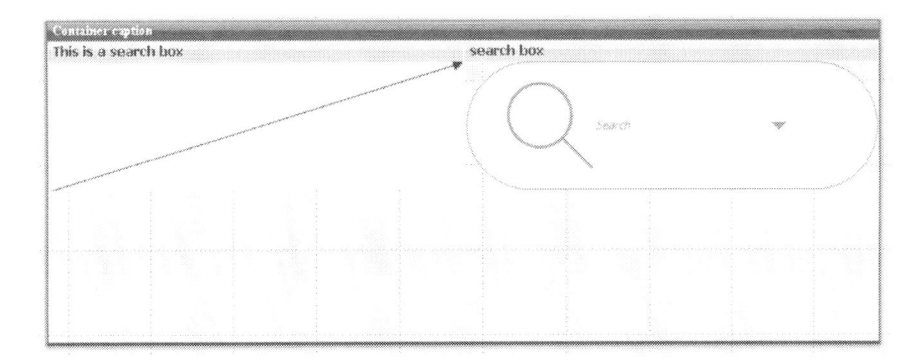

9. Return to the container properties and from the Presentation tab select a Container type of 'Single Object', then click OK. The container will look like the following screenshot:

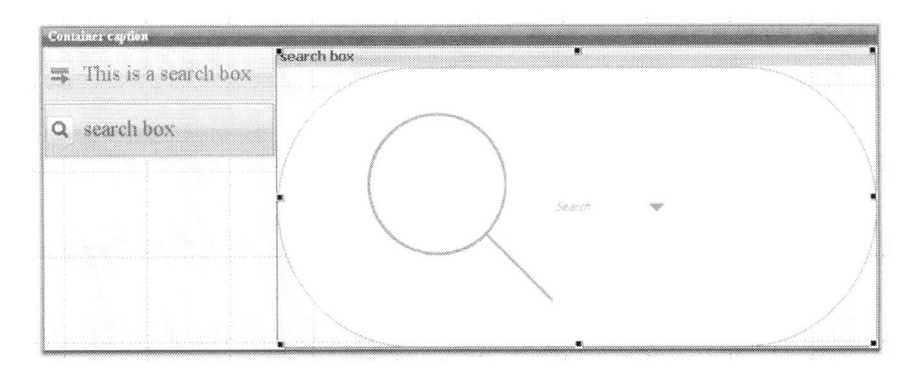

10. You can then change between objects using the buttons of the left hand side of the container below the Container caption.
11. Add some more objects to the list. Click OK to view the result :

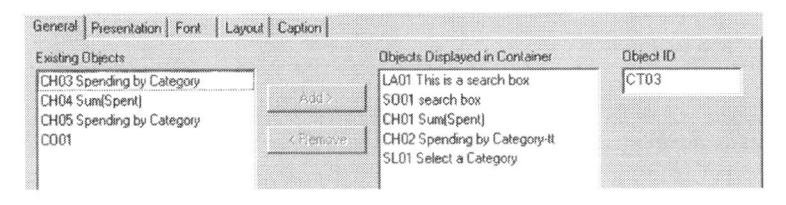

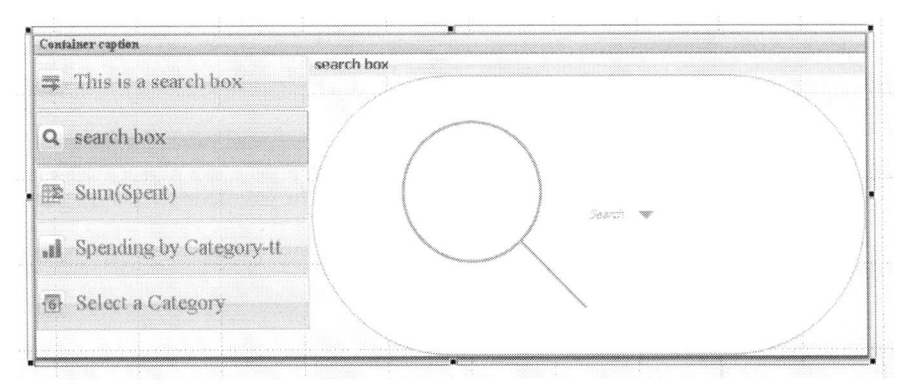

Appendix C: Useful Websites

These are some websites I recommend:

QlikView sites

- http://qlikview.com
- http://community.qlikview.com
    - Obvious first source of information for QlikView and a great community of users.

- **http://practial-qlikview.com** (also known as http://practical-qv.com)
    - The site for this book and other information about qlikview.
    - Any corrections and downloads available that can be used with this book will be on this site.

Sql Server sites

- http://Microsoft.com/sqlserver
- http://sqlservercentral.com
    - Useful for all things sql server related.

- http://Sqlmadesimple.com
    - A simple sql server business intelligence blog.
    - With tips on Sql server BI (SSRS,SSIS,SSAS).

Learning Sql

- http://w3schools.com/sql
    - A great site when you are looking to start learning sql.

Index

A
Access database, 12, 55, 56, 58, 61
Animate, 94, 95, 96
ApplyMap, 140, 141

C
Calculated Dimension, 86, 87, 123
Calendar Tables, 153
Chart, 12, 29, 30, 32, 35, 38, 66, 73, 78, 83, 84, 85, 86, 87, 88, 89, 90, 92, 94, 95, 96, 97, 98, 100, 103, 104, 107, 114, 116, 123, 131, 132, 135, 136, 141, 144, 145, 150
CrossTable, 41, 114, 115, 117, 146, 147
Cyclic Group, 88, 136

D
Drill-down Group, 90
Dual function, 152

E
Excel, 10, 12, 14, 15, 26, 27, 37, 38, 39, 41, 77, 81, 104, 108, 116, 117, 119, 143, 147, 148, 158

F
Functions, 69, 71, 72, 85, 164

G
Google Analytics, 11, 13, 143, 144
GROUP BY, 65, 66, 69, 70, 71

I
INNER JOIN, 42, 43

L
Link Tables, 63
Load Script, 37, 39, 51, 66, 67

M
mapping load, 140, 141

O
ODBC, 44, 45, 49, 50, 51, 54, 55, 57, 58, 61, 65, 134
OLEDB, 44, 51, 54, 134, 139, 142

P
Partial Reload, 146, 148, 154
Powershell, 154, 155

Q
QlikTech, 16, 159
QlikView, 9, 10, 11, 12, 14, 15, 16, 17, 18, 19, 21, 22, 24, 25, 26, 27, 29, 33, 34, 35, 37, 38, 39, 41, 49, 51, 54, 57, 59, 60, 61, 63, 65, 66, 69, 72, 73, 74, 75, 77, 78, 81, 86, 98, 99, 100, 104, 107, 108, 109, 116, 118, 120, 121, 122, 123, 129, 130, 134, 138, 141, 143, 147, 149, 151, 152, 154, 155, 156, 157, 158, 159, 160, 161, 162, 166, 169, 170, 171, 178
QVD, 160

R
Reports, 12, 38, 105, 106, 137

S
Set analysis, 149
SQL SERVER, 138
SSRS, 12, 134, 136, 178
Synthetic Dimension Functions, 86

T
Themes, 10, 14, 22, 100
Trellis, 95, 96

U
User Preferences, 10, 99

Printed in Great Britain
by Amazon.co.uk, Ltd.,
Marston Gate.